C0-AVW-060

EVIDENCE-BASED LEADERSHIP SUCCESS STRATEGIES FOR NURSE ADMINISTRATORS, ADVANCE PRACTICE NURSES (APN), AND DOCTORS OF NURSING PRACTICE (DNP)

PUBLIC HEALTH IN THE 21ST CENTURY

Additional books in this series can be found on Nova's website
under the Series tab.

Additional e-books in this series can be found on Nova's website
under the e-book tab.

NURSING - ISSUES, PROBLEMS AND CHALLENGES

Additional books in this series can be found on Nova's website
under the Series tab.

Additional e-books in this series can be found on Nova's website
under the e-book tab.

EVIDENCE-BASED LEADERSHIP SUCCESS STRATEGIES FOR NURSE ADMINISTRATORS, ADVANCE PRACTICE NURSES (APN), AND DOCTORS OF NURSING PRACTICE (DNP)

DARLENE SREDL

EDITOR

Nova Science Publishers, Inc.

New York

Copyright © 2012 by Nova Science Publishers, Inc.

All rights reserved. No part of this book may be reproduced, stored in a retrieval system or transmitted in any form or by any means: electronic, electrostatic, magnetic, tape, mechanical photocopying, recording or otherwise without the written permission of the Publisher.

For permission to use material from this book please contact us:
Telephone 631-231-7269; Fax 631-231-8175
Web Site: http://www.novapublishers.com

NOTICE TO THE READER

The Publisher has taken reasonable care in the preparation of this book, but makes no expressed or implied warranty of any kind and assumes no responsibility for any errors or omissions. No liability is assumed for incidental or consequential damages in connection with or arising out of information contained in this book. The Publisher shall not be liable for any special, consequential, or exemplary damages resulting, in whole or in part, from the readers' use of, or reliance upon, this material. Any parts of this book based on government reports are so indicated and copyright is claimed for those parts to the extent applicable to compilations of such works.

Independent verification should be sought for any data, advice or recommendations contained in this book. In addition, no responsibility is assumed by the publisher for any injury and/or damage to persons or property arising from any methods, products, instructions, ideas or otherwise contained in this publication.

This publication is designed to provide accurate and authoritative information with regard to the subject matter covered herein. It is sold with the clear understanding that the Publisher is not engaged in rendering legal or any other professional services. If legal or any other expert assistance is required, the services of a competent person should be sought. FROM A DECLARATION OF PARTICIPANTS JOINTLY ADOPTED BY A COMMITTEE OF THE AMERICAN BAR ASSOCIATION AND A COMMITTEE OF PUBLISHERS.

Additional color graphics may be available in the e-book version of this book.

Library of Congress Cataloging-in-Publication Data

Library of Congress Control Number: 2012932045
ISBN: 978-1-62081-104-7

Published by Nova Science Publishers, Inc. † *New York*

CONTENTS

PREFACE

This book provides case study analyses of actual management dilemmas and how they were resolved. Each situation is equipped with a strategy that was employed in bringing about the positive resolution; management principles that were used; a nursing and non-nursing theory that guided practice, and the evidence-base of research that helped bring all this about. This book contains scenarios from twelve different types of management problems. It can be a springboard to successful resolution of management problems by adapting the identified strategies.

LIST OF NURSING THEORIES
BY CHAPTER AND STUATION

NON-NURSING THEORIES USED
BY CHAPTER AND SITUATION

ACKNOWLEDGMENTS AND INTRODUCTION

I would like to sincerely thank all my Contributing Authors for sharing their stories, situations, and strategic successes with us in this book. Without them there would be no book. Please consider writing YOUR success situation strategy and send it to me for consideration for Volume 2 at: sredld@umsl.edu.

Many evidence-base databases exist (i.e. Cochrane Collaboration, National Guidelines Clearinghouse, etc) that only contain patient-care research and practice guidelines. While the importance of primary sources of research in these venues is undisputable, there also exists a need for a database on research dedicated to more qualitative topics within the arena of healthcare administration. This text attempts to build the evidence-base of administrative /leadership success strategies so that nurses in these challenging decision-making positions may find help to adapt and guide them through administrative problem solving.

HOW TO USE THIS BOOK

Each chapter in this book has been arranged around a specific format. First there is the SITUATION, basically a story of a leadership encounter, the problem inherent within it, and it's problem resolution. This is followed by the STRATEGY, or how the resolution came about in a concise and pithy statement. The situation is explored in more depth by an ANALYSIS in which the strategy is discussed in terms of how it brought about the resolution.

Next come leadership PRINCIPLES, or laws of nature, communication, etc. that come to mind when discussing this situation. Two sets of THEORY follow. The first is a NURSING THEORY that fits the situation. Reference is made to whether it is a grand or mid-range theory and some of the principle concepts of that theory are provided. A NON-NURSING THEORY is also provided that correlates with the situation to firm the framework of the situation and strategy. Finally, the EVIDENCE-BASE of quantifiable reference information.

HOW TO USE THIS BOOK

The idea for this text evolved from a class discussion during which one of my students said, "It is a shame that when doctors die, the secrets of their wonderful bedside manner die with them because they have not taught the secrets to anyone else." I thought about the veracity of this for a long time, finally concluding that nurses do the same thing. We teach many courses but they are mostly on techniques necessary for procedural proficiency. Rarely do we divulge secrets of what we were really thinking when faced with a complex problem that we have to solve. It is unfair to our new nurse administrators, Advance Practice nurses, and Doctors of Nursing Practice, to hire them into roles for which they may be totally unprepared to handle. My purpose in soliciting these vignettes of actual dire situations turned into success stories is not to pre-suppose that you would ever be in the exact same situation;…but…you may be in a situation in which you can ADAPT one, or some, of the strategies to use in solving the problems that *you* are faced with.

The management-leadership situations described within are real-life management dilemmas written by the professionals who lived and worked through them to effect a positive outcome from a dour situation. Inclusion was by invitation only. This author made a concerted attempt to select a cross-section of some of the more important, and apt-to-occur, management problems that a new manager might face. The Contributing Authors are/were in management positions predominately in nursing, or in other areas of healthcare, business, or academia in which similar problems were faced.

This text is arranged around a format that includes: a specific SITUATION, ANALYSIS of the situation, STRATEGY that was implemented, MANAGEMENT PRINCIPLE(s) involved, and NURSING and NON-NURSING THEORY guiding practice, as well as the EVIDENCE-BASE of research data pertinent to that management situation.

SITUATION

The situation is the 'story'. The chapter titles group situational concepts together but you will soon find that some situations could have been included in other chapters as well because the topics overlap.

It was a discretionary judgment by this author to assign them to one chapter or another. For this reason, supra-script numbers indicating which other chapters the situation might be appropriate to have been included after the SITUATION

For example, SITUATION #1.1 under Chapter 1-Goal Attainment might also have applicability in Chapters 4 (dealing with Communication Facilitators), or Chapter 6 (exploring Quality of Care), and even Chapter 11 (on how to Gather Inspiration). It would look like this:

Chapter 1 - Goal Attainment
SITUATION #1.1 Communicate your goals so that others may help you achieve them: Follow your dreams 4, 6, 11.

This means that the content addressed in this situation within Chapter 1 could also have applicability in Chapter 4 (Communication Facilitators); in Chapter 6 (Quality of Care); and in Chapter 11 (Gather Inspiration).

ANALYSIS

An analysis follows each situation. This analysis explores the basics of what the situation involves.

STRATEGY

The strategy attempts to put into a few words, a succinct way of remembering the kernels of wisdom found within the larger, situation.

PRINCIPLES

Just as educators build clinical nursing courses around broad, basic principles (such as *The Principle of Asepsis*), this Leadership/Management text distills basic principles from all fields of human endeavor and lists those that apply to each situation.

THEORIES

Each situation is accompanied by a nursing and a non-nursing theory that can be used as a theoretical framework for future research on that topic or a similar topic. Some situations lend themselves toward the use of two or three theories so I have included all that seem to apply. These may not be theories that you are used to seeing. That is because most of the nursing theories are founded upon principles of direct patient care. This text is concerned primarily with situational leadership/ management issues and, because of this, many direct patient care nursing theories do not apply. I looked specifically for theorists in nursing who originated theories on communication, fiscal responsibility, and other human resource skills. The non-nursing theories are borrowed from the scientific disciplines of psychology, mathematics, anatomy/physiology, religion, psychology, chemistry, and physics.

EVIDENCE-BASE

This text is arranged so that evidential material pertinent to that specific situation is included directly after the theories involved in that situation. I have made an effort to find Level I and II evidence wherever possible but I thought it equally important to include seminal articles and books written by the theoretical authors that explain the theories more fully as well as research performed using that theory. So, you will see dates with recent research as well as those (in some cases) over a half-century old. All the situational references are also included in the comprehensive reference list at the end of the book, which also includes other resources used in the formulation of this book's narrative.

It is my sincere wish that the lessons gleaned herein will be of value to you in your leadership/administrative nursing practice.

CONTRIBUTING AUTHORS

Betz, C.
CLBetz@aol.com.
Cecily Betz, Ph.D., R.N.
Editor-in-Chief
The Journal of Pediatric Nursing

Bogomolov, B.
bob6753@bjc.org
Barbara Bogomolov, RN, BSN, MS
Clinical Manager: Refugee Health Service
Center for Diversity and Cultural Competence
Barnes-Jewish Hospital
Washington University Medical Center
St. Louis, MO

Bovia, T.
tbovia2012@yahoo.com
Theresa Bovia, RN, MBA, MSN
Faculty
William Carey University School of Nursing
New Orleans, Louisiana

Brown, F.
fbrown1149@hotmail.com
Fred Brown, M.S.N., R.N.

Csapso-Sweet, R.
dadsweet@earthlink.net
Rita Marika Csapó-Sweet, Ed.D.
Associate Professor
Department of Theater, Dance, and Media Studies
Fulbright Fellow 2002 - 2003
Fellow at the Center for International Studies
University of Missouri St. Louis

Goddard, C.
cag2170@bjc.org
Cheryl A.Goddard RN, BSN, CPN
Clinical Educator
St. Louis Children's Hospital

Griffith, L.
lewis.griffith@yahoo.com
Lewis Griffith R.N., ACNP, WFR, M.S. Experiential Education (Ex Ed)
Critical Care Medicine
Mercy Hospital
St. Louis Mo

Gutierrez, L.
gutierrezl@graceland.edu
Lawrence Gutierrez BSN, RN, CCRN
Neuro-Intensive Brain Attack Unit

Horton, C.
horton@graceland.edu
Claudia D. Horton, PhD, RN
Dean and Professor
Graceland University
School of Nursing
Independence, MO 64050

Hughey, D.
hugheyd@umsl.edu
Douglas A. Hughey
Software Support Expert- College of Nursing
University of Missouri-St. Louis,

Hsueh, K.
hsuehk@umsl.edu
Kuei-Hsiang Hsueh, Ph.D., R.N.
Associate Professor
College of Nursing
University of Missouri @ St. Louis
St. Louis, MO

Kao, P.
kao@graceland.edu
Peter Tehua Kao, MSN, RN, FNP-C
Family Nurse Practitioner
Family Care Associates
Las Cruces, New Mexico

Krampe, Jean
jkrampe@slu.edu
Jean Krampe, PhD, RN, CPHQ
Assistant Professor,
Saint Louis University

Lenker, L.
lynn_lenker@ssmhc.com
Lynn Lenker BSN, RN, MS,BC-NE,ONC
Regional VP Nursing/ CNO
Nurse Champion Project Beacon
SSM, St. Louis

Martin, T.
rntigger2s@att.net
Theresa Martin, BSN, RN
Home Health Nurse
St. Charles, MO

Mundy, R.
rnmundy2006@hotmail.com
Rachel Mundy, RN, MSN, PNP-BC
Austin, Texas

Nguyen, L.
tanv94@umsl.edu
Leah Nguyen, BSN, RN
Neurology ICU
Barnes-Jewish Hospital
St. Louis, MO

Parrone, J.
jparrone@yahoo.com
Joyce Parrone, M.S.N., R.N.
Director of Nursing Education
Lutheran School of Nursing
St. Louis, MO

Pellerito, A.C.
NICKANEM@Charter.net
Angela Christian Pellerito, BSN, RN
Staff nurse
Barnes-Jewish Hospital South Emergency Dept.
St. Louis, MO

Peng, N.
forever_pal.lily8@yahoo.com
Niang-Huei Peng, R.N., Ph.D.,
Assistant Professor, College of Nursing,
Central Taiwan University of Science and Technology
No.666, Buzih Road, Beitun District,
Taichung City 40601, Taiwan (R.O.C.)

Pfennig, P.
plpfennig@yahoo.com
PAUL PFENNIG, Major, USAF, NC
MSN, RN-BC. ANP-BC. ACNS-BC
Adult Clinical Nurse Specialist
San Antonio Military Medical Center
Fort Sam Houston,
Texas 78234-6200

Phillips, E.
phillipse@health.missouri.edu
Eileen Phillips, BSN, RN
Infection Control Professional
University of Missouri Health System
Columbia, Missouri

Phillips. M.
majormarge@aol.com
Marge Phillips, MSN, RN
Faculty
Lutheran School of Nursing
St. Louis, MO

Ruppert, J.
ruppertj@umsl.edu
Joan Ruppert, MSN, RN, CNN
Assistant Professor
School of Nursing
University of Missouri @ St. Louis

Schneider, I.
irisschneider@onlinehome.de
Iris Schneider, MScN,
Diplom-Pflegewirtin, RN
Assistant to the Head Nurse office
Saarland University Medical Center
Homburg, Germany

Sellars, E.
esther@utm.edu
Esther C. Sellars, Ed.D, MSN, RN
Associate Professor
Department of Nursing
The University of Tennessee-Martin

Shelton, A.
Stlkshelton@aol.com
Ann K. Shelton, Ph.D., R.N.
Assistant Professor of Nursing
Southern Illinois University Edwardsville
Edwardsville, IL 62026-1066

Sredl, Darlene
sredld@umsl.edu
Darlene Sredl, Ph.D., MSN/MA, R.N.
Associate Professor of Nursing
University of Missouri @ St. Louis

Sredl, J.
jlsredl@yahoo.com
Jennifer Sredl, BSN, RN
Cardiopulmonary Rehabilitation
Alexian Brothers Medical Center
Prospect Heights, IL

Sredl, S.
Sealcoinc@aol.com
Steve Sredl
President & CEO
Sealco, Inc.
St. Louis, MO

Tanaka, L.
tanakal@umsl.edu
Lanette E. Tanaka MSN, RN
Assistant Teaching Professor
College of Nursing
University of Missouri-St. Louis
St. Louis, Missouri

Vesper, B.
busybeth@sbcglobal.net
Beth Vesper, B.S.N., R.N.
St. Louis, MO

Via, B.
bettyv@stl-psc.com
Betty Sawyer Via, NHA
Executive Director
Plastic Surgery Consultants

Wagoner, T.
traciwagoner@sbcglobal.net
Traci Wagoner, B.S.N., R.N.
St. Peters, MO

Wieland, D.
471 Ivy Wood Dr. Ballwin, MO 63011
Dortha Wieland, R.N. Retired
Evening Charge Nurse
Friendship Village West
Chesterfield, MO

Williams, L.
leawilli@graceland.edu
Lee Williams, MA, MLIS, AHIP
Library Director
Dr. Charles F. Grabske, Sr. Library
Graceland University

Wilson, D.
deann.wilson@mercy.net
DeAnn Wilson, MSN-PNP-BC, RN
Cleft and Craniofacial Team Nurse
Mercy Children's Hospital
Kids Plastic Surgery

Young-Shields, Y.
shieldy@umsl.edu
Yakima Young Shields, Ed.D(c), APRN, ANP-BC
Assistant Professor
University of Missouri @ St. Louis

In: Evidence-Based Leadership Success Strategies …   ISBN: 978-1-62081-104-7
Editor: Darlene Sredl   © 2012 Nova Science Publishers, Inc.

Chapter 1

ASSISTING TOWARD GOAL-ATTAINMENT

LEADERSHIP SUCCESS SITUATION #1.1

Cheryl Goddard

Communicate Your Goals So that Others May Help You Achieve Them: Follow Your Dreams

It was always my dream to visit Alaska! In the late 80's when the internet was new, I searched for pediatric (my clinical specialty) hospitals in Alaska. I knew that nursing re-licensure in Alaska required proof of Continuing Education Units, or CEUs. I reasoned that by providing an educational program worthy of CEU designation by the Alaskan State Board of Nursing, and combining that dream with my passion for nursing and travel, I just might wrangle an invitation to speak in Alaska- hopefully with all expenses paid.

One spring day I asked Anne, an advanced practice nurse whom I admired, if she had ever spoken at conferences outside our metropolitan area.

Casually she said, *"Yes"*.

Just as casually, I said, *"Do you want to go to Alaska?"*

Again she said, *"Yes"* and went about her work. Little did she know then how fast I would act on her affirmation!

Before long, letters went out by snail mail to Alaskan hospitals that regularly provided health care to children. Soon came phone calls asking us to speak on the Respiratory Needs of the Pediatric Patient.

After the preliminary arrangements for the conference had been made, I shared the great news with Anne.

Charting next to her at the nursing station, I said with uncontainable enthusiasm, *"OK we are booked to speak in Alaska in late August!"*

Completely shocked she said, *"I thought you were kidding!"*

Almost unable to breathe by now I whispered, *"I wasn't...well... are you going to go?"* She nodded yes.

The trip was a phenomenal experience! We met wonderful people, even some old friends of Anne's. We learned amazing things, including; some of the health care needs of Native Alaskan Indians, as well as cruise ship passengers, and the history of the area. Who knew there was a temperate rain forest in Alaska? Other learning opportunities included the variety of religious influences in the area; of particular interest was the Russian influence. We also learned to pick wild thimbleberries; how to smoke salmon, and interesting facts about the tide and floating houses. We were amazed at the profound need for recycling (they even grind glass down to pave roads)...and, we laughed and laughed, then laughed some more. Some cruise ship passengers asked funny questions, like, *"Can you use American money here"* and, *"how much does it cost to mail a letter from here?"*

Although Alaska was our first unique conference experience, it has not been our only experience. A few years ago, we spoke at the International Council of Nurses Conference in Taipei, Taiwan. Stay tuned, as we will continue to utilize strategy number one for future trips!

Analysis

What is strategy number one? Don't wait for others to do what you can do for yourself! If you want something to happen-you must *make it happen!* Take the steps (baby steps at first) toward accomplishing your objective. In his seminal text, *Law of Success*, Napoleon Hill identified fifteen personality characteristics of successful people (Hill, 1979). The most important of those personality characteristics is- having a definite chief aim. By identifying what you want to do, then keeping that goal in mind as you systematically go about accomplishing small mini-objectives toward the accomplishment of the major goal, you will ultimately accomplish YOUR MAJOR GOAL.

Leadership Success Strategy
Repeat your successes in other venues.

Principle(s)
1) Take charge
2) Define yourself and your mission
3) Support holes in your knowledge-base by working with colleagues
4) "Consider presenting as a way to share what you do" (Heinrich, 2008)

Theoretical Framework Guiding Practice

Nursing Theories
A) Virginia Henderson's 14 Components of Nursing Theory (Nursing Theory) is a *Grand Theory* in that it affects all people equally. Of the fourteen components that Henderson identifies, the first nine are physiological (as Maslow had also stipulated). Henderson also identifies psychological, communication, learning, and spiritual/moral needs which must be met among the remaining five (George, 2002).

B) Faye Abdellah's 21 Problems in Nursing Theory (Nursing Theory) (another *Grand Theory*) is also similar to Henderson's and Maslow's Theories with one major difference. That difference is that while Henderson's components focus on patient or individual behaviors, Abdellah's Theory identifies specific nursing services that should be incorporated into any determination of patient/individual needs (George, 2002).

Non-Nursing Theory

Maslow, Abraham-Hierarchy of Needs Theory

This is a *Grand Theory* that identifies the universal human physiological needs of food, water, air, and rest shared by all in the graphic base of an isosceles triangle. The hierarchy has five layers which include:

- Physiological Needs (First)
- Safety And Security Needs (Second)
- Love And Belonging Needs (Third)
- Esteem Needs (Fourth)
- Self-Actualization (Fifth and Highest)

As attention moves up from the base, those most basic physiological needs, the next level of needs that must be met is security/safety, then a sense of belonging, feelings of increased self-esteem, and finally, self-actualization.

These basic human needs MUST be met before a person can aspire toward self-actualization, or goal attainment. In the above strategy the nurse administrators/educators maintained a full-time job, so presumably their monetary needs that provided for the basic essentials of life (food, shelter, etc) were being met. The goal of a trip to Alaska was something else, however, *that* was in the self-actualization realm. Meeting that goal involved additional expense in the form of air fare, hotel and restaurant and ground transportation expenses.

By offering to trade intellectual capital for financial capital, the nurse administrator/educators were able to realize their goal and achieve the self-actualization of accomplishing their coveted trip to Alaska.

Evidence Base

George, J. (2002). Nursing Theories: The Base for Professional Nursing Practice. Upper Saddle River: Prentice Hall.

Heinrich, K. (2008). *A Nurse's Guide to Presenting and Publishing: Dare to Share.* Sudbury: Jones and Bartlett Publishers.

Hill, N. (1979). *The Law of Success.* Chicago: Success Unlimited, Inc.

LEADERSHIP SUCCESS SITUATION #2.2

Darlene Sredl

Persistence is Key

Someone famous once said "90% of success is just showing up". That was demonstrated politically in 2009 when the beleaguered Governor of Illinois appointed R. Burris to the former Senator (now President) Obama's Senate seat. Public and Senate outcry insisted that Burris not be approved. But Mr. Burris went to Washington anyway- arriving and systematically turned away for the better part of a week, until at the end of that week- he was seated and sworn in as the Senator from Illinois by Vice President Biden. THAT is tenacity of persistence!

One of my sons exhibited this trait of tenacity of persistence also when, newly graduated with a B.A. in economics, he decided to become a stock-market trader. Conventional wisdom had it that new graduates were *never* hired straight out of college into that position. Undaunted, he donned his navy pin-stripe suit, grabbed his graduation- present leather briefcase, and…armed with a thin resume, went for an interview at a prestigious investment firm. He was turned down flat.

The following week he again donned his professional suit and briefcase and went back to the investment firm. Again he was turned down for an interview but…the receptionist remembered him.

Amiable and cheerful, he repeated this unlikely rejection pattern five more times in five succeeding weeks.

By the seventh visit he was standing around one of the trader's cubicles, drinking coffee and kibitzing, when he got news that he was hired and scheduled to begin training on Wall Street the following week!

Napoleon Hill said, "Confidence in oneself and one's abilities is one of the 15 personality characteristics of a successful person."(Hill, 1979).

Analysis

Yoder-Wise and Kowalski state that leaders do not give in at the first obstacle when attempting to accomplish a goal (Yoder-Wise, 2006). Instead, the leader keeps on creating optional alternative solutions until something finally works. This approach may involve stubbornness, but it also can be seen as believing in one's goal or vision and continuing to search for alternate solutions.

Leadership Success Strategy
Transformational behaviors can be cultivated through relationship building.

Principle

Persistence can often accomplish what knowledge alone cannot.

"Think of yourself as your own company"

Kerfoot, Karlene

Theory Guiding Practice

Nursing Theory

Dorothy Johnson's Behavioral Systems Theory is a *Grand Theory* that emphasizes personal motivation as a factor in establishing successful relationships. Johnson also feels that environment influences behavior; and equilibrium affects behavior (George, 2002).

Non-Nursing Theory

Maltzman's Theory of Originality refers to evoking different responses to the same stimulus by being creative. Maltzman stated that there are three ways to increase creativity: Present an uncommon stimulus situation in which conventional responses are not available; evoke different responses to the same stimulus situation; evoke uncommon responses as text responses.

Maltzman's research is distinctive because he was one of the few behaviorists who attempted to deal with creative behavior. He provided a simple definition and methodology for studying originality, and also examined the relationship between originality and problem solving, a prelude to nursing's 'critical thinking'.

Evidence-Base

George, J. (2002). *Nursing Theories: The Base for Professional Nursing Practice.* Upper Saddle River: Prentice Hall.

Hill, N. (1979). *The Law of Success.* Chicago: Success Unlimited, Inc.

Kerfoot, K. (1997). Leadership Principles: Lessons learned. *Dermatology Nursing, 9*(4), 279-280.

Leininger, M. (2002). Culture Care Theory: A Major Contribution to Advance Transcultural Nursing Knowledge and Practices. *Journal of Transcultural Nursing, 13(3), 189-192.*

Leininger, M. (2007). Theoretical Questions and Concerns: Response From the Theory of Culture Care Diversity and Universality Perspective. *Nurse Science Quarterly, 20(1), 9-13.*

Leininger, M. and McFarland, M. (2002). *Transcultural Nursing.* New York. McGraw-Hill.

Maltzman, I. (1960). On the Training of Originality. *Psychological Review.* 67(4), 229-242.

Yoder-Wise, P., and Kowalski, k. (2006). *Beyond Leading and Managing: Nursing Administration for the Future.* St. Louis: Mosby/Elsevier.

LEADERSHIP SUCCESS SITUATION #3

Darlene Sredl

When All Looks Lost...

Few projects run as smoothly as originally planned but this one turned out to be a subversive coup! It seemed relatively simple at the beginning. As a newly licensed nursing home administrator, I was assigned to take over a 120 bed private pay/Medicaid facility from a management company that had operated it for our company.

I arrived at 10 PM ready to hang my license on the wall at midnight when the former company's administrator's licenseexpired. Good thing I got there before the change of shift. I learned from the employees that during the previous week forty private pay patients had been mysteriously transferred from the facility. Allegedly, they were transported to the new facility built by the former management company.

As if that weren't bad enough, officials representing that company told the employees not to show up for their scheduled shift when I took over tonight---or else! So, one hour before shift change I struggled with the thought that I alone might have to care for the needs of 80 sick and disabled patients!

Shaking off the initial disbelief that a healthcare management company could be/would be so unprofessional as to border on criminal behavior, I knew it was time for action. I hastily gathered the 3-11 staff together; thanked them for telling me of these events; and asked if any of them would be willing to stay over onto the night shift in case the night shift personnel chose to be absent. All said they would stay! I then placed calls to three nursing agencies for RNs, LPNs and UAPs. Although the hour was late, I did receive confirmations that one LPN and one UAP were coming.

At 11PM I was heartened to see that most of those scheduled did show up to work. So they, together with those from the 3-11 shift who wanted to stay, and the 2 agency personnel provided enough caregivers to get us through the night.

The next day I conferred with my boss and invited several shift charge people and department managers to a meeting. We got rumblings that the former management company did not plan to honor their responsibility for payroll for the previous two weeks. Together we devised a plan to get us over these rocky first few weeks. I was very cognizant of the fact that the former company had (what's a polite word for 'screwed'?) the employees and also that the employees did not know or trust me or the company I represented. We felt our best option was open and transparent communication with the staff and lots of it.

Within days I convened a meeting of all employees to let them know of the behind-the-scenes developments. We held the meeting on what was supposed to be payday, but sure enough, there were no paychecks from the former management company to hand out. Realizing that this would probably be the outcome, I had asked my boss to issue checks in the amount of $50 as a bonus so I would have something to hand to each employee in lieu of their paycheck. He agreed.

At the meeting I explained to the employees what had been going on. I also told them how their charge nurses and department managers had assisted in devising a plan to help. I told them about calling all our food service providers asking them to donate extra food to our facility. The dietary manager used that food to make a large tray of sandwiches for each shift which she put in the break room. Donuts were plentiful also. The dietary manager also made up bags of surplus groceries for employees to take home—as much as they needed or wanted. We did not want them or their families to go hungry during this transition period.

I explained what the former company had done about their pay checks, quickly adding that the company I represented was issuing a $50 bonus check to every employee. I told them we were initiating legal action against the former company to get their wages back, but that resolving it would probably take awhile.

I wrote a letter explaining these unusual circumstances and made hundreds of copies. All employees were encouraged to take as many copies as they needed to give to their landlords, utility companies, automobile loan companies, etc. so that their creditors would know it was not their fault that they could not meet their financial obligations this month.

I thanked them for standing by their ethical responsibility to continue caring for the sick in spite of this unusual twist of events and that their jobs were secure with our company.

Over the next few weeks several employees thanked me for my honesty and most stayed with the company. Eventually we garnered the employees back wages in a civil lawsuit. The criminal case for patient kidnapping has not yet been adjudicated.

Analysis

In this leadership position the nurse/administrator was required to possess many characteristics of strength in order to achieve the success that she ultimately did achieve. Like Napoleon Hill's fifteen identified personality characteristics, she needed to possess and use all of them, namely: possessing a definite chief aim; self confidence; belief in the habit of saving (money, time, etc.); initiative and leadership; imagination; enthusiasm; self control; utilizing the habit of doing more than she was paid for (there was no bonus or additional payment for taking on the responsibility of this project); possessing a pleasing personality; displaying accurate thinking; concentration; profiting from failure; tolerance; and possibly, even practicing the Golden Rule(Hill, 1979).

She needed the courage of her convictions in favor of listening to line workers who knew the job and the employees best, and were ultimately able to devise a workable solution. She knew she had the support of the CEO who delegated this big assignment to her. This upper level support is invaluable to any change agent in any circumstance.

Leadership Success Strategy
Innovators embrace change!

Principle(s):
1) Knowledge is POWER
2) Situational power can be assumed by a confident leader
3) Problems contain the seeds of their own solution

4) Problems can be solved by delegation to the right person utilizing the five principles of delegation
5) Take charge!
6) "Treat set-backs as stepping stones" Charles Garfield.

Theoretical Framework

Nursing

Wittmann-Price's Theory of Emancipated Decision-Making (EDM) is a new mid-range theory designed to increase professional women's satisfaction with decision-making about healthcare issues. The theory contains five sub-concepts: empowerment, flexible environment, personal knowledge, reflection and social norms.

Non-Nursing

1. Adult Learning Theory of K.P. Cross

(Non Nursing) *Mid-Range Theory* merges personal with situational characteristics within the dimensions of voluntary versus compulsory learning. It proposes 4 principles:

1) Adult learning should capitalize on the experience of the participants;
2) Adult learning should adapt to the aging limitations of the participants;
3) Adults should be challenged to move to increasingly advanced stages of personal development;
4) Adults should have as much choice as possible in the availability and organization of what is to be learned (Cross, 1981).

2. TriarchicTheory of R. Sternberg (Non-Nursing Theory)

It is a Grand Theory consisting of three sub-theories all underlying intelligent behavior: meta-cognitive, performance-based, and knowledge acquisition. This theory proposes that intelligent behavior involves adaptation to the environment and/or improving the present environment within a continuum of experience from novel to familiar tasks performed in a socio-cultural context. Sternberg outlines the use of this theory in skill training (Sternberg, 1977, 1983).

Evidence-Base

Cross, K. P. (1981). *Adults as Learners*. San Francisco: Jossey-Bass.

Hill, N. (1979). *The Law of Success*. Chicago: Success Unlimited, Inc.

Lewin, K. (1947). Frontiers in group dynamics: Concept method and reality in social science, social equilibria and social change. *Human Relations, 1*(1), 5-41.

Sternberg, R. (1977). Intelligence, Information Processing, and Analogical Reasoning. Hillsdale, NJ: Erlbaum.

Sternberg, R. (1983). Criteria for Intellectual Skills Training. *Educational Researcher, 12*, 6-12.

Wittmann-Price, R., and Bhattacharya, A. (2006). Exploring the subconcepts of the Wittmann-Price Theory Of Emancipated Decision-Making in women's health care. *Journal of Nursing Scholarship, 38*(4), 377-382

Wittmann-Price, R., and Bhattacharya, A. (2008). Reexploring the subconcepts of the Wittman-Price Theory of Emancipated Decision Making in women's healthcare. *AdvNursSci, 31*(3), 225-236.

LEADERSHIP SUCCESS SITUATION #1.4

Darlene Sredl

Turning Lemons into Lemonade

I was surprised at the response of a Registered (I thought she was registered) Respiratory Therapist (RRT) that I was working with when she refused my request to secure new doctor's orders on a patient we were treating. Flustered, she confessed that she could not do this since she never passed the Respiratory Therapy Boards. She had been functioning at the hospital in the informal capacity of respiratory technician, administering minor aerosol treatments, but was not fully able to function as a professional Registered Respiratory Therapist (RRT). This woman was knowledgeable, skilled, and well-liked by colleagues and patients, but had given up hope of ever achieving her registration status after failing the licensure exam 3 times. She revealed that she froze and could not think straight during exams. She further confided that she had recently lost her husband and, with the loss of his income, could not afford the exam expense. This, coupled with her lack of confidence after failing the exam so many times, gave rise to feelings of anxiety bordering on hopelessness.

Adding to this were feelings of job insecurity due to the fact that a new administration had recently come into power at the hospital and transferred her from the benign 'floor' to ICU- a unit that terrified her. She voiced concern that she might resign.

But... by the next time I saw her I had hatched a plan, and came prepared to implement it.

"Kisha", I said. "I can help you get over your exam anxiety. I am a certified hypno-therapist and by hypnotizing you and suggesting that you do not fear exams but rather, embrace them, you will not have the fear that makes you freeze during exams. But, I advise you to accept the transfer to the ICU and learn as much as you can about ICU respiratory medications and procedures, because there is something presently missing in your existing knowledge base. Undoubtedly there are some questions about those medications and procedures usually done in the ICU that are on the licensure exam. Study and know that this ICU experience will augment your knowledge because you will be working with these medications every day."

Then, I asked her the cost of the exam fee.
She said,

"One hundred fifty dollars, why?"

I asked her what the name of the organization that administered the exam was. Now, quite perplexed, she was astounded when I pulled a blank check out of my scrubs pocket, signed it, and made that check out to the Board of Registered Respiratory Therapy in the amount of $150.

Handing her the check, I counseled,

"Find out the date of the next time you are eligible to take the exam, then send in this check. This one's on me. In the meantime study like crazy focusing on ICU medications. When you are within a week of taking the exam, call me and I will hypnotize you to get over your exam anxiety."

She did all these things and passed the exam! Shortly afterward Kisha was voted 'RESPIRATORY THERAPIST OF THE YEAR' by her colleagues!

Analysis

Fear can immobilize a person. Any negative situation that is repeated starts to seem like truth; like- this is the way it will always be. One may begin thinking, why should I even try, because I won't get anywhere?

The cycle of negative self-talk must be broken before one can begin to see that there may be another, or other, outcomes possible. Usually this cannot be done by the person himself/herself alone.

That person needs a friend; someone who has one or more resources that specifically can help the person break the negative cycle of self doubt and show that they CAN achieve whatever goal has been eluding them.

In this situation I used four resources of change: verbalized confidence in Kisha's professional ability; counseling her to stretch her professional capabilities (however fearful she was) to accept the transfer to ICU and learn from it; implementing the nursing tool of hypnosis to promote confidence in her own abilities and to remove the mentally obstructing barrier she referred to as 'freezing' when taking an exam; and finally, backing it all up with the check made out to the testing Board.

By utilizing the combination of resources described above, I made it *possible* for her to succeed; and, she did!

Leadership Success Strategy
If at first you don't succeed, try, try, try-keep trying until you DO!

Principle(s)

1) Each person is a unique individual with unique needs
2) The first step in the nursing process is ASSESSMENT. Problems must be identified before a solution can be constructed
3) Belief in oneself and one's abilities underlies accomplishment
4) "Co-transcending with the possibilities is powering (empowering) unique ways of origination in the process of transforming"(George, 2002) p. 435.
5) Perception is closely related to attitudes (Assael, 1995; Jenkins, 2007).
6) Success can be enhanced by a little help from your friends-accept it.

Theoretical Framework Guiding Practice

Nursing

Reed's Theory of Self-Transcendence (1991) is a middle-range theory based on the methodology of 'deductive reformulation'of experiences over the life-span based on Roger's conceptual system.

Non Nursing

Lewin's Force-Field Analysis Framework for Change, a *Grand Theory* involves 3 phases in the change process: Unfreezing the frozen (or, initiating an awareness for the *need* for change); moving/thawing (or, identifying and exploring alternative forces of action); and finally, refreezing (or, integrating change and stabilization) (Lewin, 1947).

Evidence-Base

Assael, H. (1995). *Consumer Behavior and Marketing Action*. London: PWS-Kent Publishing Company.

George, J. (2002). Nursing Theories: The Base for Professional Nursing Practice. Upper Saddle River: Prentice Hall.

Jenkins, R., Sredl, D., Hsueh, H., Ding, C. (2007). Evidence-based nursing process (EBNP) consumer culture attribute identity: A message-based persuasion strategy study among nurse executives in the U.S. *Journal of Medical Sciences, 27*(2), 55-62.

Lewin, K. (1947). Frontiers in group dynamics: Concept method and reality in social science, social equilibria and social change. *Human Relations, 1*(1), 5-41.

Lewin, K., andLippitt, R. (1938). An experimental approach to the study of autocracy and democracy: A preliminary note. *Sociometry, 1*, 292-300.

Lewin, K., Lippitt, R., and White, R. (1939). Patterns of aggressive behavior in experimentally created social climates. *Journal of Social Psychology, 10*, 271-301.

Reed, P. (1991). Toward a nursing theory of self-transcendence: Deductive reformulation using developmental theories. *Advances in Nursing Science, 13*(4), 64-77.

LEADERSHIP SUCCESS SITUATION #1.5

Yakima Young-Shields

Help toward Goals

I encourage students to take an active role in their learning which coincides with the principles of androgogy "the art and science of adult learning" (Knowles, 1984). I encourage students from my very first encounter with them to take ownership and be self-directed in their own learning.

I also believe that it is vital to acknowledge and appreciate all previous experiences that the student/learner brings to the traditional and clinical residency areas. I also I believe it is essential to understand that students have various learning styles. Therefore I attempt to match the student's learning style to teaching instruction style. I want each of my students to know I truly care about them inside and outside of the classroom. I believe that being a facilitator for student learning also includes being a role model as well as a mentor for the student through-out the phases of learning. I don't believe there should be any barriers between the student and the teacher "that all individuals and their experiences are valuable. This, I know, can be controversial, but I believe that respect and trust between the student and teacher is what makes a difference in assisting the learner in achieving their goals /objectives and eventually life.

In closing I don't have just one teaching strategy. I draw on various philosophies and theories, but even more important, the life experiences I have had myself as a life- long learner.

Hopefully my student's will also feel the need to share similar strategies in their professional as well as personal life experiences.

Analysis

As this author states, she doesn't have just one teaching strategy-she maintains a formidable "teaching toolbox" of effective strategies depending upon the lesson to be taught and the student's objective in learning.

Leadership Success Strategy
Positive reinforcement enhances learning.

Principle(s)
Adults have a need to be self-directing and decide for themselves what they want to learn.

"You genuinely have to care for people to be a successful leader."

Kerfoot, Karlene

Theoretical Framework Guiding Practice

Nursing Theory

Nursing as Caring: A Model for Transforming Practice by Anne Boykin, Ph.D., R.N. and SavinaSchoenhofer, Ph.D., R.N. is a grand theory built upon the foundations of Mayeroff, Roach, Watson, and Parse and based upon six key assumptions:

1) By virtue of their humanness, all persons are caring.
2) People live their caring moment to moment.
3) People are whole or complete (mind, body, spirit) in the moment.
4) Personhood is defined by living life grounded in caring.
5) Personhood is enhanced through participating in nurturing relationships with other caring persons.
6) Nursing is both a discipline and a profession.

Drs Boykin and Schoenhofer agree that the best way to communicate the nursing experience in the moment is in story form.

Non-Nursing

Cognitive Load Theory by John Sweller is a grand theory concerned with cognitive processes involved in acquiring a new skill. We possess a long-term memory, a working memory, and from this we are able to form a 'schema', or way of organizing information so we can recognize new information or problems that need to be dealt with. By reducing redundancy and repetitive information a person can eliminate some stress associated with unnecessary processing of the working memory.

Evidence Base

Kalyuga, S. (2006). Cognitive Load Factors in Instructional Design for Advanced Learners *Instructing and Testing Advanced Learners: A Cognitive Load Approach*. New York: Nova Science Publishers, Inc.

Kerfoot, K. (1997). Leadership Principles: Lessons learned. *Dermatology Nursing, 9*(4), 279-280.

Purnell, M. J. (2006). Development of a model of nursing education grounded in caring and application to online nursing education. *International Journal for Human Caring 10*, 8-16.

In: Evidence-Based Leadership Success Strategies ...
Editor: Darlene Sredl

ISBN: 978-1-62081-104-7
© 2012 Nova Science Publishers, Inc.

Chapter 2

CLINICAL SPECIALTIES

LEADERSHIP SUCCESS SITUATION 2.1

Darlene Sredl

More Ways than One to...

It is important for nurse administrators to remember that unless a patient is declared mentally incompetent in a court of law, that person is considered mentally competent and capable of making healthcare decisions for herself/himself. I was Administrator of a nursing home that housed a female patient who was obviously acutely ill and running a high fever. Her oxygen saturation was in the high 80s with absent breath sounds in the lower left lobe. All clinical indications pointed to pneumonia. Since this nursing home was not licensed as a Medicare facility, we did not have the ability to treat her with IV antibiotics. She needed to be transferred to a hospital, but...she refused to go! The Director of Nurses and I were seated outside on a bench alongside the patient when the ambulance arrived. Steadfastly, she refused to go. The ambulance's back ramp was lowered to allow for easier access- but, no luck, she still refused to go. Although she had exhibited wide fluctuations in temperament before, no one had previously initiated court proceedings declaring her mentally incompetent, so the ambulance personnel had no choice but to obey her wishes; paramedics insisting they could not take her against her will. They stood helplessly by the ambulance awaiting direction. The staff was stymied by this response. At that point we could not fathom why she would choose to stay sick and remain in the nursing home when going to the hospital meant that she would likely get well. Although this lady had a nice and secure room at the facility, she packed most of her possessions onto her wheelchair each day, pushing it around the facility like one might a shopping cart in a grocery store. Suddenly the Director of Nurses sprang to her feet, took the belonging-laden wheelchair and quickly wheeled it up the ramp and into the ambulance. Just as quickly, the patient followed the wheelchair full of her precious belongings up and into the ambulance. The Director of Nurses realized the fact that the patient would go where her possessions went. Since her wheelchair went into the ambulance, she did also.

Analysis

The Director of Nurses understood a basic fact of human nature-people are reluctant to leave important (to them) possessions or relatives and friends. This is one of the fears inherent in the fear of death. Wills are made so that if a person HAS to die and leave their possessions, at least they have the last word on how they are distributed.

The elderly lady in this strategy displayed the symptom of 'hoarding' (one possible sign of mental illness) by packing her wheelchair like a big open-to-display suitcase full of items she loved.

On the chair could be found incontinent pads, washcloths, newspapers, and sometimes, more than crumbs from previous meals. She had outlived next of kin so no one visited regularly with whom the staff could discuss her bizarre behavior. Hence, there was no one to initiate a court ruling of incompetence.

The facility administration could have- but didn't. It is difficult for many health care organizations to provide federally-mandated increasing levels of care while still maintaining a profit margin. Court proceedings underwritten by the facility are usually last on the list of services provided.

Psychology saved the day in this case; as well it may in the situation you are faced with.

Leadership Strategy
Situational power can be assumed by a confident leader persuasively using the resources available in the situation.

Principle(s)
Problems contain the seeds of their own solution-analyze the root cause of the problem to find them!

Theoretical Framework Guiding Practice

Nursing

Florence Nightingale's Model of Nursing (1820-1910)
Nightingale is the Pioneer of Modern Nursing with this NURSING *Grand Theory*. She perfected her improvements to the art and science of nursing in the Crimean War during which her changes resulted in reducing wounded soldier's mortality rates from 60% to 2%. Her belief in accurate record-keeping and her background knowledge of mathematics led to the creation of the 'Pie Chart' in which the mortality statistics were demonstrated.

Other changes initiated by Nightingale included: improving overcrowded conditions; poor sanitation, waste management and odor control; improper ventilation; use of the forces of nature in assisting patient cure, and 'pet therapy' by stashing kittens in her roomy apron pockets so soldiers could pet them as she made her rounds. She lobbied for formal nursing education, and invented dumbwaiters and patient call signals.

Non-Nursing

The Plane-tree Model for Patient-Centered Care- (1985)

A (*NON-NURSING THEORY*) by Angela Thieriot focuses on 9 key areas: human interactions; emphasis on patient and family education; use of social support networks; nutrition as part of healing; tending to the spiritual needs of patients; encouraging touch; patient choice to include complementary therapies; attention to the total healing environment by architectural and interior design, and recognizing the role of the arts and entertainment in healing.

Evidence-Base

Chinn, P. and Kramer, M. (2008). Integrated Knowledge Development in Nursing (7th Ed.). St.Louis. Mosby

Dossey, B. (1999). Florence Nightingale: Mystic, Visionary, Healer. Pennsylvania: Springhouse.

McEwen, M. and Wills, e. *Theoretical Basis for Nursing (2nd Ed).* Philadelphia: Lippincott Williams and Wilkins.

McEwen, M., and Willis, E. (2007). *Theoretical Basis for Nursing.* Philadelphia: Lippincott Williams andWilkins.

Nightingale, F. (1859). *Notes on Nursing.* London: Harrison.

Planetree,Inc.Retrievedfrom http://www.planetree.org/ABOUT/ABOUT.html (Dunham-Taylor, 2010) (Frampton, 2003)

Selanders, L. (1993). Florence Nightingale: An Environmental Adaptation Theory. Newbury Park: Sage.

Tomey, A. and Alligood, M. Philosophy and Science of Caring. Nursing theorists and their work (6th Ed.). St. Louis: Mosby, Inc.

Watson, J. Nursing : *Human science and human care. A Theory of Nursing* (1st ed). New York: National League for Nursing.

Watson, J. The Philosophy and Science of Caring (1st ed). Boston: Brown.

LEADERSHIP SUCCESS SITUATION 2.2

Cheryl Goddard

Know Your Drug Calculations

My husband and I have two red- blooded adolescent American boys. In order to keep up with their extraordinary exploits during their teenage years we took turns doing frequent inspections of their habitats and frequent haunts. One of us inspected while the other kept watch.

It was my turn to keep watch while my husband was inspecting the back porch. Suddenly, he came running toward me shaking with concern, holding a vial, and yelling… " Is this insulin? Is this insulin, or is it something else?" He was holding it too close to my face to see. After pulling back and taking a long look, it did appear to be insulin as the label said. Running back to the porch, we found syringes and a box of chocolate cereal on the floor.

When the boys arrived home, we separated them before questioning, because getting to the truth was much more difficult when they were together. Our classic question to each was, "Is there anything you want to tell us?" Of course, there was *absolutely nothing* either wanted to tell us.

Finally, I simply said, to our youngest son, "Daddy found syringes on the back porch". A look of relief crossed my son's face; although I also detected a slight grin. He replied, "Oh, that! The homeless guy we've been keeping on the back porch has diabetes".

It took me a few minutes to compose myself.

"Where is the homeless guy right now"?

"On the back porch". My son said innocently. Not convinced this story was completely true, I quickly found a piece of paper and a pencil and instructed my son to get the homeless man because I wanted to talk to him.

My first question to the homeless man was, "How much do you weigh?" Followed quickly by the second question, "How much insulin do you take?" After a quick conversion of pounds to kilograms, a fraction or two and multiplication, I was sure this person standing before me had diabetes. Still curious, I just had a few more questions…

"How do you control your blood sugar?"

He replied, "I just don't drink regular soda or Kool-Aid, because it makes me feel bad."

Next, I asked, "when is the last time you saw a doctor?"

He replied, "Four years ago".

Amazed, I inquired further, "How do you get your insulin if you have not seen a doctor in four years?"

He said, "I have to save $46 dollars every six weeks to buy it".

Still not totally convinced, I said, "How do you get the prescription, if you haven't seen a doctor?"

He replied, "You don't need a prescription to buy insulin". I later found this to be a true,

My last question was to my youngest son about the coco-pops on the floor.

He asked, "Mom didn't you buy coco-pops?"

"No."

He replied, "Mom, the homeless man has a dog! It's dog food! "

Knowing your drug calculations, will help you in many ways, some of them quite unexpected.

Analysis

In this strategy a nurses' basic knowledge helps avoid what could be a nasty (and wrongful) confrontation. When one finds syringes in places where no syringes should be found, it does lead to questions. Add to this nebulous mix, exuberant teenage boys who walk a little on the wild side, and it is not surprising that a parent's thoughts naturally turn to the possibility of illegal drug usage. By using the information from her sons's explanation and coupling it with her nurse's knowledge and ability to quickly calculate drug doses, this mother is able to verify the rather surprising story that she and her husband were abruptly faced with.

A lesson in veracity can be gleaned from this story. It is always important to hear both sides of a story even when one side of the story seems preposterous. Two points of view do find a common level from which a fair solution can be developed.

Leadership Success Strategy
Be open and flexible.

Principle(s)
Significant learning takes place when the subject matter is relevant to the personal interests of those involved.

Theory Guiding Practice

Nursing
The *Theory of Unpleasant Symptoms (TOUS)* is a middle-range theory developed by Audrey Gift and Linda Pugh. It acknowledges the oft presence of multiple symptoms while also acknowledging that the management of one of the symptoms may contribute to the management of the other symptom(s) in a multiplicative rather than additive way.

Non Nursing
Baye's Theorem was originally posed in the 1700s by Reverend Thomas Bayes who suggested that 'posterior' conditions (or events) had a high likelihood of happening again- in other words he suggested prediction probabilities. If, in the scientific process, we theorize that a certain thing *should* occur, and then that thing *does* occur, it strengthens our belief in the veracity of that hypothesis. Baye's Theorem is a way to calculate 'degree of believability'.

The emerging body of scientific knowledge in the 1700's split research methodological theory into two distinct camps, Bayesian and Frequentist, according to the way in which one dealt with probability. As stated above, *Bayesian Theory* starts with observed past differences accumulated into "prior, or posterior probabilities". The Bayesian method requires the establishment of prior probability, acknowledges uncertainty, and bases outcomes on choosing the conclusion that best exemplifies the expected patient benefit. Bayesian Theory underpins the post-modern evidence-based clinical medicine model of experimental design. Evidence-based clinical medicine is concerned with probability statistics, specifically the positive predictive value (PPV) of a test or a disorder. Three estimates are required to compute PPV. Positive predictive values (PPV) are comprised of, prevalence, sensitivity, and specificity (Smith, 2000). The *prevalence* of a disorder means the pretest possibility that the patient being diagnosed actually has the disorder in question. The *sensitivity* of the clinical test refers to the probability that the test result will be positive if the person actually has the disorder. The *specificity* of the test refers to the probability that the test result will be negative if the person being diagnosed does not have the disorder. The PPV is calculated according to the following equation (Smith, 2000):

$$\text{PPV} = \frac{\text{Prevalence X Sensitivity}}{\text{Prevalence X Sensitivity} + (1 - \text{Prevalence}) \text{X} (1 - \text{Specificity})}$$

The PPV equation actually discerns the fraction of patients who have the true disorder in question among all the others whose tests yield false positives (Smith, 2000). The *Bayes Method* in its simplest form, is a likelihood ratio, a comparison of how well two hypotheses will predict the data outcome. The hypothesis with the most evidence has the maximum likelihood of predicting the observed data best (Morgan, 2000). Smith contends that in many cases, data alone are not sufficient (Smith, 2000). Current accuracy needs to be assessed against outside information and prior knowledge. Failure to take this information into account in making a differential diagnosis can lead to a serious misrepresentation of the evidence (Smith, 2000).

The Frequentist (sometimes called, Classical), method, is the most common research method in contemporary use. The Frequentist Method is a statistical analytical tool utilizing P values and confidence intervals. P values in clinical tests utilizing the Frequentist Method are analogous to false-positives, (or 1- *specificity*) of the Bayesian Method. The Frequentist, or Classical approach incorporates model parameters, such as population means and standard deviations, and a statement of the null hypothesis. P values have many limitations. P values are dependent upon sample size. P values regarding the null hypothesis may be misinterpreted, a fact that has increased the use of confidence intervals. Randomness in test statistics is elevated to 'gold standard' because Frequentists consider only the observed data in an experiment. Other data might have occurred had the experiment been repeated. These collections of data are called a distribution and are the basis for the calculation of a confidence interval. Table 1 compares Bayesian to Frequentist (Classical) Methods.

Table 1. A Comparison of Bayesian Methods to Frequentist (Classical) Methods

Bayesian Method	Frequentist (Classical) Method
Prevalence, or posterior probability	Confidence intervals
Sensitivity of test	Power of experiment
Specificity	P value
Compilation of expert opinion	Reliability and validity
Subjective	Objective
Qualitative	Quantitative
Amalgamation of subjects	Randomization of subjects

Evidence-Base

Catlin, D., and Murray, T. (1996). Drug testing in sport: Bayes Theorem meets advanced technology. *JAMA, 276*(18), 1471-1472.

Kalyuga, S., (2006). Cognitive Load Factors in Instructional Design for Advanced Learners In *Instructing and Testing Advanced Learners: A Cognitive Load Approach (pp. 1-72)*. New York, NY: Nova Science Publishers, Inc.

Kass, R. (1995). Bayes Factors. Journal of the American Statistical Association, 90(430), 773-795.

Lenz, E., Suppe, F., Gift, A., Pugh, L., and Milligan, R. (1995). Collaborative development of middle-range nursing theories: Toward a theory of unpleasant symptoms. *Advances in Nursing Science, 17*(3), 1-13.

Morgan, T. (2000). Toward evidence-based statistics *Annals of Internal Medicine 132*(6), 507.

Purnell, M.J., (2006). Development of a model of nursing education grounded in caring and application to online nursing education. *International Journal for Human Caring*. 10, 8-16.

Smith, J., Winkler, R., Fryback, D. (2000). The first positive: Computing positive predictive values at the extremes *Annals of Internal Medicine 132*(10), 804-809.

LEADERSHIP SUCCESS SITUATION 2.3

Deann Wilson

Cleft and Craniofacial Team Nurse, Mercy Children's Hospital

Looking beyond the "Obvious" to Find the Root of the Real Problem

I have worked with children my entire 30 year nursing career and learned the value of flexibility with this population, but those lessons paled in comparison to the humbling ones I learned from my current position as Cleft and Craniofacial Team Nurse. Five years ago, I began caring for children with the rare condition of Beckwith-Wiedemann Syndrome (BWS)—an overgrowth syndrome causing macroglossia, somatic and visceral hypertrophy, abdominal wall defects (omphalocele, umbilical hernia, or diastasis recti), neonatal hypoglycemia, among other less common characteristics. The tongue is so large that it frequently protrudes from the mouth and causes dental-skeletal deformities such as open and/ or anterior cross bite. The surgeon I work with has been doing tongue reductions (TR) on this population for many years, but has achieved renown in the last several years from the BWS community who now come from all over the world for the care we both provide. The TR allows children to keep their tongue in their mouth avoiding social stigma and, if done early, can allow the upper jaw to 'catch up' thereby correcting the problems and avoiding jaw surgery as a teen.

When I began my tenure in this position, these patients averaged 5 days in the hospital recovering from this surgery waiting for swelling and pain to reduce enough so that the child could return to drinking and eating. I began simply to observe them, determined to find ways to improve their recovery. The results of these observations and changes in care have resulted in 'layers' of success that collectively have translated to the average stay dropping to 3.4 days in 2008 and a greater overall comfort level expressed by both patient and families.

I first became aware of the high levels of squeamishness involved in the mere mention of the procedure—tongue reduction. Health professionals and lay people alike reacted with a variety of shocked emotions; apparently the tongue is an emotionally charged body part. I, too, reacted at the visual appearance of the newly reduced tongue as it is very swollen oozing blood for several hours after the surgery. Having had the personal experience of biting, burning or having a sore on my tongue and knowing how much these small areas hurt, I immediately assumed the child's crying and irritability was related to extreme pain. Two years into this experience, I cared for a 6 year old who was particularly agitated after surgery and assumed he also was reacting to pain and the effects of the anesthesia, yet he wasn't responding to the pain-alleviating medications given in the recovery room. Since the blood seemed to be getting in the way of our efforts to comfort him and I could not think of another way to relieve his discomfort, out of desperation, I grabbed a suction catheter to clear his mouth. He immediately quieted down. He began to simply point to his mouth when he wanted it cleared. By the time he was transferred to his room, he was suctioning his own mouth! This was an incredibly dramatic response to a simple nursing act!

My eyes were opened as I realized a big source of their "pain" was, in fact, not pain at all but the taste and feel of blood collecting in their mouth. In this immediate post-op period I started routinely suctioning their mouths. By the next morning, the patients are no longer oozing and they do not complain about the build up of saliva in their mouth-they just let it drool out. Older children were able to give me meaningful feedback. Each said the same thing: their tongue didn't hurt, but their throats were very painful. One reason for the throat pain was that these patients have a feeding tube inserted through the nose during surgery whereby liquid pain medicine and nutrition can be given post-op until the child is ready to take it orally. I realized the feeding tube itself caused an element of their throat pain, but also realized that over time a more subtle element of pain was related to a dry throat from not swallowing saliva. (You have probably experienced something like this yourself. Think back to your last head cold when you woke up in the middle of the night with a sore throat because you were mouth breathing.)

I began having the patients lie back several times a day enabling the saliva to drain to the back of the throat allowing them to swallow more easily, thereby keeping their throat moist and more comfortable. By suggesting that the parents remind the child to lay back, this strategy also makes the parents feel like they are really contributing to their child's recovery instead of just sitting back and waiting—a terribly frustrating prospect.

Pain management is an area of continued evolution. Originally patients primarily received IV morphine for pain relief and comfort during the first 24 hours post-op. Acetaminophen and codeine via the feeding tube was usually started later that evening on an every- 4 -hour scheduled basis for the first 2 days before changing it to PRN status and giving as needed. The protocol has evolved so that now the patients are given the first dose of acetaminophen and codeine in the recovery room and IV morphine is given only for break-through pain. This has resulted in a more consistent comfort level with much less need for morphine. Within less than 24 hours, these patients are now frequently able to wean to plain acetaminophen, with codeine used only for break-through pain. Since the acetaminophen can also be given in suppository form, or in a concentrated liquid form that tastes better, the feeding tube can be removed earlier along with a huge source of their discomfort. In my estimation, over the past five years, most of the children have needed very little of the codeine from that point on while being far more comfortable.

While they are usually not ready for oral nutrition at this point, their hydration status can still be maintained with IV fluids. I can usually talk the older children through the early swallowing process by encouraging them to stay relaxed. With the majority of our patients (infants and toddlers), I started to use the same squeeze bottle intended for use with our cleft-palate patients. This squeeze bottle delicately delivers formula or milk toward the back of the mouth where it can be easily swallowed instead of expecting the child with their tongue still swollen to suck on a bottle. I have found early success of children more related to the child's and parent's temperament rather than the actual tongue appearance. I saw that the more anxious and hesitant the parent; the more anxious and hesitant the child.

Another layer of success comes from developing a slide show of pictures detailing the entire recovery process. Before I had amassed these pictures, parents were so stunned at the sight of their child's tongue in the recovery room the typical response was, *"what have I done?"* Once identifying this pattern I began talking about this with them before surgery which had only a subtle effect.

A more dramatic change, however, came after several months of adding pictures to my slideshow when I began hearing, *"it's not as bad as I thought it would be."* A result of significantly reducing parent anxiety levels further helps the patient stay calm and comforted in their recovery period- an important step toward reducing the child's anxiety.

Analysis

While these strategies apply to a very specific population set's problems, what is most important to leave you with is how this has helped me solve many problems that come my way now. I observe, listen, and above all else, look beyond the "obvious" to find the *root of the real problem* as I devise solutions that more accurately address the issue. Research by Heater, Becker and Olson (2007) suggest that patient care based on evidence gleaned from well-designed studies have nearly a 30% better outcome (Bennett, 2007).

A process called CRITICAL EVENT ANALYSIS (CEA), or, ROOT CAUSE ANALYSIS (RCA) allows for data collection and investigation of original (root) causes thus allowing for implementation of corrective actions and sustainability monitoring. In a nutshell CEA/RCA is a process to analyze how a specific event happened and why to hopefully prevent the negative outcome from occurring again given similar circumstances (Rooney, 2004).

Direct care nursing costs can be reduced by improving the quality of nursing care. In this strategy the PNP improved care, reduced pain and accelerated the swallowing process which reduced the need for hospitalization, saving 1.6 patient days of hospitalization per patient (Finkler, 2008).

Leadership Success Strategy

Significant learning takes place when the subject matter is relevant to the personal interests of those involved.

Principle(s)

1) Audio-visual teaching tools reinforce the spoken word.
2) Anxiety is a barrier to learning.
3) Poor/incomplete paperwork can choke off cash flow to the organization.
4) "Vision is perhaps the most powerful principle of leadership" Dominick Flarey (Flarey, 1996).
5) Identify what you want your audience to learn through development of learning outcomes.
6) Direct care nursing costs can be reduced by improving the quality of nursing care.

Theoretical Framework Guiding Practice

Nursing

Sister Callista Roy's Adaptation Theory (Nursing Theory)

A *Grand Theory* that delves into nursing as a science that adapts to people's individual needs. The four major concepts within the theory revolve around physiological, self-concept, role functions, and interdependence. Roy was influenced by the work of Dorothy Johnson, as well as Bertalanffy's General Systems Theory and Helson's Adaptation Theory in the formulation of her own Adaptation Theory.

Roy coined the term, 'veritivity' to describe the truthfulness/ purposefulness of human existence, a concept central to her theory. Roy describes 'adaptation' as…"the process and outcome whereby thinking and feeling persons, as individuals or in groups, use conscious awareness and choice to create human and environmental integration", which is accomplished through four adaptive modes (Roy, 1999) p. 30.

Orem's Self- Care Deficit Theory

Also a *Grand Theory* at work in this situation. Orem's wholly, or partly, compensatory nursing system is represented by the child's taking responsibility for his own suctioning in the post-operative period. (George, 2002).

Non Nursing

Howard Gardner's Multiple Intelligences Theory

A *Grand Theory* that proposes nine (with one more intelligence source under study) intelligences or ways/routes by which humans gain and assimilate information, thereby learning, namely: linguistic, musical, logical-mathematical, visual-spatial, body-kinesthetic, intrapersonal (insight, meta-cognition), interpersonal (social skills, emotional intelligence), spiritual, naturalistic (recognizing patterns nature), (existential is still undergoing research). In the above success strategy, the tongue is modified (body-kinesthetic); the education is prepared with visual graphics that may include (visual-spatial) and (naturalistic) intelligences. The program is delivered by a respected nursing authority (linguistic and interpersonal built upon intrapersonal insight) and based upon the identification of a pattern of parent's behavior (Gardner, 1999).

Evidence-Base

Banning, M. (2004). Conceptions of evidence, evidence-based medicine, evidence-based practice and their use in nursing: independent nurse prescribers' views. *The Journal of Clinical Nursing, 14*, 411-417.

Bennett, C. (2007). Evidence-based practice. *Advance for Nurses, 4*(5), 15-18.

Dunham-Taylor, P., J. (2010). *Financial Management for Nurse Managers: Merging the Heart with the Dollar* (2 nd ed.). Sudbury: Jones and Bartlett Publishers.

Finkler, S. M., M. (2008). *Budgeting Concepts for Nurse Managers*. St. Louis: Saunders/Elsevier.

Flarey, D. (1996). Leading People: A Management Book Review. *Journal of Nursing Administration, 26*(12), 9-11.

Frampton, S., Gilpin, L. and Charmel, P. (2003). *Putting Patients First: Designing and Practicing Patient-Centered Care*. San Francisco: Jossey-Bass.

Gardner, H. (1999). Are there additional intelligences? The case for naturalistic, spiritual, and existentialist intelligences. In J. Kane (Ed.), *Education, Information and Transformation*. Englewood Cliffs, CA: Prentice-Hall.

Rooney, J. V. H., L. (2004). Root Cause Analysis for Beginners. *Quality Progress*. Retrieved from http://www.asq.org/pub/qualityprogress/past/0704/qp070rooney.pdf

Roy, S. C., and Andrews, H. (1999). *The Roy Adaptation Model* (2nd Edition ed.). Stamford, CT: Appleton and Lange.

LEADERSHIP SUCCESS SITUATION 2.4

Darlene Sredl

Paws for Prayer

Wild dog and I go back a number of years. I first saw him late one night in my headlights, limping across the street on three legs. That's odd, I thought, a three-legged dog-but I kept on driving. It was late, after all, and I was on the tail end of an errand that took me into a bad neighborhood.

Still, the mental image of the dog struggling to make his way across the street in front of my car froze in my mind.

The moment of truth came, as I was about to turn onto the highway for home. My conscience nudged me—do you want to go back now and check him out it asked, or would you prefer to have me awaken you at 3 A.M. to come back and try and find him? I knew the 'ole' conscience was right, so I did a 180 on the dark, and deserted (I hoped) street and headed back.

This is ludicrous, I scolded my conscience, and probably futile. How am I ever going to find that dog? It's pitch dark out here!

And, it's not a safe neighborhood…and, if the dog is hurt, he may bite me, then what if I get rabies…and, how am I going to get him in my car, anyway? I am NOT a strong person, conscience, and that's a big dog.

As I pondered these imponderables, the dog shot across my headlights again headed for a chain-link fenced lot. I pulled in after him, blocking the only exit. He was lapping muddy water out of a pothole as I approached him. In the darkness I could not see if his back leg was injured or amputated.

"Oh God…" I sent up a prayer. "I've discussed all the dangers here with your emissary, my conscience. It's late and I'm tired. What do You want me to do?"

While I waited for an answer I cleared a place on the back seat. "OK, Lord. Here's what let's do. I'll invite him into my car. If he comes in I'll know you want me to take care of him- but if he doesn't, Lord, I have to leave. I'm very tired."

With that, I opened the back door and, addressing the dog stammered, "Uh, OK dog…do you want to come in?" With not the slightest hesitation whatsoever the dog sprang three feet up and onto the backseat of my car. As I drove home in my rear-view mirror I saw him curl up into a ball and, in the warmth of the car's heater, fell fast asleep.

Once home, dog let my husband and me examine his wounded leg. Completely denuded of skin and fur, it must have been extremely painful, but he did not even whimper. Gratefully he accepted the food and water we offered, then fell asleep on a blanket that had fallen off the end of our bed. We let him sleep undisturbed.

The next day the vet theorized by the shredded pieces of dried skin hanging like beef jerky from his hip that the injury must have happened about two weeks prior to my finding him. Ribs outlined his thin frame. He probably couldn't have lived more than another day or two the way things were going for him.

As I waited for X-ray results, I heard some of the vet assistants talking outside my cubicle door. "He was lucky that she found him!" "He's one lucky dog, that's for sure!"

"Lucky" dog and I became inseparable after that. I enjoyed taking care of him. He let me bandage and apply salve to his wound and even allowed me to place one, then two lb. weights on his foot pulling down the tendons and stretching out his muscles.

Before long he walked on all fours without a limp and even jumped if his favorite blanket happens to be on top of the bed.

A few years ago I was hemorrhaging profusely from a perforated gastric ulcer that I did not even know I had. My doctor called 911 and, as the EMT's and firemen bounded upstairs to rescue me, Lucky sprang into action protecting me from the intruders.

He puffed up his fur till he looked like a lion. Literally shaking with fear, still he guarded me, baring his snarling teeth and growling business as he trembled. The fire folks stopped dead in their tracks.

"We have to mace him, M'am".

"NO, NO! Don't hurt him," I pleaded, desperately gasping for air.

Lucky was lunging forward, jab-nipping in their direction, still unwilling to let them near me when one of the firemen got an idea. He threw a blanket over Lucky temporarily disorienting him.

Then, two men carried him hammock-fashion into the shower and closed the door. Lucky's display of raw courage under fire protecting me endeared him to me even more. I saved him and now he saved me.

Now, this latest of my health problems has tightened the bond between Lucky and me even further.

I have a broken leg that refuses to heal- it having even the audacity to re-break three more times. Through one operation after another once home, Lucky stands guard on my bed. As he takes up his self- appointed station on his favorite cover next to me, we watch TV together, read, or nap.

My friend Mary came to visit recently. We were sitting by the kitchen table after lunch when Mary gently took my hand and said, "Let's pray together".

Lucky was laying under the table guarding me 'just in case'. As Mary and I held hands through our prayer Lucky suddenly sat bolt upright and put his paw on our held hands! He kept it there for the duration of the prayer! It couldn't have been a coincidence. Lucky's paw-perpendicular across our outstretched hands- completed the cross!

"God looked at everything He had made and He found it very good" (Genesis: 1:31)

Thank you, Lord!

Analysis

There are two strategies at work here; the spiritual and the importance of fuzzy creatures/pets in recovery.

Principle(s)

What goes around, comes around.

"We're all infinite spiritual beings having a temporary human experience. Find that within yourself" Dr Wayne Dyer

"Pray for each client, customer or other business contact by name asking that he may benefit from the dealings you have with him". Dr. Norman Vincent Peale.

Leadership Success Strategy

Whatever one does to further the good of another creature does not go unnoticed.

Theory Guiding Practice

For Strategy One-a Spiritual Focus

Nursing

Jean Watson's Caring Theory

This is the first nursing theory to include a spirituality component in a mind, body, spirit context. Watson's theory encompasses ten 'carrative factors:

1) The formation of a humanistic-altruistic system of human values;
2) Enabling and sustaining faith-hope;
3) Sensitivity toward self and others;

4) Seeking trans-personal connections for helping, and trusting;
5) Allowing and accepting the expression of both positive and negative emotions;
6) Developing creativity in problem-solving caring processes;
7) Enabling and supporting teaching-learning;
8) Factoring in supportive, protective, and/or corrective mental, physical, societal, and spiritual environments;
9) Assisting in the basic process of gratifying human needs amid an environment respecting human dignity;
10) "Maintaining an openness to existential-phenomenological and spiritual dimensions of caring and healing that cannot be fully explained through modern Western medicine." (Watson, 1996, p156-157)

Non-Nursing

Howard Gardner's Multiple Intelligence Theory

His last two intelligence inclusions are: existentialism and spirituality. Existentialism refers to the unexplained way that data or facts can be acquired from non-traditional sources, such as Extra-sensory Perception (ESP), Clairvoyance, and Premonition. Spirituality refers to the studies about spiritual aspects of 'knowing', some of which indicate that people who are 'prayed for' seem to achieve more positive outcomes.

For Strategy Two- Pet Therapy

Beck and Katcha's Pet Facilitated Therapy- Pet Facilitated Therapy (PFT) or animal assisted therapy was researched by Drs. Alan Beck and Aaron Katcha at the University of Pennsylvania School of Veterinary Medicine. They found evidence that petting a dog lowered blood pressure.

A larger study in Australia (1992) among 8000 participants concluded that pet owners were less likely to get heart disease, had lower blood pressure, plasma cholesterol, and triglycerides and were more likely to get more exercise than people who did not own pets.

Evidence-Base

Brodie, S., and Biley, F. (1999). An exploration of the potential benefits of pet-facilitated therapy. *Journal of Clinical Nursing, 8*, 329-337.

Hodge, D. (2007). A Systematic Review of the Empirical Literature on Intercessory Prayer *Research on Social Work Practice 17*, 174-187.

Leibovici, L. (2001). Effects of remote, retroactive, intercessory prayer on outcomes in patients with bloodstream infection: randomised controlled trial. *British Medical Journal, 323*, 1450-1451.

Watson, J. (1996). Watson's theory of transpersonal caring. In P. Walker (Ed.), *Blueprint for Use of Nursing Models: Education, Research, Practice and Administration* (pp. 141-184). New York: National League for Nursing.

LEADERSHIP SUCCESS SITUATION 2.5

Lawrence (Lance) Gutierrez
Neuro-Intensive Brain Attack Unit

Generational Perceptions on Policy

Generations play a big part on how EBP will succeed or fail. Recently I had a conflict with an ER nurse (who is older and has been at the hospital for many years) while I was getting a hand-off communication about a stroke patient ready to be admitted to our Brain attack unit.

He was giving me report and I happened to ask him, *"Did you give him something to eat?"*

"Oh yeah", he told me proudly, *"he ate the whole sandwich and drank a cup of orange juice."*

I asked him, *"Did you do a swallow assessment first?"*

Raising his voice he said, *"No, he seems fine. He can chew well and the only neuro deficit he has is Facial Droop-why do a swallow assessment?"*

I told him, *"Didn't you know that per the Brain Attack protocol all patients with symptoms of stroke should have a swallow assessment before taking anything by mouth"?*

"Well, I read it," he answered, *"but he looks just fine to me—so why do it?"*

Knowing the conflict would just escalate at that point, I told him to send the patient to my floor as soon as possible. Sure enough, while I was doing my assessment, the patient desaturated down to 82%! He was silently aspirating. We got an order for a stat X-ray and eventually sent the patient to ICU. I was really angry that night so I talked to my charge nurse and my nurse manager as well.

The next day we held a focus in-service regarding Brain Attack Protocol identifying the importance of a thorough neuro-assessment and proper swallow screen (which is using a pulse oximeter while we test and observe the patient sipping three times and swallowing a small amount of pudding. If the patient desaturates during this test he is automatically put on NPO status). I am so glad we have these guidelines rooted from Evidence-Based Practice (EBP). They really provide the best outcome for the patient.

That's how EBP works and how it will help us work-looking beyond the accepted norm and systematically and scientifically finding the solution that will produce the best.

Analysis

Utilizing the meta-analyzed research on a given diagnosis, policy/procedures can be formulated that promises to provide the best possible clinical outcomes for the patient based on a generalization of research from many combined samples. No longer can health-care professionals rely on doing things 'the way we have always done them".

Leadership Success Strategy

Two strategies are evident here:

1) Hospital policy and procedure has been developed for the purpose of providing explicit guidelines to ensure patient safety. These policies are only effective if they are followed by all professional practitioners.
2) A verbal confrontation can be avoided by halting the discussion and moving to a new venue. In this situation the patient's welfare was best guarded by prompt admission to the unit where the nurse (who was familiar with the Brain Attack protocol) could assess the patient competently and oversee the care that was necessary.

Principles

"The key to self-mastery is courage" Dr. Norman Vincent Peale.

Theory Guiding Practice

Nursing

Roper-Logan-Tierney Model of Nursing is based upon the work of Nancy Roper in 1976. It is widely used by nurses in both medical and surgical settings and is the most widely used nursing model in the United Kingdom basing activities of daily living (ADLs) as a framework for judging how a patient's life has changed due to illness or hospital admission.

Non Nursing

U.S. Army Commitment to Change Model

This model centers around seven stages to commitment: Contact, awareness, understanding, positive perception, adoption, institutionalization, and internalization. Each stage is a critical juncture in which commitment to change can either be threatened or advanced.

Evidence Base

Army, U. S. (unknown). The Communication Initiative Network: Commitment to Change Model. from http://www.comminit.com/en/node/27210/36

In: Evidence-Based Leadership Success Strategies ...   ISBN: 978-1-62081-104-7
Editor: Darlene Sredl   © 2012 Nova Science Publishers, Inc.

Chapter 3

RETAINING GOOD EMPLOYEES

LEADERSHIP SUCCESS SITUATION 3.1

Beth Vesper

A Lesson Learned

There is a lesson about service that I learned years ago when, as a graduate student, I taught classes for the first time. I learned the same lesson again later in my career while managing a team in a large corporate setting; and I would learn it yet again, in perhaps the most significant way, when I made a career change from business to nursing.

As a young teacher, I naturally had ideas about what kind of teacher I wanted to be, and I wanted to stay true to my ideals. But as my students came to see me one by one outside of the classroom, it became clear that they all expected – and *needed* – something different. Some students sought explicit instructions, some sought broader advice;, some wanted a therapist, some were looking for a mentor, and so on. Simply put, I realized in my dingy university basement office that each student needed me to be a different kind of teacher.

At first, I found this revolving door of needs disorienting. I had not expected that in order to do my job well, I would have to do it differently each time. I wondered whether I was suffering from a lack of focus or sincerity. Gradually I learned that I was uncovering an important key to providing service to people. My philosophies and personal style would always be inherently present to guide my work; but to be effective, I would also have to remain very open, literally to wait and observe, before determining how to approach each unique need.

This idea sometimes seems like it should have been ridiculously obvious, but the impact that this lesson continues to have on my behavior as a leader has been profound. *Each student needed a different teacher; each employee would need a different manager; and each patient would need a different nurse.* Since I was the same person in every case, I found that I would have to learn to be many different teachers, managers, and nurses – in short, I had to be prepared not simply to serve, but first to determine what *type* of service was most needed in each moment. When I finally arrived at the profession of nursing, I saw at once how very important this skill was going to be. Nursing is such a personal profession, one in which I find myself dealing intimately with patients and families at some of the most critical times of their lives. Surely there is no nurse who has not learned that it is just as important to assess the unique socio-psychological needs of each patient and family alongside the more clinical health assessment. We may not always get it right, but we know it is one of our most important tasks. I believe that this lesson keeps reverberating throughout my life because it always holds true when I am in a role to serve others – whether providing instruction, in management, nursing care, or parenting. Within this lesson, I have experienced some of my greatest challenges and greatest rewards. Constantly striving to match my abilities to each unique need, I occasionally find myself tapping into reserves that I did not yet know existed.

Analysis

Bandura stated that much of human behavior is learned through observation and modeling. From this observation one forms an idea of how new behaviors evolve and later on this information can serve as a guide for action. In the above situation the author forms a conclusion based on individual needs observation that requires behavioral modification on her part which she characterizes as, "constantly striving to match my abilities to each unique need." Also of note is that the author is constantly growing in abilities to match each unique need-one of the hallmarks of service learning.

Leadership Success Strategy
Each student needs a different teacher; each employee needs a different manager; and each patient need a different nurse.

Principle(s)
1) Each person is a unique individual with unique needs
2) The first step in the nursing process is ASSESSMENT. Problems must be identified before a solution can be constructed
3) Healthier bottom lines result from effective leadership
4) Within the course of serving, one may be called upon to lead

Theoretical Framework

Nursing
Servant Leadership by Greenleaf is a Mid-Range Theory arising from the premise that other people's needs should take priority and, in an effort to meet those needs, growth will take place (Campbell, 2005; Greenleaf, 1991).

Non-Nursing

The *Social Learning Theory of A. Bandura* is a *(Non-Nursing) Grand Theory* that affects people by encompassing the cognitive learning skills of attention, memory, and motivation for change, with analysis of resultant behavioral frameworks for action (Bandura, 1977, 1986, 1997; Bandura, and Walters, 1963). Bandura's Social Learning Theory is a theory proposing that people learn by observing the behavior of others. If the outcome is viewed as being positive, then people are likely to model, imitate, and adopt the behavior themselves. Behavior is goal directed-the things that we do are to gain anticipated benefits and to avert trouble.

Although a non-nursing theory the concepts apply directly to nursing in that Nursing Education includes a preceptor/preceptee relationship; role modeling; modeling behaviors in accordance with facility policies and procedures; and, adherence to standards of conduct. It also backs behavior prompting adherence to treatment regimens and disease management

Evidence-Base

Bandura, A., and Walters, R. (1963). *Social Learning and Personality Development*. New York: Holt, Rinehart and Winston.

Bandura, A. (1977). *Social Learning Theory*. New York: General Learning Press.

Bandura, A. (1986). *Social Foundations of Thought and Action*. Englewood Cliffs, NJ: Prentice-Hall.

Bandura, A. (1997). *Self-efficacy: The Exercise of Control*. New York: W.H. Freeman.

Campbell, P. R., P. (2005). Servant leadership: A critical component for nurse leaders. *Nurse Leader, 3*(3), 27-29.

Greenleaf, R. (1991). *The Servant as Leader*. Indianapolis: Robert K. Greenleaf Center.

LEADERSHIP SUCCESS SITUATION 3.2

Joan Ruppert

Coaching

As a Clinical Director at a small community hospital, the Float Pool was one of my assigned departments. Liz was an LPN in the Float Pool who was going through some life changes; a recent divorce, custody challenges, children having adjustment problems and an ex-husband who had a terminal illness. She worked on a number of floors in the hospital and had acquired a reputation for being difficult and unprofessional. I made it a habit to make rounds on the Float Pool personnel every day. I found the floors to which the staff had been assigned and visited for just a few minutes to find out how the day was going and to update them on in-services, what was going on in the Float Pool or the hospital in general.

Liz was amazed that I took the time to listen to how her day was going, and to learn of the problems she encountered. Instead of complaining and being "difficult," she began to ask my advice in problem-solving.

We discussed better approaches to problems, and what she could do differently in other situations. She said no one ever took interest in the Float Pool before and the nurses in it felt like step-children; not a real part of the hospital until I became their manager. Liz started taking more of a leadership role among the Float Pool personnel, and stopped complaining. She started problem-solving better in her home situation and decided to go back to school for her RN. Sometimes just a few minutes a day can make a difference in someone's life.

Analysis

Everyone needs to re-evaluate his/her situation periodically. Sometimes we think we are doing the right thing and have found the job of our dreams; but things change and we may discover that what worked over the last few years doesn't seem to be working anymore. We must pause and listen to our inner soul.

What really matters? Am I still meeting my goals? How does family and recreation fit into my life? Nursing is still a female-dominated profession, and as a woman, I have many hats to wear: nurse, manager, wife, mother, sister, daughter, friend, profession member and, possibly- volunteer. How will I put all these roles together to have a meaningful life and career? It's a tough job, but we all need to sort through it and ultimately do what makes us the happiest in each phase of our lives. Sometimes that means making changes and choices, sometimes difficult ones.

Leadership Strategy
Support holes in your knowledge-base with colleague's knowledge.

Principle(s)
Change is inevitable: Nurse leaders must be prepared to lead change. However…there is an inverse proportion between the amount of coaching an individual requires and that individual's value to the organization.

> "Find people who have what you want and ask them to be a mentor for your development"
>
> Karlene Kerfoot

Theory Guiding Practice

Nursing
Eugenia Eng and Edith Parker designed a *Natural Helper Model* unique in significance to health promotion practice. They identify natural 'helpers' who serve as agents complementing the practice of health professionals and thereby are more likely to. facilitate positive outcomes.

Non-Nursing

Schultz's Human Capital Theory involves the total stock of an individual's competencies, knowledge, and personality attributes coupled with the ability to work applied to an invisible yet elastic measuring tape so as to produce a product that has economic value.

Evidence-Base

Becker, G. (1993). Human Capital: A Theoretical and Empirical Analysis, with Special Reference to Education.

DiClemente, R., Crosby, R., and Kegler, M. (Ed). (2002). Emerging Theories in Health Promotion Practice and Research: Strategies for Improving Public Health. San Francisco

Kerfoot, K. (1997). Leadership Principles: Lessons learned. *Dermatology Nursing, 9*(4), 279-280.

LEADERSHIP SUCCESS SITUATION 3.3

Marge Phillips

Expecting Too Much Too Soon

On an 11-7 shift in a large metropolitan hospital, the Supervisor had assigned a new RN to orient with a preceptor. On the new RNs second 11-7 shift the Supervisor gave the new RN a choice between working with a different preceptor or working the shift as an LPN (because he had an LPN license). He chose to work with a different preceptor. When he arrived for his third 11-7 shift, the Supervisor put him in charge. The very surprised new RN accepted the charge position because he did not want to abandon his job, but after giving AM report after a particularly harrowing night shift he turned in his badge and quit!. He said he had worked too hard to lose his license so early in his career. The charge position encompassed too much responsibility and the hospital owed him the proper orientation.

Analysis

The healthcare facility has the responsibility to give a new employee a proper orientation before expecting that employee to take on any responsibility of the magnitude that a charge nurse accepts. In the above situation we might assume that the new RN voiced his dissatisfaction with the assignment to the assigning Supervisor but, to no avail.

The Supervisor did have other options to choose from rather than placing this inadequately-oriented new employee in such a precarious situation.

The Supervisor could have assumed the charge role herself; or, if unable to do that because of the scope of her other supervisory responsibilities, she could have moved another nurse of longer duration employment into the charge position and asked the new RN to assume the replacement nurse's assignment as an LPN.

Because of this thoughtless administrative act, the hospital lost a conscientious new professional by losing the trust of that person and placing his license in jeopardy.

Leadership Success Strategy

Best to move on when trust has been lost in a person or organization

Principle(s)

In order to solve complex problems one has to draw upon reserves of power within.

"Let not your heart be troubled; neither let it be afraid."

Dr. Norman Vincent Peale.

Theory Guiding Practice

Nursing

Bultemier's (1993) Theory of Perceived Dissonance is derived from the Rogerian model exploring disruptions in patterns and breaks in resonancy within the healthcare arena and during the rhythmical evolution of environmental field patterns.

It evolved from *Festinger's Theory of Cognitive Dissonance* (a non-nursing) theory in which there is a tendency for people to seek consistency among their cognitions (i.e., beliefs, opinions). When an inconsistency between attitudes or behaviors (dissonance) is noted, something must change to eliminate the discordance, or dissonance, wherein it is most likely that the attitude will change to accommodate the behavior.

Dissonance theory applies to all situations involving attitude formation and change. It is especially relevant to decision-making and problem-solving.

Two factors affect the strength of the dissonance: the number of dissonant beliefs, and the importance attached to each belief.

Dissonance can be eliminated by: (1) reducing the importance of the dissonant beliefs, (2) adding more beliefs that outweigh the dissonant beliefs, or (3) change the beliefs so that they are no longer inconsistent. Dissonance occurs most often in situations where an individual must choose between two incompatible beliefs or actions.

The greatest dissonance is created when two alternatives are equally attractive Dissonance theory is contradictory to most behavioral theories that predict greater attitude change with increased incentive (i.e., reinforcement).

Non-Nursing

Bruner's Constructivist Theory holds that learners construct new ideas based upon their current or past knowledge. Cognitive structure, or the mental models, that the learner fashions provide meaning to the individual and allow him to make decisions.

Evidence-Base

Brunner, J. Constructivist Theory http://carbon.cudenver.edu/~mryder/itc_data/constructivism.html.

Festinger, L., and Carlsmith, J. and (1959). Cognitive Consequences of Forced Compliance. *Journal of Abnormal and Social Psychology http://psychclassics.yorku.ca/Festinger/, 58,* 203-210.

LEADERSHIP SUCCESS SITUATION 3.4

Marge Phillips

Family Leave Act

As a Supervisor one also needs to consider that some things happen that are out of your control, namely that if a nurse has a life-threatening personal situation to tend to- let them go to tend to it. This life-threatening situation can involve parents, children, or very close friends. President Clinton signed that Family Leave Act legislation into place in 1993. Before this humanitarian Family Leave Act was enacted into law I experienced a situation that I will never forget. I was not allowed to leave my job (attending a meeting) to help my mother when I was notified that I needed to be with her. When I was finally allowed to leave I got word at the front desk , "Your mother died. You are too late!"

Analysis

Family has to come first in situations like these. If an employee comes to you, her/his direct supervisor, with an anxiety-causing situation that needs to be resolved by her presence, allow that employee to divide her patient assignment among two or three other nurses on that shift, give report, and go. One gains nothing in preventing a nurse from leaving when gut-wrenching things are going on in her personal life that could be handled more easily if she were present at home. This is NOT job abandonment- it is a Supervisor making a wise decision.

Leadership Strategy
Family comes first-ALWAYS!

Principle(s)
Proceed with what you KNOW in your heart to be true; let the other chips fall where they may-to be dealt with later.

Theory Guiding Practice

Nursing

Merle Mishel's mid-range Theory of Uncertainty in Illness encompasses uncertainty expressed on many fronts: uncertainty about symptoms - when the patient cannot establish a pattern to his/her symptoms; medical uncertainty – inability to be diagnosed by physician; the uncertainty of daily living in which the variability of illness causes patients to interrupt their lives and sometimes make dramatic decisions to a greater degree, i.e. quit job, avoid outside social contacts, etc. This middle range theory was extracted from and used in clinical practice and is an example of theory which educates and is formed by research.

Merle Mishel measured uncertainty with the Mishel Uncertainty in Illness Scale (MUIS) (1988), a 33 item questionnaire that asks questions valued affirmatively for uncertainty in illness. Scores range from 0 to 3300. Reliability is measured by the same questions asked at various times throughout the patient experience. Evidence from other research has supported Mishel's theoretical model in adults. Uncertainty is directly affected by social support which is thought to decrease apparent difficulties. Several studies have shown that uncertainty may have harmful effects on psychological equilibrium leading to symptoms such anxiety, depression, hopelessness.

Non-Nursing

Dr. Kubler-Ross's Theory of the Stages of Death and Dying proposes that the terminally ill patient goes through five stages of grief:

1) Denial and isolation;
2) Anger;
3) Bargaining;
4) Depression;
5) Acceptance

Dr. Ross interviewed hundreds of patients before compiling these five stages. She adds that not all terminally ill patients go through all five stages.

Evidence-Base

Decision Making Under Uncertainty in Prostate Cancer – 9/30/02 – 06/30/06 NIH/NINR
Interventions for Preventing and Managing Chronic Illness – 9/1/96 – 6/30/06 NIH/NINR
Managing Uncertainty in Older Breast Cancer Survivors – 4/1/99 – 2/29/05 NIH/NCI
Managing Uncertainty in Advanced Prostate Cancer – 3/15/98 – 2/28/02 NIH/NINR/NCI
Elisabeth Kubler Ross Foundation (n.d.) Retrieved September 15th, 2008 from http://www. elisabethkublerross.com

In: Evidence-Based Leadership Success Strategies …   ISBN: 978-1-62081-104-7
Editor: Darlene Sredl   © 2012 Nova Science Publishers, Inc.

Chapter 4

COMMUNICATION FACILITATORS

LEADERSHIP SUCCESS SITUATION 4.1

Marge Phillips

Those Who Dish It out Usually Can't Take it

This incident occurred on a very busy Medical/Surgical unit with census capacity full at 38 patients. No secretary was on duty and staffing was minimal on the evening shift (3-11PM). The Assistant Head Nurse who worked the day shift (7-3) was more interested in giving negative feedback aimed at the 3-11 shift than in any positive reinforcement even though that staff was hardworking, responsible, and gave excellent patient care.

One day the 3-11 shift was presented with a list of concerns relating to specific dates on errors in diet requisitions, an uncollected specimen, etc. *ad infinitum*- but nothing that constituted a life threatening situation.

So, the 3-11 shift personnel decided that they would identify one day shift and collect their own list of missed items. Needless to say, after that list was passed to the Assistant Head Nurse, the problem no longer existed!

Analysis

This situation describes the destructiveness of waging war against all the personnel on a particular shift and of playing 'games'. No one knows the stressors and job requirements on a particular shift better than those who work the shift. Nothing is gained when accusations are levied at an entire shift of workers. While this may be initiated under the guise of a 'quality assurance' project, let *me* assure *you* that there is no intention of quality here; it is bully behavior bordering on professional cannibalism.

My husband owned his own automobile business at one time. Two employees were particularly important to the success of the business; the Sales Manager and the Accountant, but unfortunately those two did not get along. Every day my husband heard derogatory remarks about the Accountant from the Sales Manager that got increasingly nasty as the Sales Manager pushed to get her fired.

I suggested that my husband tell the Sales Manager that he would fire the Accountant... when he (the Sales Manager) found another Accountant to replace her. Of course the Sales Manager had no interest in employee recruitment, so that ended the diatribe against her.

Personnel on each shift should be treated with respect; but since they were not, using the same game-ploy back on the perpetrators can be effective in bringing about a moratorium.

Leadership Strategy

Neutralize a negative situation with positive ricochet action.

Principle(s)

"Power can never be achieved without taking risks."(Hawkins, 1996)

Theory Guiding Practice

Nursing

Carolyn Smith-Marker's Marker Model (1987) connects quality assurance characteristics to provide a framework for dividing nursing standards into the three categories of structure, process, and outcome. She identifies these as essential to maintaining current or creating new competency as well as in responding to a quality assurance corrective action.

Non-Nursing

Hans Selye is originator of the Stress Theory, a grand theory that defines stress as the non-specific response of the body to any demand made upon it. It is about how stress affects people's ability to cope with and adapt to the pressures of injury and disease; defines stress as the non-specific response of the body to any demand made upon it; and defines the person's ability to cope with and adapt to the pressures of injury and disease through the stages of: alarm, resistance and adaptation. All of these findings led Selye to coin the term *General Adaptation Syndrome (G.A.S.)* The body goes through three phases: Alarm reaction; stage of resistance; and finally, stage of exhaustion.

Evidence-Base

Conti-O'Hare, M., and O'Hare, J (June 18, 2001). Don't participate in horizontal violence. *Nursing Spectrum, 13*(12), 6.

Hawkins, J., and Thibodeau, J. (1996). *The Advance Practice Nurse: Current Issues* (4th ed.). New York: The Tiresis Press.

https://www.us.army.mil/suite/page/doc/10713107, A. K. M. P.,

Marker, C. (1987). The marker umbrella model for quality assurance: Monitoring and evaluating professional practice. *Journal of Nursing Quality Assurance, 1*(3), 52-63.

Neylan, T. (1998). Hans Selye and the Field of Stress Research. *Neuropsychiatry Classics*, 10, 230-231.

Perdrizet, G. (1997, October 6). Hans Selye and beyond: responses to stress. *Cell Stress and Chaperone*, 2(4), 214-219.

LEADERSHIP SUCCESS SITUATION 4.2

Ann K. Shelton

Ten Strategies to Mitigate Role Conflict as a Nurse-Family Caretaker

I often feel that I am perceived as demanding and unreasonable when I try to assist other health care workers in the care of my sick loved one. It doesn't matter if my family member is in ICU, outpatient chemo, or the ER or if I am speaking to a unit secretary, physician, nurse, or tech; I always feel as if I am doing something wrong – getting in the way. To be fair, I am sure that hospital staff experience anxiety, frustration, and resentment when questioned by an outsider, particularly a nursing authority figure. My request for information on behalf of my family member could be perceived as a challenge to staff's knowledge or authority in caring for the patient. It also can be considered as a criticism that staff isn't doing its' job. I know that health care workers are, by far, caring souls. So where does this angst come from? Until we can solve the world's relationship problems; I will suggest ten strategies to increase professional courtesy among health care workers. These common sense strategies are intended to benefit the patient and further *esprit de corps* among our beleaguered ranks.

1) Step back, analyze your role critically. Has your family member notified the staff that he/she wants your help?

2) Decide what is reasonable. Define your role in writing if necessary. Try to keep other family members informed so that *you* are the point of contact between the hospital and other family members.

3) Communicate your role to staff. Do not be demanding; do not try to impress staff with your vast knowledge and expertise! Watch your body language!

4) Acknowledge the role conflict that may exist with those whom you are trying to communicate. Let staff know that you will try not to be intrusive.

5) Ask others to define their boundaries. Listen to staff, they often will tell you how they work with patients and families. Interfere with their routine as little as possible, but help as much as they will allow. (Do you really have to put the call light on to get a straw, or do you have permission to get it for your loved-one?)

6) Work with staff that is amenable to you. Without being accusatory, enlist the help of supportive staff to intervene with those who may construct barriers.

7) Adjust to staff who continue to be threatened, keep as low a profile as possible, but continue to support your loved-one. Do not be intimidated to leave because of the insecurities of some of the personnel.

8) Consider the consequences of pressing an unpopular position; but know that sometimes it is necessary to persist.
9) Attempt to set up a routine that most of the staff can work with. Some staff will welcome your help with the morning bath, some will prefer that you arrive after the bath and linen change is complete. Is that something you can compromise about?
10) Ask for feedback if problems are identified.

Analysis

Being a professional, especially a highly educated professional, can be subtly intimidating to professionals caring for your loved one even though you do not intend it to be intimidating. Nursing staff may feel inadequately prepared educationally although they may excel clinically.

They may have an abundance of 'tacit' knowledge gained from experience that is difficult to access and share verbally but easy to demonstrate it's effectiveness in practice. This realization may cause them to feel and act defensively to your suggestions.

As a family member your role is primarily one of emotional support. Although you may choose to provide direct care in addition to this emotional support, the communicative collaboration begins on admission when the 'rules' of care are first established.

Leadership Strategy
Establish a doctrine of collaboration early on.

Principle(s)
Use collaborative communication techniques.
"Every morning I ask the Lord to lead me to someone during the day whom I may help." Dr. Norman Vincent Peale.
Transformational behaviors can be cultivated through relationship building.

Theory Guiding Practice

Nursing
Comfort Theory by Katherine Kolcaba, RN is a mid-range theory. Holistic comfort is defined as the immediate experience of being strengthened through having the needs for relief, ease, and transcendence met in four contexts of experience (physical, psycho-spiritual, social, and environmental).

The comfort theory purposes that, when patients and their families are more comfortable, they engage more fully in health-seeking behaviors that include internal behaviors, external behaviors, or even a peaceful death while the institution benefits in such areas as reduced cost of care and length of stay, increased patient satisfaction, enhanced financial stability, and more positive publicity.

NURSING #2. The Theory of Care-Giver Stress by Pao-Feng Tsai, Ph.D., RN.

- This Middle-range theory proposed that the object of the burden in caregivers will be the most important stimulus that might lead to caregiver stress.
- That higher- perceived caregiver stress will result in ineffective responses in four modes: poor functioning, lower self-esteem/mastery, lower role enjoyment, and less marital satisfaction.
- Depression might be the direct outcome of caregiver stress on the four adaptive modes.

Non-Nursing

Havelock and Zotlow's Change Theory is a grand theory based on a person's moving through six stages:

1) RELATE- identify key relationships integral to obtaining change and, define your own role in the process.
2) EXAMINE- to better understand the problem. Turn desired care into solvable problems and work one on one with the person to obtain meaningful, obtainable goals. Discuss mutual benefits of changes.
3) ACQUIRE- relevant resources to help but don't be a 'know it all'
4) PUT KNOWLEDGE INTO ACTIONS- be committed to positive solutions.
5) EXTEND DEEPER AND WIDER ACCEPTANCE.
6) RENEW-solidify the new 'norm' in place, but be aware that change is on-going.

Evidence-Base

Kolcaba, K and Fisher, E. (1996). A holistic perspective on comfort care as an advance directive. *Critical Care Nursing Quarterly*, 18(4), 66-76, p. 68.]

Kolcaba, K. (1992). Holistic comfort: Operationalizing the construct as a nurse-sensitive outcome. *Advances in Nursing Science*, 15(1), 1-10, p. 6.

Kolcaba, K. (2007). *The Comfort Line.* http://www.thecomfortline.com.

Kolcaba, K., Tilton, and C. Drouin, C. (2006). Comfort theory: A unifying framework to enhance the practice environment. *Journal of Nursing Administration, 36(11), 538-544.*

Systems Implementation and Diffusion/Adaption of Innovation. (n.d.) Retrieved September 15,2008, from http://www.personal.psu.edu/mrs311/planned change.htm

Tomey, A. M., and Alligood, M. R. (2006) *Nursing Theorists and Their Work.* Philadelphia, PA: Elsevier's Health Sciences.

Tsai, P.F. (2003). A middle range theory of caregiver stress. *Nursing Science Quarterly*, 16, 137-144.

University of Arkansas for Medical Science (2008). College of Nursing. http://nursing. uams.edu/directory.

LEADERSHIP SUCCESS SITUATION 4.3

Paul Pfennig

Avoiding Confrontation

It was a busy night on our medical-surgical floor. I had 8 patients, including several post-op. Our hospital had no support staff overnight; we drew our own labs, administered respiratory treatments, completed pharmacy duties for any new admissions, and dispensed dietary needs (which consisted of going to the refrigerator/freezer for overnight nutrition). One nice aspect of the evening was that I had one medical technician who was assigned with me to care for patients. About midnight, my technician indicated all the patients were "good"; pm care was completed. She asked if she could take her meal break. I didn't mind; this technician was a great worker and pleasant. She was one that you hoped would be assigned to your team more often. Meanwhile, I was still busy with passing medications, treatments, charting, etc. After she was done eating, I noticed she was in the forms room on the phone talking to her fiancée. Her fiancée was at another base elsewhere in the world. Because the Defense Switched Network (DSN) service could connect these two without cost, I didn't mind; she was on her lunch break and it is common to utilize DSN service for morale reasons. However, the phone call stretched on and on- reaching into the 1 ½- 2 hour range.

I remained very busy, bogged down with tasks I could have delegated, had I someone to delegate them to. Finally, I entered the forms room and asked that she pass fresh water and check drains, etc. on all our patients. She quickly finished her phone call and completed the tasks as I had asked. Shortly afterwards she was back in the forms room, talking on the phone. I came back in the room and asked if she had completed all the tasks.

She replied, "Yes".

I gave her something else to do. The next thing I knew I was being asked by another technician what I had done to make my technician cry. I spoke with my technician; she was crying and frustrated with me, concerned that I thought she wasn't doing a good job.

I learned something very important that day about myself and about communication. I was actually upset that she was taking more than the time allotted for break, while other staff continued to work hard. I needed to confront this behavior directly by saying, "You have used the phone enough for tonight, you need to find something else productive to do". Instead, I chose a passive-aggressive technique to communicate my desire for her to be off the phone. This technique resulted in hurt feelings and additional time lost. In the future, I will endeavor to find the real reason I am frustrated with my co-worker's behavior and act appropriately by confronting the behavior directly.

I apologized to the technician for giving her that impression, I restated the "break" policy and reaffirmed that she was one of the best technicians we had.

(The views expressed in this article are those of the author and do not reflect the official policy or position of the United States Air Force, Department of Defense, or the U.S. Government).

Analysis

This scene demonstrates one of the most common communication errors we make as healthcare professionals and as ordinary persons engaged in communication. When it is difficult to confront the real issue that is causing the problem; and therefore we are unable to communicate the real issue, we sometimes decide to communicate another (not quite so controversial) tangential issue hoping to take the spotlight away from having to be honest about the real source of our frustration. This sends a not-so-honest message to the receiver and, oftentimes, sends the wrong message entirely as evidenced in the situation just described.

Don't beat around the bush! Phrase your verbal communication as succinctly as possible so that you are talking about the issue at hand. In the situation described above the author became increasingly annoyed when one of his assistants spent a long time on the phone with her boyfriend in the armed services in another part of the world. Although the author said that the assistant did a good job with her care for patients, she wound up thinking that he, her immediate supervisor, did not think she was doing a good job. Love is blind-sometimes even to the clock. It is possible that the time seemed to stand still as she continued the conversation-not even noticing that she had taken more than her allotted amount of break time.

Leadership Strategy

Use every interaction whether face-to-face or virtual as an opportunity to acquire and share knowledge (https://www.us.army.mil/suite/page/doc/10713107).

Principle(s)

Define the task: Right person (match task to individual's abilities; define expectations to delegate; reach agreement to accept responsibility and authority; monitor performance and provide specific feedback (Sullivan, 2009).

Theory Guiding Practice

Nursing

Ida Jean Orlando (Pelletier) conceived the mid-range theory of the Dynamic Nurse-Patient (person) Relationship Function, Process and Principle around five major concepts:

1) The organizing principle of professional nursing function.
2) The patient's (person's) presenting behavior-problematic situation.
3) Immediate reaction-internal response.
4) Deliberative nursing process of Reflective Inquiry.
5) Improvement-resolution.

Non-Nursing

Harbans S. Bola constructed a grand theory called the CLER Model. Bola was heavily influenced by Lewin, Rogers, Lippitt, and Havelock in his development of the CLER Model, an epistemic triangle.

C= configuration of social relationships within and between systems in the planner and adopter roles.

L= Linkage to carry communication between planner and adopter.

E= Environment(s) inside and around the system involved in the change transaction.

R= Resources dedicated by the planner system for enabling implementation and to the adopter system for incorporating the change,

Evidence-Base

Alligood, M. R., and Tomey, A. M. (2006). *Nursing Theory: Utilization and Application*. St. Louis, Missouri: Mosby.

Bhola, H. S. (1994). The CLER Model: Thinking Through Change. *Nursing Management, 25* (5), 59, 62-63.

Lehman, K. J. (2008). Change Management: Magic or Mayhem? Journal for Nurses in Staff Development, 24 (4), 176-184.

Sullivan, E., and Decker, P. (2009). *Effective Leadership and Management in Nursing (7th Edition ed.)*. Upper Saddle River, NJ: Pearson: Prentice-Hall.

LEADERSHIP SUCCESS SITUATION 4.4

Traci Wagoner and Darlene Sredl

Silence Is Not Always Golden

I was asked by my unit director to participate in a committee to implement and improve new computerized charting. In preparation, I immersed myself studying the new database and asked the staff on my floor how they felt about the change. By the time of the first meeting I felt very prepared with plenty of ideas and constructive criticism.

But, I was dismayed by one team member who was negative about almost every suggestion I had. Needless to say, I was disappointed and a little angry after the meeting.

Now...I am not a newcomer to managing people. I have a broad base of experience in management within people-intensive jobs. In addition to a BSN, I also have a degree in business and had previously worked several years in database development. I was a Sergeant in the Marine Corps spending half my time in surveillance/ reconnaissance and the other half processing new military applicants. Later, I worked within a global company as an Account Coordinator. I knew how to work with people and had the education and experience to back up my ideas. The question was, how do I convince the naysayer of this?

I decided that the best course of action was to be direct. I asked her to join me for lunch one day. Through the course of our conversation, I brought up my disappointment at the last meeting and asked her what her motivation was. She was surprisingly taken aback. She explained that she was not aware that she had come off so negatively. She went on to explain that she was extremely nervous about the upcoming change because no one on her floor was comfortable with computers including her. So, she wasn't trying to dismiss my ideas; she was desperately trying to keep things from changing and moving forward.

I was so glad that we had this conversation. Not only did I get to express my feelings, I also had a much better understanding of some of the barriers other floors' personnel would experience in the transition. I offered to help her and her staff as much as needed and we ended up collaborating on other projects in the future.

The moral of this is SPEAK UP! Only you can allow yourself to feel belittled. If you don't stand up for yourself, no one will.

Analysis

Co-workers who have had limited exposure to research principles, or in developing critical thinking skills to use in new situations may resist change. It is the nurse leader's responsibility to integrate all the elements of evidence into user-friendly information that co-workers can absorb and assimilate into their own sphere of comprehension.

Leadership Strategy
Anticipate barriers to idea acceptance and use non-judgmental knowledge sharing to overcome them.

Principle(s)
Avoid turf-based opposition to change by recognizing that knowledge is power when it is shared.

Reject rejection!

Theory Guiding Practice

Nursing
Nathaniel's Moral Reckoning in Nursing (A Grounded Theory) identifies a three-stage process in confronting and engaging conflict. First there is a Stage of Ease embodying comfort and congruence of values. When a situation arises that challenges the nurses' core beliefs it forces the nurse into the Stage of Resolution through which the nurse must choose among values to either give up lobbying for or to make a stand in defense of them. The final, Stage of Reflection involves examining the process through memory, story-telling, conflict resolution examination, and living with the consequences of action(s).

Non-Nursing
Patricia Cross's Adult Learning Model holds that for effective learning to occur one must capitalize on the experience of, adapt to the aging limitations of the adult learner, and challenge the adult learners to move to increasingly advanced stages of personal development. Adult learners need choices in the availability and organization of the learning programs. This theory includes adults as managers needing choices among alternatives when

pondering management decisions. Cross devised two conceptual frameworks in further development of the original model for adult learning. The first is called the Chain of Response (COR) model that explores personality types, self actualization and expectation of reward as composites of motivation. The second is called the Characteristics of Adult Learners (CAL) model that compares differences between adults and children regarding personal and situational issues that would be involved so that alternative teaching strategies could be developed.

Evidence-Base

McCarthy, J., and Deady, R. (2008). Moral Distress Reconsidered. *Nursing Ethics, 15*(2), 254-262.

Zuzelo, P. (2007). Exploring the moral distress of registered nurses. *Nursing Ethics, 14*(3), 344-359.

LEADERSHIP SUCCESS SITUATION 4.5

Jenn Sredl

Hostile Communications that Have their Place!

I work as an RN in Cardiac Rehab. One day a patient came in with his adult daughter who became belligerent requesting her father's stress test results, since the doctor had not given the results to the patient.

The RN stated she could not release these results to her and that she needed to call the doctor for that permission. The daughter then requested a copy of the stress test since it was in her father's chart. The RN said she could not do that either. The daughter began yelling and pointing her finger at the nurse demanding that she make a copy for her! She also wanted the unit manager's name and phone number. Rehabilitation patients were exercising within full earshot of this disruptive scene. The daughter then escalated the situation by raising her voice louder and swearing, making the nurse so nervous she was visibly shaking!

I stepped in to corroborate what the other nurse told her, however she kept getting louder and louder. There is no security at this cardiac rehab unit because it is off-site from the hospital. I said, "Do I need to call the police?" loudly enough for the daughter to hear and, hopefully, leave. But…that did not work and she kept up her tirade against the nurse. Finally, more authoritatively, I picked up the phone and announced, "I *am* calling the police!"

"No, don't do that." The daughter replied. "We are leaving." With that, she left.

Analysis

Bullies come in all shapes and sizes. What they want is whatever they want and they usually are prepared to strong-arm (at least verbally) whoever gets in their way. Nurses know that test results are confidential and that chart documents cannot be copied at someone's request or whim.

Nurses must stand their ground in living up to their ethical responsibilities...but they do not have to stand that ground alone. Police are the champions of our safety and should be called upon in a disruptive situation such as the one described above. Verbal assaults sometimes escalate into physical confrontations-possibly with dire consequences. Keep the situation from escalating by calling upon the authorities entrusted with keeping the peace. You may see, as in the situation above, that the act and the verbalized intention of calling the police is enough to dissipate the threat.

Leadership Strategy
Speak softly but carry a big stick—and be prepared to use it.

Principle(s)
Know that you are under attack;

- Identify what kind of attack you are facing;
- Know how to make your defense fit the attack;
- Follow through confidently.

Theory Guiding Practice

Nursing
Butcher's Theory of Kaleidoscoping in Life's Turbulance (1993) was originally derived from Roger's Science of Unitary Human Beings, Chaos Theory, and Csikszentmihalyi's Theory of Flow. It is concerned with focusing on and maintaining harmony and positive patterns amid life's turbulent events and transforming them into a state of equilibrium when possible.

The visual image invoked by a kaleidoscope is meant to symbolize the shifting flow of patterns, sometimes turbulent patterns, that one experiences when looking through a kaleidoscope. The theorist hopes the kaleidoscope image conjures images of scattered patterning, forging a solidifying resolve and once again restoring harmony.

Non-Nursing
Donohew, Palmgreen and Duncan's Activation Model of Information Exposure which evolved from studies of sensory deprivation, holds that humans seek change and newness in moderate amounts. When an individual is engaged in information-seeking behavior and the situation goes beyond his 'processing state' (high arousal state), he will reduce his input need for variety.

Evidence-Base

Butcher, H. (1994). The unitary field pattern portrait method: Development of research method within Roger's science of unitary human beings. In Madrid and Barrett's (Ed.), *Roger's Scientific Art of Nursing Practice* (pp. 397-425). New York: National League for Nursing.

Butcher, H. (1998). Crystallizing the process of the unitary field pattern portrait research method. *Visions: The Journal of Rogerian Nursing Science, 6,* 13-26.

Butcher, H. (2005). The unitary field pattern portrait research method: Facets, processes and findings. *Nursing Science Quarterly, 18,* 293-297.

Butcher, H., and Parker, N. (1988). Guided imagery within Martha Rogers' science of unitary human beings: An experimental study. *Nursing Science Quarterly, 1*(103-110).

Donohew, L., Palmgreen, P., and Duncan, J. (1980). An activation model of information exposure. *Communication Monographs, 47,* 295-303.

Quine, L. (1999). Workplace Bullying in NHS Community Trust: Staff Questionnaire Survey, *British Medical Journal 318*(7178), 228-232.

LEADERSHIP SUCCESS SITUATION 4.6

Peter Tehua Kao

Addressing Hostile Communication

Julie was always hostile to me. No matter what I did, I could not please her; so, I chose to avoid her. I had hoped that the trouble would go away as long as I did not take it seriously, but that was just "wishful thinking". I wondered if my silence was the message telling her that her behavior was acceptable.

I knew I would lose my temper sometime soon, but I tried to avoid that. I knew that would destroy my professional image, making people think that I was unable to solve a conflict. Moreover, she might exact revenge, and this could create more battles in the future.

Someone said, "Hostile people hate themselves. That is the only reason why they behave in that way." First, I became empathetic and offered to help her. Second, I knew I needed to be kind. Chinese people say, "Nobody will slap a smiling face." Dale Carnegie said, "A spoonful of honey will catch more flies than a gallon of poison." Both kernels of wisdom support the idea that kindness is the key to open or disarm someone's heart.

Third, I looked for a "magic moment" that would provide me an opportunity to let Julie know how I felt about her hostility to me. Finding such a moment takes time. People usually cannot "schedule" that moment. One has to remain open to the opportunity as it presents itself.

One day I saw Julie in a grocery store. I smiled as I greeted her and gave her a hug. My conversation started casually, talking about her family and pastimes. At the beginning of the conversation, Julie did not really "open herself up." Her use of sporadic "mean language" was evidence of her defensiveness. As the conversation lingered, she began to disclose that her single-parent life was very hard on her recently.

As I listened to her, her disclosure confirmed my first assumption: She was not happy about her own personal situation, and her hostility to other people was a "transformation" of unhappiness. I wanted her to be sure of one thing: I was eager to know what I could do to make her life easier. When I observed Julie's appreciation non-verbally, I knew I had the "moment" I was seeking. I frankly told Julie that I wanted her to be my best friend, but there was something standing in our way, making us unable to be close to each other. "What is it?" She crossed her arms in front of her chest and did not make eye contact with me. Regardless of her offensive "style" as usual, I took my perseverance, talking to her to send my message: "Julie, I want to be your friend and see you succeed."

Julie has never been hostile toward me since, and I never abandoned my promise to her. Like watering a plant, I never stopped caring about her. It might be easier for me to find other people who do not like Julie, and "circle" with them trying to push Julie out of this working environment. However, someone like "Julie" is everywhere. We might be able to get rid of our Julies, but we will surely come across another one in the future. A positive attitude helps us learn how to get along with hostile people.

The way I cope with hostile communication is to take the courage to confront it, and my goal is to dissolve the hostility permanently, not just temporarily. The success of achieving my goal needs the cooperation of the right moment and right approach. Instead of being judgmental, I use empathy. "Be a friend if you want a friend." Helping each other is to create a win-win situation, and pushing someone to be out of business is to claim a war. "Love conquers everything" and is the best policy for hostile communication.

Analysis

There are many reasons why a person appears to be aloof or 'uppety' and we cannot expect to know those reasons. For an isolated incident we may conclude that the person is having a 'bad day', or has just received some distressing news. For a chronic issue in which the person appears to be aloof or hostile most of the time, we may conclude that the attitude prevents the person from having to get too close emotionally to the other person initiating the conversation. It could also be that the aloof person does not trust people-possibly having been emotionally hurt earlier in life and has since built up a wall in order to isolate herself from that painful experience occurring again. Best not to personalize the issue. Try, sometimes repeated trying is necessary, to demonstrate by your words and actions a pattern of consistency. This will help the person come to trust you.

Leadership Strategy
Smiles are contagious-start an epidemic!

Principle(s)
People don't care how much you know until they know how much you care.

Mentally see quietness and calmness starting in your head, draining all tensions from your mind. In turn consciously rest each muscle and visualize automatic emotional control taking over. (Paraphrased from Dr. Norman Vincent Peale).

Theory Guiding Practice

Nursing

Conti O'Hare's Q.U.E.S.T. Model of Reflective Practice is an acronym that stands for:

- Question - Identification of the trauma
- Uncover - Reflect on the experience of the trauma
- Experience - Recognize feelings about the experience
- Search for meaning - Determining the meaning of the experience in one's life
- Transform and transcend - Resolve the trauma and become a "wounded healer"

This model centers on the nurse as a 'wounded healer'-one who has experienced some sort of trauma or sadness and is able to use that experience in the process of caring for another.

Non-Nursing

Filley's Interpersonal Conflict Negotiation Model advocates striving for a 'win-win' resolution among conflict participants.

Evidence-Base

Conti-O'Hare, M. (2002). Walking wounded to wounded healer. *Nursing Spectrum*, 14, (10), 26-27. (May 20, 2002).

Conti-O'Hare, M., O'Hare, A., Scarolla, L., Greco, P. and Murray, T. (2000). Transforming nursing with love: Nurses caring for themselves and each other. *Beginnings: The Official Newsletter of the American Holistic Nurses' Association*, 20 (4), 1, 13.

Conti-O'Hare, M. (1996). A descriptive analysis of the therapeutic use of self with addicted clients in early recovery: The expert nurse's perspective. *Journal of Addictions Nursing*, 8, 81-84.

Miller, E. and Conti-O'Hare, M. (1998). An evaluation of a patient centered care model. *Federal Practitioner*, 4, 52-61.

LEADERSHIP SUCCESS SITUATION 4.7

Lanette Tanaka

Advice for Administrative Personnel/Managers Planning Effective Meetings (with Special Content for Staff Members Who Don't Want to Comply with Policy and Procedures)

Getting "difficult staff members" to comply with policy and procedures can be a challenge for any nurse manager. In one of my creative moments, I tried something new.

Realizing that just "telling" the staff member, who resists following policy and procedure was not always effective, (and it sometimes made them feel like I was "picking on them."), I called a mandatory meeting of all nursing staff in which I asked all members to sign-in (which holds everyone accountable for information that is shared). I then distributed my planned agenda, which included a copy of the new policy and procedures for our unit so they could be reviewed before the meeting. In my pre- planning, I took my senior nursing staff members aside ahead of time and asked them to bring up specific questions and ideas regarding the new policy and procedures (that I specifically wanted them to address during the meeting).

By doing this, in addition to planning the agenda, I also planned what would be addressed before the meeting so that the discussion would emphasize major points *brought up by the staff*, while relieving me of some of the administrative responsibility of doing all the talking. I found that very often, challenging staff members find it easier to get on board and comply (with new policies, etc.) when they identify with positive-attitude staff members who want to follow the policies and procedures as they have been laid out. The difficult /non-compliant staff member realizes for themselves they had better "get on board with doing things right" based on positive peer pressure.

Analysis

This method involves not only planning the agenda but also "planting" material and questions that will be covered by others during the discussion. There are times when the message from a single presenter tends to be discounted in the minds of some attendees, but it is more difficult to 'tune out' on several different colleagues who are offering a fresh perspective on the content.

Leadership Strategy
Plan your work, then work your plan.
Identify positive personality characteristics of people you admire, then, emulate them.

Principle(s)
The adult has a need to know why they should learn something. The adult has to consider it important to apply the effort to acquire a new skill, knowledge or attitude.

Champions, or early adopters, are helpful in conveying an attitude of acceptance to new ideas, skills, knowledge or attitudes.

THEORY GUIDING PRACTICE

Nursing

Brian Hodges' Health Career Model is concerned with the person within a social context whether that person is a patient or a colleague. The 'person' in question has already established a biography and that biography influences his physical and psychological frame of reference.

Non-Nursing

Bion's Countertransference is a Theory that posits the claim that groups often employ psychologically-rooted organizational maneuvers designed to divert attention from more anxiety-producing topics and can be used as a tool of "deepened understanding of the psychological reality of organizational life." (Stein, P10).

Evidence-Base

Hodges, B. (1997). Hodges' Health Career Model.
Jones, P. (2004). Viewpoint: Can informatics and holistic multidisciplinary care be harmonised? *British Journal of Healthcare Computing and Information Management, 21*(6), 17-18.
Stein, H. (2007). Insight and Imagination: A Study in Knowing and Not-Knowing in Organizational Life. Lanham: University Press of America, Inc.

LEADERSHIP SUCCESS SITUATION 4.8

Steve Sredl
President/CEO, Sealco, Inc.

Social Communications

"Learn as you go, but act like you know."

Analysis

Leaders must project confidence and authority. They have the authority to make decisions and must take responsibility for the decision's consequences. In attempting to acquire knowledge/evidence pertinent toward solving a problem, a leader may have to compromise on time devoted to fact-finding and just move forward with the decision process. We call this 'satisficing'. It is not 'satisfying' as it might be if enough time were allowed to ferret out more evidence. Satisficing is a management term for 'making do and making decisions with what you have learned thus far."

Leadership Strategy
Project confidence while keeping an open mind.

There are those who do not know that they do not know for they are asleep;
There are those who know that they do not know for they have awakened;
There are those who know that they know for they are enlightened– follow them.

An old Persian saying- Author unknown

Principle(s)

Attitudes can turn problems into blessings:

Comes the Dawn by Veronica A. Shoftstall

After a while you learn the subtle difference
Between holding a hand and chaining a soul,
And you learn that love doesn't mean leaning
And company doesn't mean security,
And you begin to understand that kisses aren't contracts
And presents aren't promises,
And you begin to accept your defeats
With your head held high and your eyes open,
With the courage of a man (the grace of a woman), not the grief of a child
You learn to build your roads
On today-because tomorrow's ground
Is too uncertain for plans, and futures have
A way of falling down in mid- flight.
After a while you learn that even sunshine
Burns if you get too much.
So, you plant your own garden and decorate
Your own soul, instead of waiting
For someone to bring you flowers. And you learn that you really can endure,
That you really are strong
And you really do have worth
And you learn, and learn,…and you learn,
With every goodbye you learn.

Ann Landers
St. Louis Post Dispatch March 30, 1985

Theory Guiding Practice

Nursing

Fitzpatrick's Rhythm Model combines recognition with communication patterns permitting thoughts to be shared through language. Recognition means that new observations are mentally placed into previously classified categories based on observed characteristics. Those categories are constantly changing based on new input, hence, "learn as you go".

Non Nursing

Collins and Stevens' Cognitive Theory of Inquiry Teaching involves a method of discovery instruction. Discussion and trial statements used in discussion help expose inaccuracies and misconceptions in the topic under discussion. Positive examples lead to a shift in thinking. This theory follows the Scientific Method in the following format:

Question→ hypothesize→investigate→analyze→model→evaluate

Evidence-Base

Collins, A. (1983). A cognitive approach to inquiry teaching *Reigeluth, C.M. (Ed). Instructional Design Theories and: an Overview of their Current Status* (pp. 247-277). Hillsdale, NJ: Lawrence Erlbaum Associates, Publishing.

In: Evidence-Based Leadership Success Strategies …
Editor: Darlene Sredl

ISBN: 978-1-62081-104-7
© 2012 Nova Science Publishers, Inc.

Chapter 5

BECOMING AN ARCHITECT FOR MORAL GOOD WITHIN YOUR SPHERE OF INFLUENCE

Author wishes to remain Anonymous[*]

LEADERSHIP SUCCESS SITUATION 5.1

Another Point of View about Rape and Abortion

One evening she and her friend double-dated, drank some alcohol, and she wound up unconscious on a couch in one of the men's apartment. Her friend hurriedly woke her up and said "We have to get out of here". Once safely in the car, the friend told her that she witnessed her date taking advantage of her. When the girl's friend tried to stop him, he threw her down and proceeded to have his own way. The friend then took a frying pan and knocked him out cold. They went to the police station to file a report but no follow-up was ever carried out by the police.

Several weeks later she found out she was pregnant and knew it must have been due to this encounter because she had not had sexual relations with any other man. The police were of no help, telling her that there was no way that they could prove that it wasn't consensual (even though there was a witness!) and that it was basically the man's word against hers. The following is in her words:

"I was upset thinking that my first child was going to be a child conceived by date- rape and not with a man that I loved. I contemplated an abortion, but decided that no matter what he had done to me I would love this baby no matter what. This was a very hard decision because I knew I might have to deal with the man that did this horrific thing to me for the rest of my life, but I did not care. I cared more about this little thing growing inside of me. So, I did not get an abortion, and my son is now a handsome, smart, pre-schooler!" Since that time, as a nurse, I have had an opportunity to share my thoughts with other girls in similar situations providing a real-life story that rape does not have to end in abortion!

---

[*] This story was told to me by a young woman who did not want to be identified.

Analysis

This situation is certainly reprehensible. It changed a young girl's life forever. But…instead of rushing into a major decision (possibly, like having an abortion) this young woman contemplated the effects that such a rash move would have on her, on her life, and on the life of her unborn child. She chose life and went on to give birth to her baby. As she says, "my son is now a handsome, smart, pre-schooler! Since that time, as a nurse, I have had an opportunity to share my thoughts with other girls in similar situations providing a real-life story that rape does not have to end in abortion!" It bears repeating.

Leadership Strategy
Do no harm.

Principle(s)
Aspire to higher things or a higher purpose.

Theory Guiding Practice

Nursing
1) *Corley's Theory of Nurse Moral Distress*-Moral distress has been defined as psychological disequilibrium associated with knowing the right course of action to take in a given situation but possibly being forced to act in a manner that contravenes personal and professional values. In a professional situation nurses' unresolved ethical problems are often linked to high staff turnover and burnout. In personal situations it may lead to emotional exhaustion, powerlessness, anxiety and dread. Situations of ethical conflict leading to moral distress can be alleviated somewhat by discussing proposed interventions with trusted colleagues. Many places of healthcare employment have counseling benefits offered free of charge included in their benefits package. This can be one option used to explore alternatives of action before action.

2) *Polk's Theory of Resilience*- Resilience involves the capacity to maintain competent functioning in the face of major life stressors. There are two essential components in the development of resilience:

   a) The presence of biological, psychological, and environmental risk factors that increase an individual's vulnerability.
   b) The presence of protective factors that help an individual counter and resist the effects of personal vulnerabilities and hazards.

In addition to the rape situation above, the resilience theory can be applied in multiple situations such as, substance abuse, victims of terrorist attacks, refugees from war torn countries, and migrant families and adopted children from a long-term institutionalized setting.

The major constructs (or, defining characteristics of) resilience are:

- *The dispositional pattern*-Pattern of physical (Constitution and genetic factors) and ego- related psychosocial (sense of self and personal compete) attributes.
- *The relational pattern*- Pattern of roles and relationships which includes both intrinsic (placing value on intimate or close relationships), and extrinsic (placing value on broader social network aspects) relationships.
- *The situational pattern*-Pattern of problem solving skills, cognitive skills and attributes that indicate a capacity for action in facing a situation.
- *The philosophical pattern* -Pattern of personal beliefs marked by a sense of self understanding, a belief that self knowledge is valuable, and a belief that lives are worthwhile and meaningful

Non-Nursing

Greenleaf's Servant Leadership expands from the traditional nursing principles of caring, service, growth and serving the health and needs of others. Servant leadership occurs when, in the course of serving, other people's (or, in this case the fetus's) needs take priority over our own. Servant Leadership means that even the least advantaged in our society benefit from the Servant sacrifices.

Evidence-Base

Ahern, N (June 2006). Adolescent resilience: an evolutionary concept analysis. *Journal of Pediatric Nursing, 21*, Retrieved February 3, 2008, from http://www.journal ofpediatric nursing.com

Campbell, P., and Rudisill, P. (2005). Servant leadership: A critical component for nurse leaders. *Nurse Leader, 3*(3), 27-29.

Corley, M. (2002). Nurse moral distress: A proposed theory and research agenda. Nursing Ethics, 9, 636-650.

Corley, M., Elswick, R., Gorman, M. et al,. (2001). Development and evaluation of a Moral Distress Scale. *Journal of Advanced Nursing, 33*, 250-256.

Greenleaf, R. (1991). *The Servant as Leader*. Indianapolis: Robert K. Greenleaf Center.

Grojean, M., Resick, C., Dickson, M. et al. (2004). Leaders, values, and organizational climate: examining leadership strategies for establishing an organizational climate regarding ethics. *Journal of Business Ethics, 55*, 223-241.

Gutierrez, K. (2005). Critical care nurses' perceptions of and responses to moral distress. *Dimensions of Critical Care Nursing 24*, 229-241

Hart, S. (2005). Hospital ethical climates and registered nurses' turnover intentions. *Journal of Nursing Scholarship, 37*, 173-177.

Kaplan, C.P., Norman, S, and Stillson, K Promoting resilience strategies: a modified consultation model. *Social Work in Education, 18*, Retrieved February 4, 2008, from http://web.ebscohost.com

Polk, L (2000). Development and validation of the Polk Resilience Patterns Scale. In L Hoskins (Ed.), (pp. 1-25). Washington DC: Pro Quest.

LEADERSHIP SUCCESS SITUATION 5.2

Angela Christian Pellerito

Advocating Takes Guts!

As an older student in the nursing program I am aware that I have a great impact on many of the young (as well as, older) students in my classes. Because I come from a psychiatric background and I am the age I am with the personality that I have, I am often an advocate for my younger fellow students. I have been instrumental in helping them to learn the importance of being honest in their practices and standing firm, as a nurse, on what they know and believe to be true. We have one particular young woman in one of my clinical groups that really works at balancing nursing with the needed aggression that it sometimes takes to get done what needs to be done. I try hard to reason with her regarding her obligation as a nurse and helping her understand the difference between needing to be aggressive to get done what needs to be done, and purposing hurting or aggravating a patient. As a nurse you can't spend a lot of time negotiating care with patients. There are certain procedures that have to be done; although unpleasant, you know as a nurse that you are doing them for the greater good of your patient. If you haven't been around a lot of patients, that lesson is sometimes hard to learn.

I spend time listening to my fellow students and making myself available to them. My fellow students truly feel that they can come to me about most anything without fear of being judged or criticized. I am a very open and honest person and nothing is off the table if they need to talk about it! I help direct them and make sure they themselves are not being treated unfairly or taken advantage of. Sometimes they present difficult situations assuming they simply have to take what life throws them. They don't have to take what life throws at them! Yes, they will learn most of that over time, but as nursing students, they are currently overwhelmed and need someone to watch their backs.

There is no one that I go to school with or work with that wouldn't see me as a very honest person, a person that will do the best or right thing for another. I work to be an advocate at school for my fellow school mates and at work for my patients.

Case and point - I had a very ill women come into trauma one day a few months ago. She was elderly, septic, had fallen and laid on the floor for several days before being found-not a good picture. It was my job to undress the women and place a cath. Once I had her undressed I noted extreme excoriation around her genital area. It was very disturbing. I am a nursing tech in this job, so I mentioned what I saw to my fellow tech and to the nurse, both of which seem to not be too concerned. Mind you, we didn't know why this woman had been on the floor for the last couple of days, so I am thinking anything was possible. I mentioned it to the doctor, who also seemed unconcerned. At this point I am becoming livid with the idea that no one in a position of power is asking this woman why her genitals are in the shape they are. I wanted someone to ask if she had been assaulted and I didn't think with those more highly educated professionals standing around me that it was my place to do so! When I said something to the doctor about my assumption, she said it might be possible, but still didn't ask. With my fellow tech standing there, I leaned over the face of the women and asked her if someone had hurt her or had done this to her. The room fell silent. My colleague couldn't believe that I would ask something like that. I explained to her that the only way of knowing was to ask! It wasn't an improper question and I was tactful in my questioning- but I wasn't leaving that patient's side until I had an answer! Many issues hinged on the women's answer and I wasn't letting it go.

Needless to say, I am often called upon when there is a situation that requires guts and information is needed. You can't help someone without getting information and sometimes, even though it's uncomfortable, you just have to push through for the sake of your patient.

So, in a nutshell, I put myself out there for the sake of others. Right is right and you can't get past that. My actions encourage others around me to act in the same manner or avoid taking shortcuts in my presence. They know I am not likely to just let something go without good reason.

Analysis

The author of the above situation was the only healthcare professional with enough 'guts' to ask the tough, but very important question. This is especially disturbing since the physician was a 'mandated' reporter who needed the answers in order to notify the state Division of Aging that a case of suspected abuse had been uncovered at the hospital. In cases like this, the reporter could not face prosecution even if the allegation turned out to be untrue after investigation. If, however, the suspected abuse WAS TRUE and not reported by the mandated reporter (in this case the physician)- that physician could face prosecution for not reporting her suspicions.

Leadership Strategy
The client is *always* the main focus of care.

Principle(s)
Use every interaction whether face to face or virtual as an opportunity to acquire and share knowledge.
Speak with confidence!

Theory Guiding Practice

Nursing
Marlaine Smith's Theory of Unitary Caring is a middle-range theory that was formulated with heavy undertones from Martha Roger's Science of Unitary Human Beings theory. It is comprised of five distinct assumptions/concepts that make up the core of the theory. The first is of 'manifesting intentions' or, creating or holding thoughts and beliefs concerning bettering the well-being of humans. The second assumption/concept is that of 'appreciating patterns' or acknowledging patterns without attempting to change it. "Attuning to dynamic flow" is the third assumption/concept, meaning identifying and utilizing the rhythms of relating in the

'moment'. The fourth assumption/concept is experiencing the Infinite, or a realization of the presence and coexistence of a spiritual union. The fifth assumption/concept is inviting creative emergence. This speaks to a transformative emergence of the self and a calling to a deeper realization of the patterns of life.

Non-Nursing

Howard Gardner's Theory of Multiple Intelligences posits ten separate ways of knowing or, 'intelligences' through which one comes to know, information via a distinct route. In this theory Gardner identified three intelligences that coincide with Smith's Theory of Unitary Caring. He noted the importance of 'patterns in nature' as one of the ten intelligences in his Theory of Multiple Intelligences. Gardner also identified "Spirituality" as a provisional intelligence for his Theory of Multiple Intelligences. He also brought forth Intra-personal intelligence as a way of reflecting deeper into oneself for meaning.

Evidence-Base

Gardner, H. (1999). Are there additional intelligences? The case for naturalistic, spiritual, and existentialist intelligences. In J. Kane (Ed.), *Education, Information and Transformation*. Englewood Cliffs, CA: Prentice-Hall.

Sherwood, G. (1997). Metasynthesis of qualitative analysis of caring: Defining a therapeutic model of nursing. *Advanced Practice Nursing Quarterly, 3*(1), 32-42.

LEADERSHIP SUCCESS SITUATION 5.3

Fred Brown and Darlene Sredl

Crisis on the Horizon-Professional Outrage!

When most healthcare professionals think of the state of California, they think of top-notch, cutting edge healthcare and one of the country's best boards of professional nursing. However, as a traveling nurse in the state of California for many years now, I have found this not to be accurate.

The crisis in question stems from the compromises the Board of Nursing is forcing on its nurses, putting the nursing profession in jeopardy.

For example, in California a member of the military who holds a variety of specific documented certificate(s) of healthcare training can present this to the Board of Nursing along with a college transcript of other courses, and then can *challenge* the professional registered nurse (RN) National Council Licensure Examination-Registered Nurse (NCLEX), examination to become a RN! The state Board of Nursing does not require these individuals to have had a formalized list of nursing courses of training from an approved and accredited National League of Nursing (NLN) program; a specific number of hours of clinical experience; or any prerequisites from a board-certified college or university. Obviously the state believes it is helping solve the state's nursing shortage and low staffing ratios by allowing individuals with specific healthcare training from the military to enter the profession without going through a formal nursing training program.

Herein lies the problem, this state can approve nursing programs or individuals with minimal training and courses far different from those of other states that have criteria nurses must meet in their nursing program.

This is also reality for certified nursing assistants (CNAs). These individuals can go through a one-, three-, or six-month CNA program; work for four years in a healthcare setting; pass a state-approved pharmacology course; and then challenge the board of Licensed Vocational Nurse (LVNs) to become an LVN without going through a formalized, state- or NLN-certified nursing program. This state also has an over-abundance of licensed vocational nurses (LVNs) working in critical care areas, a situation strictly not allowed in other states because, as technical healthcare members, the scope of practice of these individuals is very limited. The following are nursing functions routinely prohibited by LVN and/or LPN registration in most states: administration of any intravenous- push drugs, IV drip medications, blood products, assessment, and re-assessment of the patient status/condition.

It's interesting California's hospitals allow these technical healthcare members (LVNs)' to function in a nursing role in many high acuity areas. This is an attempt by the state, hospital, and administration to offset the legal woes of low patient –to- staff ratios mandated by state law.

From a public relations standpoint, the situation in California is causing many people to deduce that nursing is not a true profession. What if people took some classes, and then challenged the medical board examination to become a licensed physician? Due to the fact that nursing is a predominately a female occupation; the individuals involved in the diluted occupation have not understood nursing's fundamental theories, standards, and philosophies that make nursing a profession unique from other occupations. Professionals receive a highly-structured education, clinical and ethical training, and a strict licensure examination before entry into the profession. Although most programs have similar courses, the profession hierarchy is very specific about who can become a member of that profession by training and examination. Members of the nursing profession should be outraged by this reality!

The society/community these nurses serve should demand better standards for their healthcare professionals charged with delivery and implementation of their healthcare in this highly technical global system.

Analysis

This essay speaks about a dilution of the standards that we, in nursing, have been trying to build for the past 150 years. The criteria of a profession that includes: Code of ethics, specific body of knowledge, and practice autonomy, could in no way apply to a person who is allowed to be called a nurse by endorsement of a limited health -care background. We, as nurses, should be outraged at this not-so-subtle attempt to erode our professionalism. Mr. Brown's question- "What if people took some classes, and then challenged the medical board examination to become a licensed physician?" Or, one may substitute the word, 'electrician', or, 'dentist', or any other number of professions that involve a strict combination of study and practice in controlled situations. Would you want such a person performing neuro-surgery, or wiring your home, or pulling your teeth? Advocate against this travesty!

Leadership Strategy

Stand up for your beliefs.

Principle(s)

Possessing a comprehensive knowledge base and applying it utilizing critical thinking skills is an essential skill for nurses and nurse leaders.

Advocate FOR nursing as well as WITHIN nursing!

Theory Guiding Practice

Nursing

Carr's Vigilance Nursing Theory was comprised from her qualitative research among family members staying at the bedside of hospitalized relatives. It is an appropriate theory for the professional outrage felt by this author because those family members have a right to know the professional qualifications of the caregivers assigned to their relative's care. Used in this context the vigilance needed to keep the profession of nursing at the minimum set of standards determined by NCLEX licensure exams must be borne by professionals themselves.

Non-Nursing

The Theory of Constraints (TOC) by Eliyahu M. Goldratt is a dynamic organizational systems philosophy based on the assumption that every organization has at least one factor that inhibits the organization's ability to meet it's objective(s): profit maximization is the objective usually cited. This inhibiting factor, once identified as a production-limiting factor, must be used most efficiently in order to overrule it's inhibiting function. TOC analysis can be used to increase a company's profit margins.

Evidence-Base

Buerhaus, P. (2009). The Future of the Nursing Workforce in the United States: Data, Trends, and Implications. Sudbury, MA: Jones and Bartlett Publishers.

Donaldson, N., Bolton, L., Aydin, C., Brown, D., Elashoff, J., and Sandhu, M. (2005). Impact of California;s licensed nurse-patient ratios on unit-level staffing and patient outcomes. Policy Polit Nurs Pract, 6(3), 198-210.

Health Resources Services Administration: What is behind HRSA's projected supply, demand and shortage of registered nurses? 2004 from http://bhpr.hrsa.gov/healthworkforce/reports/behindrnprojections/index/htm

Jha, A., Duncan, B., and Bates, D. (2002). Evidence report/technology assessment, No 43: Making healthcare safer of patient safety practice from www.ahcpr.gov/clinic/ptsafety/index.

In: Evidence-Based Leadership Success Strategies …   ISBN: 978-1-62081-104-7
Editor: Darlene Sredl   © 2012 Nova Science Publishers, Inc.

Chapter 6

QUALITY OF CARE

Theresa Martin and Darlene Sredl

LEADERSHIP STRATEGY 6.1

Making a Difference

Do you ever wonder if you make a difference as a nurse? In the Home Health Nursing field, I make a difference! I am on a Cardiac Home Health Nursing Team and we all make a difference. Not only do we perform as clinical nurses but we wear many other hats also. Some of these hats include Social Worker, Counselor, Chore worker, Friend, Advisor, and Teacher. These are all skills that we learn in nursing school but are not necessarily given the time to perform in a hospital setting. In the home, there is time for that one- on-one care that most patients need to better understand and cope with their illness.

Recently I was hired to work in a more affluent area of our city, but because another nurse left the position, I ended up being assigned to the poorest and roughest area of the city. I will admit I was very nervous entering this area as I am of a very different race and culture than the majority of this area's population. I did not believe that I would be able communicate effectively with the people living in this area; causing me great concern. Well, I decided that I had to get in there and just do the best I could with the situations I found.

I am proud to say I am making a difference in the situations I found.

My patient populations all have major co-morbidities. The prevalent diseases include diabetes, hypertension, obesity, COPD, congested heart failure (CHF), and renal insufficiency/failure. The majority of the patients want to be compliant with their treatment plan, but due to their lifestyles they end up non-compliant for a variety of reasons. But…this is exactly where my job becomes fun and interesting! I love a challenge. Every time one of my patients meets a goal/accomplishes a task, I feel I have played a major part in that accomplishment and I rejoice in the joy right along with them and their family.

I have a patient (we will call him Roger) who is a diabetic, with hypertension, COPD, obesity, and CHF. Roger has been non-compliant with medications, diet, and disease management. Over the past few years, he has been in and out of the hospital regularly. I began taking care of Roger when he was discharged from the hospital after his fourth visit in the past 6 months due to CHF exacerbation.

When I interviewed him and asked why he believed he was having so much trouble, he shrugged his shoulder and said, "I don't know and really don't care. I cannot do anything to change this. I am sick and I just have to accept that."

After further investigation, I found that Roger was not taking his medication, following his diet, and was still smoking. He told me that he could not afford his medication, and that healthy food was too expensive when you have other family members to feed. I did some research into area food banks and other sources for food funding and was able to set up a continuous source of fresh, healthy foods using funding from state and local sources. Then, I arranged supplementation from area food banks and meals on wheels for Roger and his family. I the spent the next several visits going over reading labels, identifying healthy food choices, and proper food preparation to get the most per serving and to keep it healthy.

Roger and his family all began to lose weight and starting feeling better. Because of the weight loss, they all began asking about exercise to enhance their health and weight loss efforts. On each visit, when weather allowed, I began spending time involving some form of outdoor activity with Roger and his family. I also gave them suggestions for other family activities they could enjoy together thereby getting them up and moving and spending quality time together as a family.

I then petitioned to the local YMCA for a family scholarship membership to the facility close to the patient's home. The family received a 1-year renewable scholarship with incentives. As I further investigated his situation, I found that Roger is a veteran and was eligible for veteran benefits including prescriptions at a much-reduced rate through the VA. He is now receiving all of his medications and taking them as prescribed because he can afford a full month supply instead of having to make one-month's worth of medications last 2-3 months. This is also giving Roger a more hopeful outlook on his illnesses. He realizes he can control them and, with the ability to control his diseases, he feels more in control of his life.

He states he is happier and now has the desire to quit smoking. I pointed out that by not smoking he will reap even more health benefits that will help him and his family. He has agreed to put the money he saves from not buying cigarettes into a kitty to be used for something special for him and his family. Currently he is trying to decide what it is he wants to save up for and is having fun coming up with possibilities. This also gives him hope and purpose to his life.

Roger has been able to stay out of the hospital and is now dealing with medication dosage reductions as he loses weight and gets control of his diabetes and hypertension. He agrees this is good for several reasons, including the fact that he is also saving money. We are currently working on assisting Roger in finding gainful employment and getting his landlord to make necessary repairs to the home making it safer and more energy efficient.

As you can see from the above story, we *do* make a difference in people's lives every day if we just try. I will agree that it can become very taxing. Sometimes you just want to give up on the person and let them continue to go down the broken path they have chosen. But…if you do, what difference have you made in their life? None! You just become another non-believer in their minds and they become more depressed and even less willing to try to change. Then they give up completely, become even more ill, and may have to return to the hospital as the cycle begins again. I am not saying that you have to give your all to every patient, because some truly do not want help and until they are ready to accept the help you will be beating a dead horse.

Therefore, I say to you-go out and find a person who is truly in need of something and help them get it. It may be a simple thing like a smile, a hug, or a gentle touch. Maybe they just need a bag of trash taken out to the dumpster and they are unable to walk that far-encourage them to walk *with* you to their limit and then you go the rest of the way for them. Next time maybe they can walk a little further for you. Encouragement goes a long way in a person's life. If you believe they can and continue to instill this belief into them, soon they, too, will believe they can and then they do!

There is also the difference that a nursing supervisor or administrator can make that has an impact not only on the nursing staff but also on the patient's well being. This difference comes when a supervisor takes the time to speak to the nurses as if they are human and have feelings and needs just the same as a patient would have.

When management praises a person for a job well done it gives that person a sense of pride in accomplishment. It makes them feel good about what they are doing and may strive to improve even more. In addition, when others see praise and comments on a co-worker's job well done, they also want to try harder. Morale lifts in the work place.

I have a supervisor who actually speaks to each of the nurses on staff at least weekly letting them know what a great job they are doing. She expresses sincere appreciation when we go that extra mile or perform a task that is not part of our job description. Each month at the team meeting she makes a point of recognizing the whole staff for a job well done.

She has an open door and gives her work and personal cell- phone and home phone number to each employee so she can always be reached if we have a question or concern. We all know that no matter how little or big the problem, question, or concern we can call her at any time. She will freely admit if she does not know the answer; then direct you to someone who might have the answer, or she will find the answer for you. She is always open to suggestions, ideas, and encourages conversation about any concern whether about nursing, or anything else personal that you wish to discuss.

I was hired into this department as a novice nurse with very little cardiac experience. I was scared and worried that I would never learn all there was to learn to be a Home Health Cardiac Nurse. Supervisory and support staff has taken the time to teach me what I need to know and continues to encourage me even when I feel defeated. This agency's policy is-orientation takes as long as necessary. They want to ensure that you are truly comfortable with what you are doing before they take you off the orientation/training status and give you a full case load.

I had believed that I was to that comfort point and took on the full load that was expected of the staff.

After a few weeks I was overwhelmed. Instead of ignoring my problem, management actually stepped in and helped me. I had supervisors offer to go to patient's homes for me when I could not make all of my appointments in a day; and staffing called nurses and asked for their help in covering my patients. The staffing personnel also moved some of my case-load to other nurses who had a lighter load to help me. I was allowed to have other nurses go on visits with me to give me tips on how to be more efficient and to verify for me that I truly was assessing a situation correctly.

I was still not comfortable reading an EKG strip, but paid for a telemetry class. When I finish the course, I will take this knowledge back to my company teaching what I learned to the other nurses that I work with. By teaching, I will be reinforcing what I have learned while helping others. This will make a difference in all our lives.

Making a difference for one person can make a difference for all. The difference that the administrative and support staff has made for me is huge. I have gained confidence in my abilities as a nurse and this has given me a more confident outlook on myself. This new confidence is spread to my patients who then gain confidence in their abilities to become compliant with their healthcare needs.

Then, this confidence spreads to their family building confidence in helping the patient maintain compliance and continue working on improving their health status. When neighbors see the difference in that patient's health status, they also get a renewed sense of confidence that maybe they could make changes in their own life to become healthier. The next thing you know the whole community becomes healthier! With this renewed health the community begins to heal itself by cleaning up the streets and getting more involved in activities and helping each other.

A Difference Has Been Made!

Analysis

This poignant situation involves the best of nursing. Not only does this nurse analyze her patient's need for basic comforts: i.e food, water,safety- she works with them in finding the needed resources to get the care that is needed. She also recognizes the power of a positive collegial relationship with her immediate supervisor. In research entitled, (Sredl, D., and Peng, N., 2010).

CEO-CNE Relationships: Building the evidence-base of Chief Nursing Executive Replacement Costs. *International Journal of Medical Sciences*), it was discovered that the following qualities enhanced working relationships: Chief nurse executives who respect their CEO (r= .694, p<0.01) (Sredl, 2005); believes the CNE and CEO share common goals for the facility (r=.782, p<0.01); that their relationship is better than average (r= .718, p<0.01); take time each week to mutually problem-solve (r=.437, p<0.01); believe that their job is interesting and exciting (r=.406, p<0.01); share similar interests outside of the work environment (r= .346, p<0.01); content themselves that the roles of CEO and CNE are specific with little overlap (r= .261, p<0.05); enjoy the income range that they earn (r=.251, p<0.05); are willing to actively seek new ways to improve their relationship with the CEO (r=.254, p<0.05); and are, (from the results of this study), more likely to maintain a positive relationship with their CEO boss, hence more likely to remain in their CNE position.

Leadership Strategy

Think through the patient's situation and uncover via root-cause analysis simple precedents that need to be addressed first before more complex issues can be tackled.

Principle(s)

The client is the main focus.

Theory Guiding Practice

Nursing

Dorothea Orem's Self-Care Deficit Theory is a grand theory incorporating three theories within it:

- The Theory of Self Care;
- The Theory of Self Care Deficits;
- The Theory of Nursing Systems. The basis of her theory is, if self care demands are identified but the provider of those needs is inadequate, then needs are not being met.

Non-Nursing

B.F. Skinner's Theory of Operant Conditioning posits the idea that behavior is determined by its consequences (either reinforcement or punishment). He believed that positive reinforcement is more effective at promoting change than is punishment. Linking the two theories-positive reinforcement will generally be more beneficial in teaching self care to patients and their families.

Evidence-Base

Sredl, D., and Peng, N. (In Press). CEO-CNE Relationships: Building the evidence-base of Chief Nursing Executive Replacement Costs. *International Journal of Medical Sciences.*

LEADERSHIP SITUATION #6.2

Dortha Wieland

Quality of Care in Long Term Care

I have long believed that long term care facilities could improve the quality of care, and save themselves a great deal of money with some very simple changes. Here is my "How to improve quality of care in long term care list"

1) Schedule nurses meetings on a regular basis with the Director and the Administrator. Ask the staff what they would like to change and what works well- then implement worthy changes.
2) Provide good supervision to make sure that policies are followed correctly.
3) Establish a good orientation for newly hired; preferably with one nurse doing the orientation. Assess that newly hired employees thoroughly understand their duties and the policies of the facility.
4) Insist that physicians treat nurses as professionals.

5) Nurses and nurse assistants should be given an individual report about their residents. No one can do intelligent care if they don't know about the patients. They should be given frequent praise, verbal and written, for a job well done. One of the things my aides told me late in life that I did well was that I always went to see for myself when an aide told me about a problem. They said that gave them respect in my eyes and they appreciated it…and, it opened communication so that they probably told me more than they otherwise might have. Telling them 'thank you' at the end of a shift was also a pleasant way to end the day. Nurse assistants play a very important part in the Resident's lives and in upholding the good reputation of the facility. Nurse assistants should be made to feel valued.

6) Maintain comfortable working conditions. Keeping the staff intact on the same assignment schedule if they are comfortable working with each other. They won't leave, even for more money somewhere else, if they like their bosses and the environment they work in.

Analysis

Sometimes the best and wisest critical thinking is ole' fashion common sense. The above list of ways to improve quality of care in a long term care facility would work equally well in another healthcare venue.

Mutual respect for all healthcare workers; hands-on supervision to help when help is needed; opportunity to work with compatible co-workers is not fairy-tail Camelot , but it can make working conditions at YOUR facility a lot nicer IF you take the time and make the effort to make it happen.

Leadership Strategy
Authority carries responsibility with it.

Principle(s)
The 14 principles of management by Henri Fayol state that these principles serve as guidelines for the decisions and actions of managers derived through observation and analysis of events that occur in practice.

Theory Guiding Practice

Nursing
The Eden Alternative to the Planetree Model p. 137 in Dunham-Taylor(see situation 2.1 for Planetree Model). This model was developed by Dr. William Thomas that utilizes four of the five important drivers of culture change encouraging nursing homes to physically alter the facility to create a more home-like environment. There are approximately 270 registered Eden Alternative homes in the United States.

Non-Nursing

Principles of Management (Henri Fayol) includes:

1) Division of work-specific personal and professional development to increase productivity.
2) Authority and responsibility- commands/orders, followed by responsibility for consequences.
3) Discipline-proper conduct, respect for authority.
4) Unity of command- every subordinate should receive orders and be accountable to one supervisor.
5) Unity of Direction-all related activities grouped together and all employees pursue the same objectives.
6) Subordination of individual interest-goals of the organization must prevail over personal individual interests (also taken from the management method of 'Quality Circles' used in Japan's automobile industry.
7) Remuneration-Sufficient pay is a chief motivation factor among employees. Remuneration should be reasonable and rewarding of effort.
8) Degree of Centralization-aim towards a balance of 'centralization' which is power conferred by top management; and 'decentralization' which is the sharing of authority with lower levels- also known as 'Shared Governance'.
9) Scalar Chain-also called 'chain of command'- a clear line of authority linking managers at all levels.
10) Order-social order ensures good communication; material order ensures workplace safety and efficiency.
11) Equity-fairness and justice in all employee dealings. When employees feel that they have a definite 'stake' in the organization they are more willing to make necessary changes to ensure success.
12) Stability of Personnel Tenure- also known as 'job stability/security' which means affording a proper length of time in the position for the employee to become accustomed to the job and comfortable in performing it, and non-intimidating future employment.
13) Initiative-Listening to and utilizing the ideas and initiative of employees is a source of organizational strength infusing the organization with new ideas. If their ideas are accepted and championed the employee is more likely to take a greater interest in the organization.
14) Esprit de Corps- This refers to the manager's responsibility to improve and continue to develop morale in the workplace in an atmosphere of mutual trust and team spirit.

Evidence-Base

Henri Fayol137.216.208.99:02,24 November 2009 (UTC)ls 14 Principles of management.

LEADERSHIP SITUATION # 6.3

Paul Pfennig

Ensure They Have Adequate Supplies

It was a busy night at the Aeromedical Staging Facility (ASF) at Scott AFB, IL. A larger than normal patient load was arriving from a C-17 Aeromedical evacuation mission due to the Andrews AFB airshow.

I had volunteered to help settle the patients and complete nursing assessments due to the small number of staff assigned to the ASF. After completing an assessment on one patient, I asked a "Phase II" student (a technician doing her clinical practicum) to flush the patient's IV with normal saline. Minutes later, I observed this technician drawing up normal saline from a medicine cup that she had poured from a bottle of normal saline irrigation solution on the table next to her.

Alarmed, but not wanting to jump to conclusions, I asked her what the normal saline was being drawn up for. My heart sank as she told me; "To flush his IV." I asked her if this is how she learned to flush an IV. "No, we always take it from those little vials, but I can't find any." In an effort to do the right thing, to help the nurse and the patient, she had found some normal saline. I reviewed with her, in detail, the bottle that read, "for irrigation only" We then found some sterile, injectable normal saline that read "for injection". I reported this incident to her supervisor so she was aware of this breach in critical thinking.

I learned two valuable lessons that night.

The first lesson is to make sure that the people that work for you have adequate supplies to get things done. The second lesson is to know who you are delegating to, the training level of the person delegated to, the proper way to delegate, and the importance of supervisory follow-up.

(The views expressed in this article are those of the author and do not reflect the official policy or position of the United States Air Force, Department of Defense, or the U.S. Government).

Leadership Strategy

Problems can be solved by delegation to the right person utilizing the 5 principles of delegation.

Analysis

Don't beat around the bush! Phrase your verbal communication as succinctly as possible so that you are talking about the issue at hand. There are five principles of delegation. Knowing that the person to whom you are delegating a task has the proper training to complete the task safely is one of the most basic.

The lesson learned in this scene involves a manager's duty to have the proper and necessary supplies on hand when delegating a task.

Principle(s)
5 principles from Sullivan and Decker.

1) Define the task;
2) Decide on the delegate;
3) Determine expectations for the task;
4) Reach agreement;
5) Monitor performance and provide feedback
   (Sullivan, 2009)

Theory Guiding Practice

Nursing
Artinian's Intersystem Model. This model explores the concept of a sense of coherence within the construct of specific situations. It is a structure for evaluating the effectiveness of interactions and interventions within healthcare.

Non-Nursing

Thomas and Kilmann's Conflict Mode Model
This model is based upon the theory author's assumption that the first step in conflict resolution should be to determine the causative party's intent in causing the conflict whether cooperativeness or assertiveness.

The theory's authors also identified five conflict resolving strategies: competing, accommodating, avoiding, collaborating, and compromising. Each dimension has strengths and limitations while recognizing that no one mode is ideal.

Evidence-Base

McEwen, M. W., Evelyn. (2011). *Theoretical Basis for Nursing* (Third ed.). Philadelphia: Wolters Kluwer/Lippincott/Williams and Wilkins.

Sredl, D. (2005). Evidence-based nursing practice (EBNP) meta-paradigm: A crystallized synthesis of apperceptions, beliefs and efforts toward EBNP implementation among contemporary nurse executives in the United States of America (pp. 166). St. Louis, MO: Doctoral Dissertation, University of Missouri- Saint Louis.

Sullivan, E., and Decker, Phillip. (2009). *Effective Leadership and Management in Nursing* (Seventh Edition ed.). Upper Saddle River: Pearson/Prentice Hall.

LEADERSHIP SITUATION #6.4

Rachel Mundy

Overcoming Resistance to the Adoption of Evidence-Based Practice

The human race in general does not accept change very well. People become used to their routines and they like to keep a schedule. As healthcare providers, nurses have always had to have some sort of acceptance for change. Whether it is because of the demand to switch shifts from days to nights or the fact that nursing and medical information is always in transition, nurses are surrounded by change.

Even though change surrounds us, we still attempt to push it away. Nurses do things that their preceptors taught them to do and if you ask the justification for certain interventions or practices, the answer will most likely be something along the line of "It's always been done this way." I am not saying that tradition is not important; it is very important to the history of nursing and to the future of nurses so that they may respect how much our profession has grown.

Growth in a profession is crucial if that profession is to be taken as seriously as other professions. Today, our patients, the consumers of our care, are much more informed than previous generations. This is due in great part to the internet. In order to provide the best care and to have our care accepted satisfactorily in our patients' minds, we must have justification and reasons for the procedures and assessment we perform. When a patient questions you and you do not have the resources to find an ,appropriate answer, nursing's professional reputation suffers. I am very proud to be a nurse and I admire how our profession continues to expand and take on ever more responsibility than before. I definitely believe that through evidence-based practice (EBP) and more acceptance to the changes that (EBP) will bring that the nursing profession will continue to grow and thrive.

Evidence Based Practice provides the nursing profession with validation for justifiable actions and interventions. EBP combines the clinical knowledge, the aesthetic knowledge, and the empirical knowledge into policies and procedures- established and clarified through the synthesis of evidence. This allows nurses to provide more effective, satisfying, and safe patient care. Utilizing EBP through the periodic revising and editing of guidelines, policies, and procedures will continue to make the nursing profession thrive and flourish. By teaching and involving staff nurses in the EBP process, patients will benefit by having more knowledgeable care provided.

Nurse administrators can suggest utilizing EBP, but the staff nurses, the ones directly involved with patient care must get on board for this movement! The nurse administrators must be role models for their staff nurses. If the staff nurses only hear about EBP, and do not utilize their resources (or, do not HAVE resources) to practice using EBP, then the nursing profession will remain at a standstill.

In order to encourage the use of EBP, the staff nurses must be informed of the importance of utilizing it in practice. They must be shown how and why nursing policies are changed to include EBP. This information could be shared during staff meetings or provided throughout the year in mandatory education settings.

Not so long ago I became the head of a unit- based committee on my floor. We are in charge of patient, employee, and physician satisfaction and safety. We have taken it upon ourselves to revise certain policies including EBP guidelines and interpretive reasons for doing so. A lot of our staff is involved in unit -based committees; however, I made sure to include a policy showing those not committee involved how to go about including EBP in their personal practice. We were aware that not all RNs have a BSN; therefore they may not have had research or statistics as nursing background knowledge. This policy allows every staff RN to become involved in EBP anyway, hopefully to use these evidential practices by utilizing a format.

This movement toward adoption of EBP was not meant to overwhelm nurses who already have a lot of tasks to do; rather , the evidence-base process *should be slowly integrated throughout the year* as policies come up for revision or as questions arise.

I have included a policy presently under review to demonstrate how this works. It is possible to assign an established committee the duty of encouraging EBP because many committee titles are interchangeable with other titles.

On my floor I have noticed nurses asking more questions about why we do things certain ways? Questions like this open the discussion on how EBP benefits us as nursing professional leading to the search for knowledge and, benefits our patients by allowing us to provide optimal patient care!

Example- Policy:

A) An established technique or structure will be implemented for each EBP subcommittee.
   - The Unit Practice Committees will be the Evidence- Based Practice group. These Unit Practice Committees or the UPC are unit- based groups run by involved staff nurses.
   - The UPC will report staff nurses' questions and concerns to the Clinical Practice Committee. The Clinical Practice Committee is a more hospital- based committee rather than unit- based. Each unit would have a representative at the Clinical Practice Committee, or CPC to assimilate staff questions.
   - The CPC will report these questions to the EBP committee.
B) The EBP committee will report to Nursing Research. (This involves a large infrastructure, if that does not apply to your facility the UPC can implement this EBP routine on a smaller scale on its own particular floor.)
   - The EBP subcommittees will encourage interest in EBP.
   - The UPC will initiate communication about EBP. This can be done by email, bulletins, or verbally through practice, especially while training a new team member.
   - Unit based seminars, a journal club, or monthly postings can be used to emphasize EBP.
C) Staff nurses should learn the PICO format to submit questions to the EBP team.

Example of PICO question format:

P =   Patient Population
I =   Intervention/Issue of Interest
C =   Comparison intervention
O =   Outcome

"In adult cardiac surgery patients (P), is morphine (I) or fentanyl (C) more effective in reducing postoperative pain (O)"

- Implementation of EBP and knowledge of EBP will be evaluated during performance appraisals for the staff nurse.
- Access to Pubmed or other data sites should be available in your facility; there is also a center for research that offers consultation.

D) The Clinical Nurse Specialist and the UPC will revise policies based on EBP.
  - Revisions will take place annually unless an issue is brought to the attention of the committee, at which time the policy may be revised before the annual revision date.
  - Announcements of revisions and EBP changes will be announced at staff meetings.
  - EBP knowledge will be evaluated with the staff nurses during their performance evaluations.

Leadership Strategy

Evidence-Based Process (EBP) enhances nursing's professionalism by acknowledging and integrating theoretical and practical research, collegial expertise, available resources, and patient preferences into a cohesive plan of care.

Analysis

The fact that the nurse administrator/Chief Nursing Executive/Director of Nursing or whichever title is conferred upon the top nursing leader in a facility, must lead the way in becoming a role model supporting EBP cannot be overstated.

Research has shown that one of the most effective drivers in implementing the evidence-base process is administrative support. Other research has indicated that many Chief Nursing Executives in 300+ bed facilities believe in the Evidence-based process but have been slow to implement it.

The above situation acknowledges some of the barriers of implementing EBP and suggests a slow implementation approach by revising policies with an EBP point of view as they come due.

Principle(s)

Practice what you preach.

Theory Guiding Practice

Nursing

Melnyk and Fineout-Overholt's theories on Evidence-Based Process and instruments: EBP Belief Scale ©and the EBP Implementation Scale ©.

Non-Nursing

The *Belmont Principles* of beneficence, respect for persons, and justice was a phrase coined by the U.S. National Commission for the Protection of Human Subjects of Biomedical and Behavioral Research in the Commission's Belmont Report as a 'shorthand' way of thinking about ethical values in research.

Evidence-Base

ASU College of Nursing and Healthcare Innovation. (n.d.). Retrieved November 22, 2008, from ASU: http://nursing.asu.edu/index.htm

Banning, M. (2005). Conceptions of evidence, evidence-based medicine, evidence-based practice and their use in nursing: independent nurse prescribers' views. *Journal of Clinical Nursing* , 411-417.

Block, V., and Sredl, D. (2006). Nursing Education and professional practice: A collaborative approach to nurse retention. *The Journal for Nurses in Staff Development* 22(1), 23-30. CE TEST.

French, B. (2005). The process of research use in nursing. *Journal of Advanced Nursing* , 125-134.

Gawlinski, A. (2008). The Power of Clinical Nursing Research: Engage Clinicians, Improve Patients' Lives, and Forge A Professional Legacy. *American Journal of Critical Care* , 315-326.

Jenkins, R., Sredl, D., Hseuh, K., and Ding, C. (2007). Evidence-based nursing process (EBNP) consumer culture attribute identity: A message-based persuasion strategy study among nurse executives in the United States of America. *Journal of Medical Science,* 27(2), 55-62.

Melnyk, B. M., and Fineout-Overholt, E. (2005). *Evidence-Based Practice in Nursing and Healthcare.* Philadelphia: Lippincott Willaims and Wilkins.

Newhouse, R. P., Dearholt, S., and Poe, S. (2007). Organizational Change Strategies for Evidence-Based Practice. *JONA* , 552-557.

Schiemann, D. (2006). Expert Standards in Nursing as an Instrument for Evidence-based Nursing Practice. *Journal of Nursing Care and Quality* , 172-179.

Sredl, D. (2005) Evidence-Based Nursing Practice (EBNP) Meta-paradigm: A Crystallized Synthesis of Apperceptions, Beliefs, and Efforts toward EBNP Implementation among Contemporary Nurse Executives in the United States of America. University of Missouri-St. Louis. (Dissertation).

Sredl, D. (2008). What nurse executives in the United States *really* think about evidence-based nursing process. *Nurse Researcher*, 15(4), p.51-67.

Sredl, D., Aukamp, V. (2006). Evidence-Based Nursing Care Management for the Pregnant Woman with an Ostomy. *Journal of Wound, Ostomy and Continence Nursing. 33*(1), 42-51 CE TEST.

Sredl, D., Werner, T., Springhart, D., Watkins, D., Shaner, M., and McBride, G. (2003). An evidence-based pilot study exploring relationships between psychologic and physiologic factors in post-lung transplant adolescents with cystic fibrosis. *The Journal of Pediatric Nursing 18*(3), 216- 220.

Stone, P., Stone, C., Curran, C. and Bakken, S. (2002). Economic evidence for evidence-based practice. *Journal of Nursing Scholarship, 34*, 277-282.

U.S. Dept of Health, E., and Welfare,. *Ethical Principals and Guidelines for the Protection of Human Subjects of Research (The Belmont Report). Publication no. OS 78-0012.*

Wimpenny, P., Johnson, N., Walter, I., and Wilkinson, J. E. (2008). Tracing and Identifying the Impact of Evidence-Use of a Modified Pipeline Model. *Worldviews on Evidence-Based Nursing*, 3-12.

LEADERSHIP SITUATION 6.5

Niang-Huei Peng

New Program Development Barriers

I was employed as a nurse on neonatal intensive care unit in 1994. A new nursing caring initiative to cover and keep darkness inside of incubators, was applied in my work place. In the beginning, some of our nurses refused to keep the inside of incubators dark for preterm infants even though the head nurse asked us to do this. We were also confused about WHY it was now important to keep environmental bright lights dimmed for preterm infants. We worried about the safety of covering the incubators, keeping the inside of incubators dark, and not being able to readily see the infant. Most importantly we were concerned because we did not understand the reasoning behind this intervention.

On this issue, I stood in the middle side between these opinions from my co-workers and the manager in NICU. I didn't worry too much about a blanket covering the incubators while I was working with my preterm infants in NICU. I have enough confidence to maintain the preterm infants' safety even though I have to keep the darkness inside of the incubators. However, I could not get an answer from my manager that satisfied my wanting to know the benefits of applying this (supposed) developmental care intervention on the preterm infants. The manager just told us that she learned about this and other interventions during some continuous nursing education conferences (I suspected that she herself was not clear about the reasons for applying this intervention).

Therefore, I reviewed the literature to better understand the benefits of applying this developmental care intervention in preterm infants. I shared what I learned from these readings with my co-workers and also convinced them to apply this intervention in preterm infants in NICU.

As a result, I have also done empirical research on this topic entitled- "Exploration of the influence of light illumination on physiological parameters and behavioral states of preterm infant in the incubator" while I wrote my Master's thesis. Now, I totally understand the importance of applying the developmental care interventions to preterm infants, and I also teach neonatal clinicians and nursing students about new knowledge and skills of caring the preterm infants in the clinical. I also translated one related textbook from the English to the Chinese version for our clinicians who worked in the NICU.

Continuing learning is a good way to deal with any confusion in your working situation. Remembering the phrase "don't quit" is another other way to improve my career in nursing. My belief is "don't quit over doubts and questions, for there is always something we may learn."

Analysis

Professionals have a 'need to know'. In patient care situations wherein they are providing care and putting their license on the line they want to know reasons that drive the practice. This is one of the reasons evidence-based practice is now becoming so popular. Delving into research and utilizing research that has affected positive outcomes streamlines the care delivery process and eliminates time wasting, ritualistic practices.

The above situation describes one nurse's quest for knowledge in response to a superior's order that a procedure be instituted without the staff's understanding of how this procedural change would benefit the patient.

As this author stated: "Continuing your learning is a good way to deal with any confusion in your working situation. Remembering the phrase, "don't quit" is another way to improve a career in nursing. My belief is, "don't quit over doubts and questions, for there is always something we may learn."

Leadership Strategy
Rely upon yourself!

Principle(s)
Self-initiated learning is the most lasting.

Theory Guiding Practice

Nursing
Theory of Health as Expanding Consciousness by Margaret Newman. She felt that disease gives insight to already existing life patterns; that environment and the person make up a single pattern of consciousness; we are continually discovering new ways for growth. Movement (self awareness and decision making) among time (allowing for recognition among patterns), space (discovery of identity), and patterns (expands the consciousness).

Non-Nursing

Knowles- Principles of Adult Learning (Andragogy). The following are significant to understanding Knowles principles of Andragogy:

- Adults who connect learning experiences to past experiences can make the learning experience more meaningful and assist in acquiring new knowledge.
- Adults have a need to know why they should learn something;
- Adults have a need to be self-directing and decide for themselves what they want to learn.

Evidence-Base

Gordon, I. E. (1997). *Theories of visual perception* (2nd ed.). England: John Wiley and Son, Ltd.

Marchione, J. (1993). *Margaret Newman: Health as expanding consciousness*. California: Sage Publications.

Newman, M. A. (1986). *Health as expanding consciousness*. St. Louis: The C.V. St. Louis: Mosby.

Newman, M. A. (2008). *Margaret newman's biography*. Retrieved September 12, 2008, from http://healthasexpandingconsciousness.org/home/index.php?option=com_http://healthase xpandingconsciousness.org/home/index.php?option=com_contentandtask=viewandid=12 andItemid=26contentandtask=viewandid=12andItemid=26

Yantis, S. (2001). *Visual perception: Essential readings*. Philadelphia: Psychology Press.

LEADERSHIP SITUATION 6.6

Frederick Brown and Darlene Sredl

The Magnet Factor

The new momentum pushing healthcare toward excellence and evidence-based practice will come from the industry's hospitals and insurance companies and the need to achieve and maintain Magnet Status as a provider. Magnet Status is achieved through a recognition program for nursing excellence and scientific-based research by nurses in their practice and at their place of employment. A Magnet hospital has chosen to endure an extensive review process and a systematic evidence-based evaluation of its nursing practices and is awarded Magnet Status by the American Nurses' Credentialing Center (ANCC), an affiliate of the American Nurses Association (ANA), because the facility satisfied a set a criteria that is determined to measure and indicate its level of nursing care (ANCC: The Magnet Recognition Program Overview, 2010).

Magnet Status is awarded to healthcare institutions in which nurses deliver excellent patient outcomes and the majority of staff nurses are either degreed and/or certified in critical care, emergency nursing, and/or any number of specialty areas. Magnet facilities also report a high level of job satisfaction among their nurses. Furthermore, other issues that are explored throughout the Magnet program certification are as follows: safety of facilities; hospital policies to protect and support nurses, strengthen nursing, and strengthen nursing managers; staffing; employee benefits; media exposure; plan to strengthen the credentialing process over time; and evidence of collaboration between the all healthcare professionals.

What Type of Facility Achieves Magnet Designation?

Hospitals that are awarded the Magnet designation are referred to as Magnet Hospitals. Magnet hospitals are healthcare facilities that value strong, quality nursing and strive to provide excellent care to all patients. The national Magnet Hospital Recognition Program was developed by the ANCC to identify and recognize excellence in nursing services at such healthcare facilities. The Magnet Hospital Recognition Program is based on quality indicators and standards defined by the ANA. It is indeed the highest honor a hospital can receive for its nursing services (ANCC: The Magnet Recognition Program Overview, 2010).

Characteristics of Magnet Hospitals!

Magnet designation fosters a sense of pride among the nursing staff, thereby creating positive attitudes in the workplace. Core values, such as empowerment, mentoring, nurturing, respect, integrity, and teamwork, must be evinced in Magnet hospitals. Additionally, such hospitals must demonstrate the following: concern for the patient, high nurse satisfaction ratings, high rates of staff retention, a reputation for quality nursing care as indicated by patient satisfaction scores, identification by nurses as a good workplace, and evidence of a high degree of teamwork (ANCC: The Magnet Recognition Program Overview, 2010).

What Are the "Forces of Magnetism?"

The "Forces of Magnetism" refer to fourteen characteristics that were identified in early research as those that set outstanding nursing institutions apart from the others. Each Magnet hospital must demonstrate that they possess 14 standards based on the "Forces of Magnetism," which include: quality nursing leadership, effective organizational structure, effective management style, promotional opportunities for personnel, professional models of care, quality care, quality assurance, expertise available to staff, high level of autonomy, active community outreach, positive teaching experiences for nurses, positive perception of nurses, positive nurse-physician relationships, and a high emphasis on personal growth and development (ANCC: The Magnet Recognition Program Overview, 2010).

What Makes Magnet Hospitals Special?

The Magnet designation helps patients identify healthcare organizations with a proven level of nursing excellence. It also attracts quality nursing staff who will likely maintain the high-quality standards of care. Independent studies show that patients who receive care at Magnet hospitals experience a shorter length of stay and indicate higher satisfaction rates (ANCC: The Magnet Recognition Program Overview, 2010). Furthermore, one benefit that patients who receive care in a Magnet hospital can expect includes a lower patient to nurse ratio, thereby ensuring that nurses have enough time to give patients the attention that they deserve. Additionally, Magnet hospitals are typically involved in research because research participation has led to medical breakthroughs and the acquisition of the most advanced medical technologies along with the knowledge to apply it. Magnet facilities must also demonstrate a proven patient safety record as part of a "culture of caring" that is fostered when nurses believe in the exceptional quality of nursing care that they provide.

Magnet hospitals are also concerned with the level of education that their nurses have obtained. Why should employers (i.e., hospitals) hire associate-degreed nurses when they can hire bachelor-degreed nurses for almost the same rate of pay? Why should a nurse who does not have at least a four-year degree within the profession be paid between $20 to $50 per hour? Why do communities allow their loved ones to receive care in their most critical moments from healthcare practitioners who work at non-Magnet facilities and have less education than the individuals who run their laboratory tests (i.e., most laboratory technicians have four-year degrees in laboratory science or medical technology)? These are questions that the Magnet status designation will be forced to answer as the trend continues to move toward some form of national accreditation for all healthcare organizations by an independent group, e.g., the Joint commission, which was formerly known as the Joint Commission on Accreditation of Healthcare Organizations (JCAHO).

Indeed, the concept of Magnet Status is very similar to the founding principles of The Joint Commission. Today, the Joint Commission offers accreditation standards throughout the country for all healthcare-related institutions, i.e., hospitals, nursing agencies, etc. If an institution is not accredited, it will not receive Centers for Medicare and Medicaid Services (CSM) funds, and insurance companies will not allow their clients paid access to that facility (Centers for Medicare and Medicaid Services, 2010). Estimates indicate that Magnet Status will be the national standard for medical facilities in the United States by 2025. Magnet status is indeed a renowned indicator of quality (The Joint Commission, 2010).

My Role

When I think back over my career in nursing, I easily recall the time when obtaining JCAHO accreditation was "the big push" in most healthcare facilities. Presently, JCAHO accreditation is considered the standard for most healthcare facilities because with the JCAHO "stamp" or "seal of approval," Medicaid, Medicare, and insurance companies are more apt to fully reimburse each JCAHO healthcare facility its services. Clearly, Magnet recognition could become a similar standard in the healthcare industry.

Anecdotally, having worked for a Magnet hospital in the greater Kansas City, MO, area, I was privy to the inner-workings related to the role that nursing administration played in their direct relationship with the hospital administration in their joint commitment with the then evolving Magnet system. I now clearly see that along with the Magnet "designee status," this hospital believed strongly (and still does) that a Bachelor of Science in Nursing (BSN) is fundamental for the professional Registered Nurse (RN). The hospital more easily acquired ANCC-related Board Certification of Nurses because of this belief. Magnet Status also helped nurses to increase their earning potential, and the recognition as a Magnet Status facility increased the potential for new career opportunities and the advancement of its nurses. (ANCC: Board Certification of Nurses Makes the Difference, 2010) In addition, nurse educators at the facility also found BSNs were far better qualified for critical care and leadership training. This proved to also be true for the facility nurses because they had been trained in the ICU and were required as educators to have an advanced degree either in nursing or education. The hospital hired 40 new BSN students throughout the medical center primarily in critical care areas for the first time that very same year.

For the most part, nurse educators have the task of implementing the Magnet standards within their facility. For example, in this Kansas City, MO, Medical Center, nurse educators with nursing administration approval immediately put a halt to every nursing school training program for nursing students coming from associate degree programs. These changes were felt throughout the neighboring junior colleges in the form of a panicky concern for its nurses and their "nursing school" programs. Simultaneously, the hospital administration, informed nurse recruiters that the hospital would only hire nurses that had a BSN at minimum from this point forward.

Amazingly, this medical center changed its nursing philosophy while developing a new mission statement to bring about a paradigm shift toward excellence in patient care in accordance with its shift to Magnet status. Specifically, BSN nurses facilitated the following within the hospital facility:

- Improvement of specific product lines, such as cardiovascular services, in its critical care service areas;
- Increased customer service excellence through the implementation of mandatory customer services, leadership, and management courses;
- Improved professionalism overall as a result of requiring a minimum four-year education for nurses credentialed in their area of specialty, which led to an increase in the national core measures of the medical center;
- Understanding better the implementation of evidence-based research based on a background of a scientific research based courses at the university level; and
- Implemented of the National Patient Safety Goals for the prevention of sentinel events, including a decrease in hospital-acquired infection rates and deaths throughout the facility (The Joint Commission, 2010).

In conclusion, magnet hospitals, on average, compensate better, and the majority of nurses appreciate the degree to which other healthcare providers esteem and honour their contributions to the care of patient (customer). For a vast majority of nurses employed at Magnet facilities, they denote greater job contentment and lesser burnout rate because of a correspondingly lower nurse to patient ratio that is being implemented at a non-magnet hospital (ANCC: The Magnet Recognition Program Overview, 2010).

In addition, the status of nurse employment at a magnet hospital can be very attractive in building one's resume. Moreover, I believe the focus should be on future success of magnet facilities by improving upon lowering hospital acquired infections (i.e., MRSA and VRE); having a strict adherence to the facility nursing policies and procedure; the continuous building and implementation of better working condition for its greatest and costly accesses (i.e., the registered professional nurse); the improvement of well educated nursing leaders; well trained supportive staff for the nursing to provide better and safe nursing practices; specific nursing remuneration program hospital wide; the improvement and implementation of better educated and trained credential nurses; and hospitals and/or medical centers should be institution, predominantly operated by well trained registered professional nurses from the CNO to CEO and even to its governing board members (Nursing Advocacy. 2010).

Analysis

Insurance companies, Medicare, and Medicaid will likely require that healthcare institutions and facilities demonstrate the standards associated with Magnet status, such as the tracking of outcomes, and such standards will become increasingly necessary for the ability to compete in the evolving global healthcare market. Magnet hospital facilities will be an additional standard required of hospitals in their pursuit of being the best through being accredited, just like the various accreditation awarded currently by the Joint Commission.

Leadership Strategy
Always reach toward your maximum potential.

Principle(s)
Nurse leaders must be prepared to lead change.

Theory Guiding Practice

Nursing
The *McGill Model of Nursing*-previously known as the Allen (after Dr. Moyra Allen) Model, The Developmental Health Model, and the Strength Model was developed in the 1970s to showcase the complementary role of the nurse.

Non-Nursing
Human Capital Theory based on the work of Schultz (1971), and refined by Sakamota and Powers (1995), and later by Psacharopoulos and Woodhall (1997) holds that formal education increases the productivity and efficiency of workers due to an increase in the level of cognitive abilities resulting in economically productive human capability. Education is an investment in human capital.

Evidence-Base

Freeley, N., and Gottleib, L. (2000). Nursing approaches for working with family strengths and resources. *Journal of Family Nursing, 6*(1), 9-24.

Gottlieb, L., and Feeley, N. (1995). Nursing intervention studies: issues related to change and timing. *Canadian Journal of Nursing Research, 27*(1), 13-29.

Gottlieb, L., and Feeley, N. (1996). The McGill model of nursing and children with a chronic condition: Who benefits, and why? *Canadian Journal of Nursing Research, 28*(3), 29-48.

Olaniyan, D., and Okemakinde, T. (2008). Human Capital theory: Implications for Educational Development. *European Journal of Scientific Research, 24*(2), 157-162.

LEADERSHIP SITUATION #6.7

Jean Krampe

Everything You Always Wanted to Know about Blending Quality Improvement and Research but Never Thought to Ask

As many nurse administrators do, I was wearing two hats, leading the Quality Improvement (QI) department at my practice, and continuing my education as a graduate student. I was challenged with identifying an annual data driven QI strategic goal, along with it beginning a graduate school project. Both projects were focused on fall reduction in older persons. Multiple strategies to prevent falls had either been tried or were currently in place in my practice. I was intimate with the prolific body of published research on fall reduction. I was also concerned with the emerging economic crisis resulting from injurious falls, compounded by the aging "Boomers". Barriers addressing this situation, common to all nurses, were scant resources and buy-in from the "powers that be". A wise Medical Director once told me that, based on his experience, it is difficult to *change a QI project into research.* But...I decided this may be the exact opportunity to *change a research project into QI.* A dual research/QI project was conceived with the goal of moving the predicted positive outcomes into a new QI program.

There are numerous common denominators between research and QI projects, with research undeniably containing the most rigor due to Institutional Review Board requirements, methodological approaches to data acquisition, and statistical analysis. Using the approach of matching similarities, I enlisted a key academic partner closely aligned with the values of the practice organization. An academic partner helped address the resource barriers and added additional accountability to the project. I received support launching an innovative fall reduction program from both practice and academic leadership. The practice resource issue was addressed by submitting an internal grant and appointing dedicated point persons.

One year later, thanks to the support of all involved with the project, a dance-based therapeutic activity pilot study was completed, with outcomes showing positive trends , for older persons in reducing fall risks, specifically by increasing gait and balance. Most importantly, the older persons found this program enjoyable; 100% stating that they would recommend it to others. This research project is now a new QI program, translated into practice based on the positive evidence.

Affordable programs that can move quickly into practices add tremendous value to research. Pilot intervention research studies with the dual role of QI initiatives can move into practice with minimized barriers. Programs that are initially thought of as research and QI have sustainability power. The broad scope of these dual projects extends beyond the facility. The opportunities for dissemination are likewise expanded, with both practice and research conferences to present our findings, and professional journals within which to publish our experiences, lessons learned and outcomes. This is a viable approach to the quest for moving evidence-based research into nursing practice expeditiously in the future!

Analysis

The economic stranglehold that has gripped our economy has left its mark by diminished funds for research. National Institutes of Health (NIH), the government's largest research funding source has gone on record as stating that research grant proposals that can translate into clinical care positive outcomes will receive priority for funding.

Leadership Strategy
Challenge the status quo!

Principle(s)
Focus on strengths;

- Vary approaches to achievement

Theory Guiding Practice

Nursing

1. Martha Curley's Syngery Model
Martha Curley's Syngery Model creates a practice infrastructure integrating evidence-based practice with quality improvement based upon health services research. Nurse scientists are challenged to align their program of research with clinical problems in order to advance the science of nursing as well as contribute value to healthcare facility they are a part of- this is called 'translating research into practice (TRIP)'.

According to Dr. Marita Titler, "translation research is the scientific investigation of methods and variables that affect adoption of evidence-based health care practices and operational decision making." Kovner, A., Elton, J., and Billings, J. (2000). Evidence-based management. *Frontiers of Health Services Management*, 16(4), 3-24.One of the nurse competencies cited in the Synergy Model, also cited as a component of EBP, is professional collaboration. The Synergy Model can be used as a theoretical framework for patient care, administration and research.

2. Sredl's Theory of Amalgamethodology
Sredl's Theory of Amalgamethodology (unpublished manuscript) provides a template for a research methodology unique to nursing combining quantitative with qualitative methods.

Non-Nursing
Gibson's Theory of Information Pick-up includes the following concepts:

Awareness of self existence while being part of environment;
Stored memory is unnecessary;
Perception begins with environment, not the senses;
Perceptual system differs from senses;
Coined the term "affordances" – action possibilities;

Evidence-Base

Alligood, M. R. and Tomey, A. M. (2002). *Nursing theory: Utilization and application* (2nd ed.). St. Louis: Mosby, Inc.

J. J. Gibson. (2008). In *New World Encyclopedia online.* Retrieved September 12, 2008, from http://www.newworldencyclopedia.org

Sredl, D. "Amalgamethodology: Building the Educational Evidence-Base for a Research Design Unique to the Science of Nursing". 11th Annual Nurse Educator Institute. North Arkansas Partnership for Health Education. Branson, MO March 15-15, 2011.

Titler, M. (2002). Use of research in practice. In J. Haber (Ed.), *Nursing Research* (5th ed.). St. Louis: Mosby-Yearbook, Inc

Titler, M., and Everett, L. (2001). Translating research into practice: Considerations for critical care investigators. *Critical Care Clinics of North America, 13*(4), 587-604.

In: Evidence-Based Leadership Success Strategies …   ISBN: 978-1-62081-104-7
Editor: Darlene Sredl   © 2012 Nova Science Publishers, Inc.

Chapter 7

CHANGING CORPORATE CULTURE

LEADERSHIP SUCCESS SITUATION 7.1

Claudia Horton
University School of Nursing, US

Change Is Good!

The times, they were a changin'. After revising our foundational documents such as mission, philosophy and theoretical framework, the faculty decided that we needed to update the School of Nursing (SON) bylaws. At that time the dean had *always* convened and chaired the monthly faculty business meeting. Faculty volunteered, or were appointed to, committees by the dean.

Under the new bylaws, a faculty chair was elected by the faculty as well as members of the standing committees, and new standing committees were formed with designated membership of each committee also determined by ballot. Some committees included members from the undergraduate and graduate faculty, while other committees were restricted to faculty from only one level. The new bylaws have been in place for two years and, while some tweaking of membership has occurred, overall everything is running smoothly.

My dilemma was related to the fact that I had operated under previous deans in the old system for 14 years. Suddenly, *I* was the dean of the school but not the chair of the faculty meeting. I wasn't "running the show." It was awkward trying to find my place in this new structure. I was not following in my role models' shoes. What was I supposed to do at the meetings? How was I supposed to "lead" the faculty if I wasn't at the head of the table?

Over time I learned that the new structure was best for the school, the faculty and for me. The new system holds the faculty to a much higher level of accountability. Undergraduate and graduate faculty work together more closely. Faculty are responsible for routing the policy changes through the appropriate committees. Faculty are responsible for working with the secretary to create the agenda, complete with all attachments. Faculty are responsible for sending policies back to the committees if they are not ready for the vote. It is positively liberating! I can still submit items for the agenda. I can still vote since I have faculty status. I am given time at the beginning of each meeting for announcements. I can interact as much as I want or need to.

Through our new bylaws I can empower faculty with the tools and the authority they need to make the process work smoothly. We have a number of new forms that they must use to track changes through the approval process. All forms, policy manuals, faculty handbooks are on a private School of Nursing computer drive. I have used time in the faculty meeting to remind faculty how to utilize the forms to expedite the process. We have become so efficient at completing our business that we now have time for faculty development!

The structural changes have resulted in a win-win situation for all of us. The changes have helped us all use our time more wisely to "run a better show."

Analysis

Although the above situation occurred in a School of Nursing, the same strategies and principles are inherent within the Shared Governance concept. Shared Governance recognizes caregivers as local experts. The Shared Governance movement (also called TPS), is an acronym for Toyota Production System, the automobile giant that originated the quality control/cost and waste-cutting concept that now has adopted and advocates for 'lean' healthcare- 'lean' meaning cutting unwanted fat from an organization and improving the muscle or critical thinking.

Leadership Strategy
Empowerment is liberating!

Principle(s)
- Critical thinking is an essential skill for nursing leaders.
- Change is constant-might as well get used to it.
- Keep expectations realistic
- Self-fulfilling prophecies often self-fulfill
- Focus on strengths

Theory Guiding Practice

Nursing
Fiedler's Contigency Theory was formulated in 1967 stating a basic premise that leaders are most effective when the leader's leadership style is matched to surrounding situational factors. Those situational factors can include: the relationship between manager and follower, the task structure, and the manager's power quotient.

Non Nursing

Filley (1975) identified nine situations that could lead to conflict: ambiguous jurisdiction, goal incompatibility, communication barriers, one-party dependence, organizational differentiation, personal specialization of involved parties, interpretation of behavioral regulations, and unresolved prior conflicts. Resolution may result in a 'lose-lose', 'win-lose', or (preferably) a win-win outcome.

Ausubel's Theory of Subsumption incorporates the idea that believes new material is learned based upon relevant ideas existing in the cognitive structure in a substantive, non-verbal way. Ausubel describes 'cognitive structures' as the residue of all learning experiences. A major mechanism within the theory is that of 'advance organizers'. These organizing phrases are abstract and general and introduced in advance of the learning itself so that the learning can be substantively adhered to a broader concept.

An example of this can be seen in a call that came into a local police station. The caller started out by describing a series of mishaps on connecting flights that led to the loss of her luggage, etc. The call receiver had no idea of what the caller was talking about. The caller gave no 'frame of reference' that the facts could be applied to. Advice was given that suggested she call back stating, "I am calling to report a felony larceny at the airport," then the details could be subsumed, categorized, (and used) by the organizing structure.

Evidence-Base

Sare, M., and Ogilvie, L. (2010). *Strategic Planning for Nurses: Change Management in Health Care*. Boston: Jones and Bartlett Publishers. www.davidausubel.org

Stone, P., Bakken, S., Curran, C. and Walker, P. (2002). Evaluation of studies of health economics. *Evidence-Based Nursing, 5*, 100-104.

Sullivan, E., and Decker, P. (2009). *Effective Leadership and Management in Nursing (7th Edition ed.)*. Upper Saddle River, NJ: Pearson:Prentice-Hall.

LEADERSHIP SUCCESS SITUATION 7.2

Lewis Griffith
Acute Care Nurse Practitioner

Changing Corporate Culture

There are a lot of players on a high volume orthopedic floor in a Level I trauma center: Surgeons, Residents, Nurses, Physical Therapists, Occupational Therapists, Social Workers, Pharmacists, various techs, students, families, and the patients. Everyone has a hand and a stake in the patient's care, as well as the expected outcome of the patient's full-recovery to pre-surgery status, if not better.

The various individual visions of the patient's recovery were often nebulous amorphous concepts lost among all the players on our floor. Everyone working in a hospital knows the time-crunch and demands placed upon staff to complete patient care within a specified shift. On top of students from every discipline asking questions, road-trips to imaging, surgery, therapy, etc., there is a lot of jockeying for the patient's time as well as the nurse's time. Care plans and experience were being overrun by students, turnover, and lack of communication. Some of this is to be expected at a large teaching institution, but the demanding pace was slowly eroding floor morale, professionalism and collegiality among the disciplines.

The unit manager encouraged our request for a sit-down meeting involving all the players. Free lunch was a major enticement toward making it happen as well as the promise of an open forum to voice concerns over "where we are headed." I suggested the activity "Puzzles" which was used as an ice- breaker starting point to reinforce the mission and/or help develop a new culture for our floor. "Puzzles" is a visual representation of not only the "work" that happens on a clinical unit, but it can also serve as an example of how the work is performed.

The activity needs three 20 piece puzzles similar in appearance. Children's- themed puzzles are easiest to find and work with, such as Sesame Street, Bob the Builder, Dora, etc. A room large enough for up to 20 people to sit and maneuver around without being able to see one another's "puzzle" work is also necessary.

Directions: Split all three puzzles into an equal number of pieces and mix-and-match so that there are three piles of pieces from each puzzle. Split the participants into 3 teams with each team taking a "puzzle". Inform the groups that the goal is to put the puzzles together in 20 minutes. The groups can not walk around or look at one another's work, nor are they allowed to talk to the other groups, only to one another. They can at any time "Call a Meeting" to exchange puzzle pieces to aid in the completion of their puzzle. When a meeting is called the other 2 groups have 5 seconds to give a verbal "OK" to attend the meeting. The meeting takes place at the front of the room with the leader of the activity with each group bringing 3 puzzle pieces to trade as they see fit. The group leaders are not allowed to speak to one another at the meeting, only to bring their 3 pieces and trade. If talking occurs, everyone returns to their group with their original pieces and no meeting can be called for one minute. The groups are allowed to call meetings till the puzzles are completed or time expires. Remember that every group must verbalize an "OK" for a meeting and must attend every meeting, even if they have completed their puzzle.

Discussion Questions

What Was the Purpose of the Activity?

You can relate this question to the purpose of the floor. At the hospital the purpose is often to get the patient well enough to go home. This takes several groups (therapists, doctors, lab, nurses, etc) to make this happen often with one group unaware of what the other is doing.

Did it Matter Who Finished First?

Each health care worker likes to think that his job is important, often more important than the next person's job but, this attitude can be at the expense of the patient. There are situations where it is important to accomplish certain tasks before another, but not always. To have awareness of other's work and purpose can increase one's ability to complete their work and purpose.

How Was the Activity Completed?
What skills, abilities and methods are used by the floor/culture?

Who Was the Team Leader?
Whydid there need to be a team leader? Why? What purpose did each team member serve? Who called a meeting? Why? Who took the puzzle pieces to the meeting? Was it the same person every time, or did they change roles? Why?

Staff members can unwittingly fall into "roles" at work and play them out whether they want to or not. Allow team members a moment to reflect on what roles they play on the floor and whether or not they want to change those roles.

When framing the activity you can be as focused or general as you would like. The 3 work groups can represent: executive management, physicians, and other staff (nurses, therapists, lab, housecleaning, etc.); or be focused specifically to your floor: floor manager, nursing staff, and patient techs (care partners, house cleaning, etc.). This activity can be used in the class room too, and the students can be assigned group roles as the instructor thinks appropriate. Each puzzle can represent a commitment or pillar of the culture. Allow time for the group to "lay-out" a new culture or mission statement for the organization.

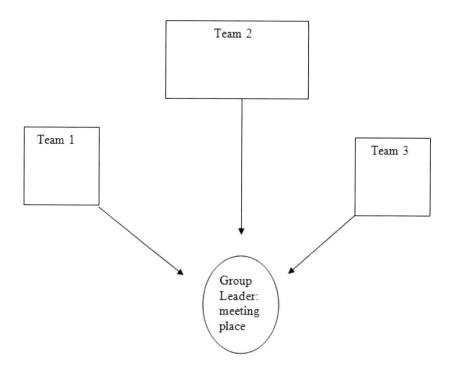

In our session once the activity was completed, the disciplines each talked about how tunnel vision was creeping in with many of us thinking that one's work was more important than another's. In the ensuing discussion we began to realize that just because "our" work was completed that did not necessarily mean that the patient was getting "well" faster.

To resolve this newly identified problem, twice weekly group rounds were established to clarify patient issues, establish schedules (for therapy, tests, care, etc.), and coordinate services. Expectations for all staff on all shifts were established and published so that all involved knew what to expect from one another. The overall vision of the patient's outcome and the road to get there by each team was built with the commitment and shared responsibility of all the teams.

Corporate, or floor, culture is not built over night, nor it is easily changed. A floor can spend years building an acceptable culture that can be undone in a moment if commitment to the culture is not strong. The foundation of the culture is not only the mission of the organization, but the mission of the floor or department.

The following are three models of organizational change cited by Melnyk and Fineout-Overholt: The Change Curve Model (2002); Kotter and Cohen's Model of Change (2002); and, the Transtheoretical Model of Behavior Change. (Melnyk, 2005) (Duck, 2002).

Analysis

Clinical units, especially high acuity units like ICU and EU, can get very intense at times placing the employees under duress stress. Once this is recognized the stress-load can be dealt with in a number of ways. This Author initiated an educational yet fun 'game' that all unit participants could take part in.

The 'game' evidently provided stress relief while teaching some valuable lessons as well. Other clinical improvement outcomes surfaced from the staff afterwards.

Leadership Strategy

Griffith employed principles of Shared Governance by mandating active participation in the proposed changes so that the nurses could tap their own expertise in establishing those policies.

Principle(s)

"Difficulties stimulate invention"

Dr. Norman Vincent Peale

- Communicate often
- Be open and flexible
- Concentrate on continual improvement
- Focus on the future-lose the baggage of the past

Theory Guiding Practice

Nursing

Turkel and Ray's Theory of Relational Complexity is a scientific theory of dynamic systems in play based upon the idea that opposing things can happen at the same time, in the same space, without necessarily contradicting each other. This theory looks at the inter-relationship of mind and matter and the interconnectedness of choice and moral responsibility, in bringing order into a chaotic world.

Non-Nursing

Drucker's Equity Theory and Employee Motivation is a balance between what workers feel they *contribute* to a job (assigning values to each of the various contributions) and what they will *get* from a job. The most highly motivated employee is one who feels that his/her rewards are equal to his/her contributions.

Evidence-Base

Cory, C. Retrieved from http://www.motivation-articles.com/motivate/equity-theory-and-

Duck, J. (2002). *The Change Monster: The Human Forces that Fuel or Foil Corporate Transformation and Change*. New York: Crown Business.

Marchionni, C., and Richer M. (2007). Using appreciative inquiry to promote evidence-based practice in nursing: The glass is more than half full. *Nursing Research, 20*(3), 86-95.

Melnyk, B., Fineout-Overholt, E. (2005). *Evidence-based Practice in Nursing and Healthcare*. Philadelphia: Lippincott Williams and Wilkins.

Parker, M., and Smith, M. (2010). *Nursing Theories and Nursing Practice* (3 rd ed.). Philadelphia: F.A.Davis.

Sullivan, E., and Decker, Phillip. (2009). *Effective Leadership and Management in Nursing* (Seventh Edition ed.). Upper Saddle River: Pearson/Prentice Hall.

LEADERSHIP SUCCESS SITUATION 7.3

Darlene Sredl

Saving Face

The administrative team had assembled in the Administrator's conference room for the weekly advisory council meeting. Present were the Administrator and her assistant, the chief financial officer (CFO), the heads of IT, grounds/maintenance, dietary, library service , housekeeping, and nursing (me).

During discussion I noticed something peculiar about some of the reports. The Administrator kept referring to the 'physical year' quite pronouncedly, instead of the 'fiscal year'; and to the necessity of obtaining a 'Notary Republic,' instead of a Notary Public. At first I thought that she said this as a cute-ism but as time went on it became painfully obvious that she was woefully, totally serious. She obviously thought that these were the correct phrases to use. The next time she said 'physical' year (with heavy emphasis on the second syllable) I glanced at the CFO. He winced momentarily. Succeeding administrative meetings bore out the fact that this verbal administrative gaffe was indeed noticed by those in attendance; but equally obvious was the fact that no one had the courage to tell the

Administrator about the errors. Laughing, of course, would never do; it would only serve to embarrass the Administrator.

One of the meetings ended with an unresolved problem. I decided to put forth a suggestion for a way to resolve the problem. I put my suggestion in the form of a typed memo to the Administrator that included the phrases 'Fiscal year' and 'notary public'. With this message I intended to let her know the correct phrasing without having to confront her with her mistake. My hope was that if she read my suggestion she might see that I spelled the phrases differently than she had been pronouncing them. But...I also recognized that she could think that *I* made the mistake in which case she would either reprimand me or ignore my "mistake" and keep on calling for a Notary Republic in this Physical year. Hopefully, if she didn't assume that I was wrong, she would examine the phrases further and change how she pronounced them in the future, saving face for all of us.

She obviously did read my letter and never again did we hear about the "Physical year" or the "Notary Republic."

Analysis

It is never a good idea to initiate a confrontation with one's boss especially over small details or other inconsequential things. It is important, however, to alert one's boss to gaffes like the ones described above because they lead to embarrassment for the superior. It is also a good idea to make the correction sooner rather than later because the longer the situation goes uncorrected the person involved realizes that many, many people have heard this and will wonder why no one told him/her before this and will be very embarrassed.

Leadership Strategy

"Saving face" or, not saying or doing anything overtly to embarrass another in a social or business communicative encounter is to be prized. Also, it is just plain smart never to embarrass your boss!

Principle(s)

Using communication techniques to 'save face' (or save from embarrassment) for all involved in the conversation are very important.

Theory Guiding Practice

Nursing

Barrett's (1989) Theory of Power and Theory of Power as Knowing Participation in Change Tool (PKPCT) concerns the nurses knowing participation in the change process. Use of the PKPCT tool identifies a power score determined on four sub-scales: awareness, choices, freedom to act intentionally and direct involvement in bring about change. The word 'power' is not used, instead mutually identified 'patterning strategies' are discussed to induce change.

Non-Nursing

Face-Negotiation Theory postulated by Stella Ting-Toomey (1985) asserts that 'face' is an entity comprised of the public image of an individual or group that the public evaluates based on cultural norms and values. Because Face-Negotiation Theory is considered a cross-cultural theory, it attempts to explain differences between cultures and differing approaches to conflict. The theory has seven assumptions from which twenty-four propositions expand.

Evidence-Base

Barrett, E. (1996). Canonical correlation analysis and its use in Rogerian research. *Nursing Science Quarterly, 9,* 50-52.

Barrett, E., and Caroselli, C. (1998). Methodological ponderings related to the power as knowing participation in change tool. *Nursing Science Quarterly, 11,* 17-22.

LEADERSHIP SUCCESS SITUATION 7.4

Darlene Sredl

Power Communication

The nursing workforce had that brow-beaten, defeatist attitude on their faces. They had been at the mercy of the insecure, ill-tempered, irate 'club' of physicians for so long that they accepted it as a matter of fact. Many had worked at the small rural hospital most, if not all, of their professional lives -so they thought that this was supposed to be a nurses' lot in life-humiliation and verbal onslaught at the mercy of anger-management-challenged doctors. As the new VP of Nursing, I began to hear stories of horrific tongue-lashings that my nurses had been subjected to. In one staff meeting, I made the nurses a promise-I told them: "whenever one of the doctors starts on one of these rampages (which were usually in full earshot of patients, visitors, and staff) call me. I will leave anything I am working on; any meeting I am attending, and will come to your side and confront that doctor with you."

Like Hiroshima and Nagasaki, it took two instances of confronting two doctors before they started communicating with the nurses in a more professional manner and tone—but the confrontation did work!

Analysis

Confrontation can be unpleasant but it is sometimes necessary. When that necessity appears, do not back down! Remember you are in a position to support your colleagues. They are looking to you for help. Give it to them. Oddly enough you will be remembered as stronger for having done it (even if you may be shaking in your boots).

Leadership Strategy

As a nurse leader, your staff look up to you AND look to you for support when the going gets rough. Do not disappoint them.

Principle(s)

- Challenge what needs to be challenged!
  "Be bold and mighty power will come to your aid."Basil King
- Take Charge!
- Define yourself and your mission!

Theory Guiding Practice

Nursing

Porter O'Grady and Malloch's view of Quantum Leadership is actually based upon the concepts inherent within Chaos Theory holding that reality and levels of complexity are constantly changing. Porter O'Grady contends that Quantum Leadership demands a different type of leader and a different way of thinking about leadership. Challenges must be met head-on and dealt with.

Non-Nursing

House-Mitchell Path-Goal Theory smoothes the way for others to reach high levels of productivity and performance because of the leader's insight in removing barriers and obstacles to goal attainment that had previously laid across the worker's path. This theory facilitates the process by which employees can reach goals.

Evidence-Base

Porter-O'Grady, T., and Malloch, K. (2002). *Quantum Leadership: A Textbook of New Leadership*. Gaithersburg, MD: Aspen.

LEADERSHIP SUCCESS SITUATION 7.5

Lynn Lenker

The SSM Story of Nursing Strategy to Restructuring

This is about strategic response to the implementation of the Electronic Health Record (EHR) and Patient Satisfaction by Nursing. As health care organizations grow and change with demands of the regulations, patient needs, and the developing technology, restructuring was necessary in our organization moving toward a network solution- 1200 beds in 7 locations -acting as one organization. Since organizations (even those within a larger, umbrella organization) may view each other as competitors, this was a tall order.

Process

The nursing response needed to implement a care-model that would bring the people caring for patients together while integrating use of technology. Although the two concepts are diverse (almost polar opposites), co-existence was necessary in our vision of health care transformation.

The selected care-model was Relationship-Based Care. The easily understood concept is implemented using relationships with patients, care team members, and families to cooperate in providing direct care.

A group of 70 team members were brought together to develop the direction of the model. This team included nurses, environmental service employees, case managers, physicians and human resources personnel.

Using Appreciative Inquiry as a research methodology, team members were asked to reflect on a time when they were involved in the assisting of great/exceptional care delivery. Stories were shared and themes emerged from the work. The themes were then used in developing actions for implementation.

The model of care research findings indicated a strong relationship among our workers and leaders toward developing a role for the Clinical Support Nurse (CSN). This new role was intended to support the nurses at the bedside in their care delivery efforts. Support was anticipated to occur in the through- put of patients on the busy units, as a mentor-expert for novice team members and, in guiding the ongoing work of care delivery.

It was anticipated that the new position would be filled by RN's who had clinical competence in the respective clinical area; who could demonstrate the ability to lead people in a positive direction; and who could coach team members in a manner that advanced quality clinical practice.

This role was intended to replace the current role of the Care Team Coordinator since the duties would be redefined within the model.

Implementation

Like a chain, the CSN links the team members together on the units. CSNs were selected by unit members in peer review. We were surprised by the amount of time it took to locate RN's who both met the criteria and were willing to serve in the role. In areas where the 24/7 CSN position was implemented, there has been added value reported for the team members and support for their patient care. Team members report that the CSN role is a great satisfier in their work.

The implementation of the Electronic Health Record (EHR) was equally as important as instituting Relationship-Based Care. The Clinical Support Nurse integrates the use of the Electronic Health Record (EHR) technology reports to assist in coaching team members in the important work of the day- which may include missing documentation, core measure support and focus on safety. Other strategies that emerged from the work of the design team included- bedside report sharing of the daily agenda. The technology of the EHR provided team members a better method of shift hand-off. Electronic communication tools at the bedside, along with the printed copy of the daily agenda, provided the care team at the time of shift hand-off an opportunity to converse with the patient and family so they could be more involved and aware of what is in store for the day.

This is when discussion regarding laboratory testing, medical imaging, therapy (respiratory, physical, occupational, etc.) that will be taking place for the day occurs. The ongoing roll- out of the EHR continues throughout the restructuring among the network of hospitals in our system. Implementing the nursing model enhanced the workflow of the electronic health record and has allowed the two concepts of technology and care/compassion to become closer.

Results

Turning the organization in a new direction with new leaders has been slower than expected. The overall adoption of the EHR continues to move in a positive direction. Relationship Based Care is a model that grabs the nurse where they are - what they are about - having good relationships to accomplish providing the care that they love to provide. The overall forward movement of organizational change is slower than personal change adoption; so our work continues in the direction of hardwiring processes. Focused work is being done to implement the other strategies for the model.

These include an admission blitz; where no one admits alone, rounding with physician colleagues and more. The good news is that team members relate to the model created by colleagues, who understand the work and the workflows. Patient satisfaction also continues to improve slowly. Like all cultural changes, there needs to be careful monitoring of the results and rounding to assure that all elements are being accomplished routinely.

Analysis

Changing corporate culture in one's healthcare facility is always a unique and demanding challenge; but changing it within multiple facilities held together by a common corporate bond is even more difficult. The Chief Nursing Officer (CNO) cannot be present an equal amount of time in each of the facilities. It is imperative that the CNO develop strong leaders (champions) of the proposed change in each of the facilities.

These strong champions must be fully invested in the vision, the mission and the implementation strategy so that their knowledge and enthusiasm for the project infects others with an equal amount of commitment.

Leadership Strategy
Vary approaches to achievement. Situational power can be assumed by a confident leader

Principle(s)
"Vision is perhaps the most powerful principle of leadership"R. Rosen

Stakeholders are more positively committed to success.

"Think great thoughts. You will never go any higher than you think.

Lord Chesterfield.

Theory Guiding Practice

Nursing Theory

Myra Levine's Theory of Conservation, is a grand theory based on Nightingale's idea that nurses create an environment in which healing can occur. There are four principles associated with her theory:

1) Principle of conservation of energy.
2) Principle of conservation of structural integrity.
3) Principle of conservation of personal integrity.
4) Principle of conservation of social integrity.

Non-Nursing Theory- Appreciative Inquiry (AI)

Appreciative Inquiry (AI) is theory, methodology and philosophy that utilizes social interactions to promote changes within the system by emphasizing what is best about the organization Identified by Cooperrider in 1987 AI is considered more innovative than traditional action approaches. AI carries a greater capacity to spur change particularly when implemented by advanced practice nurses because they are considered credible opinion leaders (Marchionni, 2007).

Evidence-Base

Auerbach, D., Buerhaus, P., and Steiger, D. (2007). Better late than never" Workforce supply implications of later entry into nursing. *Health Affairs, 26*(1), 178-185.

Cooperrider, D. S., S. (1987). Appreciative inquiry in organizational life In W. P. R. Woodman (Ed.), *Research in Organizational Change and Development* (pp. 129-169). Greenwich: JAI Press.

Marchionni, C., and Richer M. (2007). Using appreciative inquiry to promote evidence-based practice in nursing: The glass is more than half full. *Nursing Research, 20*(3), 86-95.

Melnyk, B., Fineout-Overholt, E., Feinstein, N., Sadler, L., Green-Hernandez, C. (2008). Nurse practitioner educators' perceived knowledge, beliefs, and teaching strategies regarding evidence-based practice: implications for accelerating the integration of evidence-based practice into graduate programs. *Journal of Professional Nursing, 24*(1), 7-13.

Rosen, R., and Brown, P. (1996). *Leading People: Transforming Business from the Inside Out* New York: Viking Penguin.

Sredl, D., Melynk, B., Jenkins, R., Hsueh, K., Ding, C., and Durham, J. (In Press). Healthcare in crisis! Can evidence-based nursing practice (EBP) be a key solution to healthcare reform? *Journal of Teaching and Learning in Healthcare.*

LEADERSHIP SUCCESS SITUATION 7.6

Lanette Tanaka

How to Earn Your Subordinate's Respect from Day 1

I joined the Air Force Reserves as a young 2nd Lieutenant shortly after graduating from nursing school and assigned as Officer- in -Charge of the Pulmonary Ward at Scott Air Force Base, Illinois. To my surprise, I was much younger than the majority of the enlisted personnel that I was in charge of. Very early on, I realized that just being in-charge didn't mean telling people what they need to do. *I needed to show* my subordinates that no task was beneath me. I feel that I earned their respect every time they saw me clean up, put-away, and/or stay after assigned hours to get whatever job done that needed to be done. I knew I had earned their respect, when my subordinates would check –up on me and ask "is there anything else that needs to be done before I go home?"

Later on, as I moved up in rank to Lieutenant Colonel, I realized that leading by example is truly the only way to lead effectively, especially when the territory is brand new to everyone involved (whether being trained in a new institution, or when deployed to war). When I was asked to train my medical technicians at the John Cochran Hospital in St. Louis, Missouri , I realized I needed to learn how this organization was run first-hand.

I scheduled time with the 1st Sergeant to jump in and assist with patient care, bed baths, dressing changes- everything that needed to be done. I have to say, I have always enjoyed "bed-side caring for the patient" as a nurse best of all.

To be effective in the nursing administrative role, I realized I needed to see what was going on at the patient care level, in order to make good decisions in planning the training for our medical technicians. As some of the young enlisted medical technicians later told me, they realized I not only cared, but also knew what I was doing; and realized I was also learning how to function in the new situation right along with them.

Analysis

This is Advice on Leadership Style from my Air Force Reserve Career. Leaders in any walk of life are people just like you and me. They don't always know everything that they will be required to know but if they make an honest effort to learn those things, they will be respected for it. In the above situation, Second Lieutenant Tanaka worked alongside her company in completing their missions whether in the kitchen or on the battlefield.

Leadership Strategy
Lead by example. Spread the credit around.

Principle(s)

A manager's job is to take care of employees. When you take care of your employees they *will* take care of the patients.

Theory Guiding Practice

Nursing

Erickson, Tomlin and Swain's Theory of Modeling-Role Modeling (MRM) has, of late, been mainly fostered by Helen Erickson, daughter-in-law of famed psychiatrist Milton Erickson**.** The MRM theory promotes an awareness of emotions, fears, needs (met and unmet), and goals that the client is anticipating having to face. These emotions, fears and needs are also being experienced by co-workers.

The Modeling and Role-Modeling Theory was adapted for use in a theoretical management application. Study aims used respect as a dependent variable as well as an initiator of trust, positive orientation, strength, control, and goals. MRM serves as a useful pattern for nurse managers and staff nurses, alike. The interventions also affirm that the value of respect is a fundamental principle that should be upheld by every health care organization. One question that arises from a staff relationship with a manager is: does the staff have, desire, and/or need a nurturing relationship with the manager? Use of the MRM Theory might be one way to achieve it.

Non-Nursing

1) *Fiedler's Contingency Theory (1967)* postulates that a leader is most effective when matching his/her leadership style to the relevant situational factors.

2) *Hershey, Blanchard and Johnson (2007)* expanded upon Fiedler's Contingency Theory by transformationally factoring in the follower's willingness to perform the assigned task.

Evidence-Base

Society for the Advancement of Modeling and Role-Modeling. (2006, Jan). 16(1).

LEADERSHIP SUCCESS SITUATION 7.7

Iris Schneider

Reoganization Issues

I got the order to evaluate, modify, and reorganize the nursing standards that were validated at my hospital 10 years ago. This is a hospital with 4 facilities in 4 different cities;

all of which had their own nursing policies. So, my job was to reach a consensus among all these facilities to arrive at policies that would be valid in all facilities within the organisation.

I knew that one unit in the facility where I work most of the time, would fight against whatever new issues were planned to be implemented. I knew the strongest person in this group as well. So, I thought, what could I do to get this unit on the way toward accepting the new issues?

There were, I felt, two ways to do this. One, I could just implement the new nursing standards and fight with that unit a long time until they accept them; or I would have to order this strong-willed nurse out of the unit and into the project group. If I did the latter, I would have to fight with her anyway but at least she would have helped to work out the new nursing policies and then she could help to implement them at the unit level.

I asked my co- workers at the other facilities, to look for nurses with strong leadership ability and the ability to influence their co-workers. Project completion was expected to take nine months. As with many conflict situations, meetings in a highly emotionally charged atmosphere usually resulted in creative activity as well. All these nurses saw the chance, and were very motivated, to present their ideas and experiences....and they had very good ideas and a lot of experiences!

The implementation worked without further problems in all of the four facilities. The group members brought the worked-out issues into their part of the hospital company and presented their work to the other units and co-workers. So, they started to sense personalization in the modification of the policies. And, they felt part of the big organization. The looked out of the box and saw the bigger picture.

Analysis

Everyone wants to shine. Sometimes, however, the peer group culture prevents an individual from bringing forth her/his best talents. There is an emotional undercurrent of 'sameness' in which an individual who stands out whether academically, intellectually, or in an activity of some sort is looked down upon.

I saw this negative (and often, jealous) attitude in action while visiting Australia when I overheard two nurses discussing a third nurse who had recently applied for a leadership position at the hospital within which they all worked. "She wants to be a 'tall puppy' doesn't she?" one of the nurses said sarcastically. I asked what that meant, wanting to be a tall puppy?

One of the nurses explained: grass grows very high on the plains in Australia. Some of the smaller ground animals have evolved and taken to standing on their back feet attempting to look up and over the tall grass in order to spot predators. This, then, gives them an advantage because by standing on their back feet they become 'tall puppies', more able to spot predators and, hence, better able to survive. This action phrase then was personalized and applied to those wanting to 'get ahead'.

Leadership Strategy

My strategy here was to take these nurses out of their group with it's strong and safe background. With their participation I gave them the opportunity to showcase their own work.

Principle(s)

- Life is all about letting go and moving on.
- Support holes in your knowledge-base with colleague's knowledge.
- Learning, threatening to the self (new attitudes or perspectives), is more easily assimilated when external threats are kept to a minimum.

Theory Guiding Practice

Nursing

Imogene King's Conceptual System and Theory of Goal Attainment (King, 1981) have led to the development of seven theories:

- Theory of Goal Attainment (King, 1981)
- Theory of Social Support and health (Frey, 1989)
- Theory of Departmental Power (Sieloff, 1991, 1995)
- Theory of Perceptual Awareness (Brooks and Thomas, 1997)
- Theory of Personal System Empathy (Alligood and May, 2000)
- Theory of Empathy, Self-Awareness and Learning Style (May, 2000)
- Theory of Decision-Making in Women Eligible for a Cancer Clinical Trial (Ehrenberger et al, 2002)

Non-Nursing

One of Knowles Principles of Andragogy

Adults who connect learning experiences to past experiences can make the learning experience more meaningful and assist in acquiring new knowledge.

Evidence-Base

Alligood, M. (2000). A nursing theory of empathy discovered in King's personal system. *Nursing Science Quarterly, 13*(3), 243-247.

Brooks, E., and Thomas, S. (1997). The perception and judgment of senior baccalaureate nursing students in clinical decision making. *Advances in Nursing Science, 19*, 50-69.

Ehrenberger, H., Alligood, M., Thomas, S., Wallace, D., and Licavoli, C.. (2002). Testing a theory of decision-making derived from King's Systems Framework in women eligible for a cancer clinical trial. *Nursing Science Quarterly, 15*(2), 156-163.

King, I. (1981). *A theory for nursing: Systems, Concepts, Process*. New York: John Wiley and Sons.

May, B. (2000). Relationship Among Basic Empathy, Self-Awareness, and Learning Styles of Baccalaureate Pre-Nursing Students within King's Personal System. Unpublished Dissertation Abstracts International, University of Tennessee, Tennessee.

Sieloff, C. (1991). *Imogene King: A Conceptual Framework for Nursing*. Thousand Oaks, CA: Sage.

Sieloff, C. (1995). Development of a theory of departmental power. In M. S. Frey, C (Ed.), *Advancing King's Systems Framework and Theory of Nursing* (pp. 46-65). Thousand Oaks, CA: Sage.

LEADERSIP SUCCESS SITUATION 7.8

Darlene Sredl

How to Start Your Own Business

I remember awakening that fateful day feeling positively energized-like somehow I must have been struck by lightening as I slept, yet suffered no ill consequences. I felt like something momentous was going to happen …but I knew not what it might be.

As I entered Thunderhead Flight School for my weekly flying lesson, Carl, the manager greeted me warmly asking, "Darlene, what kind of nurse are you?" Rather taken aback by this abrupt question, I retorted, "A very good one, why?"

He chuckled, "Don't get yer dander up. I mean-are you an RN or an LPN?"

"An RN…why?"

"I just wanted ta know cause sometimes we get a call fer an RN to fly with a patient whoz been in an accident or somethin'. I wuz wonderin' if you'd be interested?"

BINGO! The light bulb over my head lit up! This was IT! An obvious need had been established for a new practice specialty for nurses-flight nurses! And, it was obviously not organized. Carl said that as need arose, flight centers around the country sent out 'feelers' for RNs who might want to earn extra money by accompanying patients on air transport.

I knew instinctively that I was a natural for this. I had almost completed my flight training, and during flight training had noticed my own body experiencing physiologic changes that puzzled me. No one seemed able to answer the questions I asked about this. Remembering my energized feeling earlier this morning, I knew I should capitalize on this idea right away. I called a lawyer in my neighborhood and asked if he could be available for an incorporation meeting later that very evening. He said he could. I called an accountant with the same request. He, also, pledged to be present. Then, I called my best friend and asked if she would be the Secretary-Treasurer of my newly conceived corporation and she agreed. With all hands on deck that evening, AV-NURSE INTERNATIONAL was born!

That was the easy part. I still had to complete all the requirements of flight school: putting in the required number of flight hours (by day and by night), and taking the written and final flight checks. In addition, I now had to write up articles of incorporation and job descriptions for my flight nurses. And…I began to worry…now that I was a corporate entity…what would happen if something tragic occurred? Would I lose my house? My family's savings? I knew this needed more study. So, I got corporate insurance and went dormant for two years while I researched, researched, researched. I was allowed access to

NASA's and the Air Force's research. They had some of the answers I was seeking about those physiologic changes at altitude that I was feeling that no one (in my circle of acquaintances) could explain.

I began to see that now, if indeed I were to operate a dispatch service for flight nurses, I would first have to educate those nurses on how body physiology at altitude differed from physiology on the ground (or, at sea level).

In order to educate the nurses to these differences, I would first have to identify the differences and organize the concepts into an understandable whole.

An incredible journey ensued. I isolated concepts of barotrauma, vacuolization, ozone toxicities, radiation hazards, and acceleration trauma, and organized them into a textbook for flight nurses: *AIRBORNE PATIENT CARE MANAGEMENT: A MULTIDISCIPLINARY APPROACH.* Once published, the government of Chile translated the text into Spanish and adopted it as their country's official air evacuation manual. I was invited to teach this content as a Master's level continuing education course at a local university. I used my flight experiences as a backdrop for fiction in "PILOT QUEST." I was invited to consult for major businesses such as Monsanto and Utah's Holy Cross Hospital. I formulated the Aerohemodynamics Theory designed to be used by flight nursing personnel and flight crews.

If you let a snowball roll down a mountain, you will see that it picks up more snow as it rolls-so that by the time it reaches the bottom, it is much bigger than the handful of snow you started with. Like that snowball, my efforts in starting this business kept on adding new potential as it rolled along the way.

On it's journey, the snowball rolls over jagged rocks, sometimes bumping into trees and losing volume as it goes because things do not always run smoothly. But...anything worth doing is worth doing well and worth taking risks for.

Analysis

Not every good idea will present itself cloaked in mystery such as the above situation; but it is important to recognize and seize upon a good idea or opportunity when one comes along. Surrounding yourself with people who are supportive of you and your ideas is also important, especially at the beginning of a new venture. There are many nay-sayers in the world who thrive on insisting, "that won't work", while they sit back and do nothing. Tune a deaf ear to them and proceed to show them how your idea CAN work by MAKING it happen!

Leadership Success Strategy
Capitalize *immediately* on opportunities that fit your goals and expertise, or apathy, inertia and/or self-doubt may prevent you from accomplishing them in the future.

Principle(s)
- Think of success as a journey-not a destination.
- Worthwhile goals are usually *progressively* realized.
- Self-fulfilling prophecies often self-fulfill.
- See failure as temporary
- See failures as isolated incidents

- Be resilient-bounce back
- Enjoy the ride!

Theory Guiding Practice

Nursing

The *Aerohemodynamics Theory* is a grand theory by this author that correlates the concepts of Acceleration/deceleration, vacuolization, barotraumas, gaseous toxicities, radiation hazards and thermo-stability with psychological factors into a cohesive guide that can be used as a template for airborne patient care.

Non-Nursing

Rosen's Relational Complexity Theory arose from his research proposing a methodology he called 'Relational Biology''. In biology the relationship among the parts and the effects of interactions among them must, according to Rosen, be considered as additional 'relational parts', or, 'structure-functionality relationships''. Rosen's attempts at establishing a taxonomy of these structure-functionality relationships fits well with the establishment of a taxonomy of concepts related to the Aerohemodynamics Theory.

Evidence-Base

Baianu, I. (2006). Robert Rosen's work and complex systems biology. *Axiomathes, 16*(1-2), 25-34.

Rashevsky, N. (1969). Outline of a unified approach to physics, biology, and sociology. *Bulletin of Mathematical Biophysics, 31*, 159-198.

Rosen, R. (1960). A quantum-theoretic approach to genetic problems. *Bulletin of Mathematical Biophysics, 22*, 227-255.

Sredl, D. (1979). Acceleration phenomena: Effect on pregnant women *Point of View 16*(4), 6-7.

Sredl, D. (1979). Top flight care in the air. *Emergency, 11*(11), 58-60.

Sredl, D. (1979). Up in the air. . *Nursing '79, 8*(10), 110-116.

Sredl, D. (1980). Aerohemodynamics. *Point of View, 17*(3), 11.

Sredl, D. (1981). Aviation opportunities for occupational health nurses. *Occupational Health Nursing 29*(4), 20-21.

Sredl, D. (1983). *Airborne Patient Care Management: A Multidisciplinary Approach.* St. Louis: Medical Research Associates Publications.

Sredl, D. (2005). Evidence-based nursing practice (EBNP) meta-paradigm: A crystallized synthesis of apperceptions, beliefs and efforts toward EBNP implementation among contemporary nurse executives in the United States of America (pp. 166). St. Louis, MO: Doctoral Dissertation, University of Missouri- Saint Louis.

Sredl, D. (2007). *Pilot Quest.* Frederick, MD: PublishAmerica

Sredl, D. (2008). Conceptual Model: The Aerohemodynamics Meta-Theory. *Journal of Teaching and Learning in Nursing, 3*, 115-120.

Sredl, D. (2009). Multi-attribute Multidisciplinary Concept Analyses related to the Aerohemodynamics Conceptual Model *Journal of Teaching and Learning in Nursing 4*(3), 98-103.

Sredl, D. (2011). Evidence-Based Process (EBP) Considerations of Hypoxia During Flight for Flight Nurses: The Aerohemodynamics Theory Revisited *Airline Industry: Strategies, Operations and Safety*

Sredl, D., Aukamp, V. (2006). Evidence-Based Nursing Care Management for the Pregnant Woman With an Ostomy. *Journal of Wound, Ostomy and Continence Nursing, 33*(1), 42-49.

In: Evidence-Based Leadership Success Strategies …   ISBN: 978-1-62081-104-7
Editor: Darlene Sredl   © 2012 Nova Science Publishers, Inc.

Chapter 8

HARASSMENT

LEADERSHIP STRATEGY SITUATION #8.1

Frederick Brown

Harassment Prevents Retaining Good Employees

Being employed as a Clinical Emergency/Trauma Nurse III at two of the nation's finest level- one trauma centers in the country (Georgetown and John's Hopkins University Medical Centers), resulted in some of the most rewarding experiences any nurse could ever ask for. I returned to the Midwest due to family obligations and continued my nursing career at the city's local university teaching hospital, a level one-trauma center at my alma mater. I was thrilled to join the team of some of the industry's highly trained trauma professionals.

It was during my hospital orientation that I came to understanding how gossip is a factor in the work place, an understanding that stayed with me throughout my tenure at the institution. My colleagues warned me about a doctor in our department that the administration allowed to demean, curse at, harass, and actually assault the nursing personnel. The nurses stated that their working relationship with this physician was strained at best, and they suspected that he had a classic case of bipolar disorder. At this point I became extra vigilant with regard to this physician and discovered the importance of maintaining a good working relationship with all of the physicians in the department.

Once I began my unit- based orientation, my immediate supervisors, department director, and preceptor warned me about this physician, cautioning me to keep out of his way. During my initial training within the department, as he extended a glare in my direction, he asked my preceptor about me. My preceptor explained that I was a new trauma registered nurse team member from the East Coast with a great deal of emergency room and trauma experience and that I held a master's degree in education.

It was when I began working independently in the department that problems began with this physician. I overheard him tell one of the charge nurses that I was not implementing his orders in a timely fashion and that he felt as though I was too self-confident in my knowledge. I informed my supervisors and director about my feelings and concerns about the situation.

They responded that he is the physician; that he was just that way; and that the physicians worked for a contractual physician agency, so there was nothing that could be done concerning his behavior. I felt somewhat defeated and overwhelmed, despite the fact that I loved my work at the institution. I held the medical center/university mission, values, and philosophies dear to my heart. I was afraid of this physician, and knew that the negative-but staff-accepted working relationship in the department might cause a problem for me in allowing my real personality- entertaining, polite, kind, and uncomplicated-to come out freely.

Unfortunately, a few months down the road, the nightmare from hell began. I noticed that when the patient acuity was extremely high and we were short staffed with all trauma bays full with the department on standby, this physician began cursing and being very rude to everyone in the department. Almost every patient I cared for involved over 30 written physicians' orders that needed to be implemented. There was difficulty in establishing vascular access on some of my patients, and all of my patients required critical-care nursing measures (for example; blood administration, IV pressor medication, and/or mechanical ventilation assistance for respiratory problems). In one instance the physician in question asked if I had seen and completed those orders on one of his critically ill patients. I responded that they had not yet been completed, but I was doing the best that I could under such circumstances. I asked him to please have patience with me and work with me tonight because it is busy, chaotic, and short staffed. As the night progressed, I noticed words being exchanged at the nurses' station. The charge nurse then informed me that the doctor wanted to speak with me in the supply room. I proceeded to the supply room to meet him. At this point, the physician verbally assaulted and cursed at me, asking me who I thought I was, and demanding that I complete his tasks immediately. He finished his tirade by stating, "I am the physician, I have been here for five years and will be here when you are gone. I have seen nurses like you come and go." I was astonished and in disbelief that this doctor felt that he had the authority to curse at me and talk to me as though I were something less than human.

I explained the situation to the house supervisor on duty only to later learn that she misrepresented the situation making it appear to be my fault. I then brought the occurrence to the attention of my charge nurse and unit director, and they said that they would look into it and talk with me later. I demanded a meeting with the physician; my boss, the ER dept nursing director; and his boss, the medical director of the ER. An agreement was reached that he would work with me and other staff, but I was held responsible in not carrying out his orders in a suitable manner.

As weeks and months passed, he and another charge nurse scrutinized my charts, looking for mistakes, since they could not find fault with my clinical skills and nursing knowledge. The pressure, constant scrutiny, and distrust finally became too great. Coupled with the continual backlash that I endured for being outspoken about the behavior and verbal abuse of this physician, I felt the need to resign from this position.

I later realized I did not quit the medial center; *I quit my manager because she allowed this type of behavior from the physician and did nothing to stop the abuse.* She could have had me transferred or lodged a formal department-wide grievance against this physician, but she did not.

Being an emergency room trauma nurse is work that I truly love. It is my life's calling and passion. I strongly feel that if the institution had valued its staff members, there would have been a system in place to curtail problems with physician-related abuse before it could rear its ugly head and before it could cause irreparable damage to a staff member. Furthermore, if the medical center had had a system for retaining good employees, it would have been able to retain well-trained, educated, and dedicated staff members like myself. Department transfer would have given me the opportunity to retain my seniority yet work with a different staff. The outcome could have been much different.

Analysis

Remember...people do not quit jobs; people quit managers!!

All new employees should have an assigned buddy (preceptor) with significant organization input. There needs to be effective, clear, written facility and dept orientation schedules of working hours, shifts, and days of the week, working conditions (i.e., group nursing report, snack time). Employees and team-workers who participate in the Shared Governance model – empowers the manager and/or supervisor who is pro-employee, friendly, and easy to work with to foster your success, department success, and companies success.

Foster a collaborative working environment.

Adopt user-friendly computerized state- of- the- art patient chart apparatus. Arrange patient care items conveniently in the patient's rooms. Open lines of communication between staff members and management. Advocate for an open door policy by nurse manager. Career ladder benefit options should include recognition and acknowledgment of achievement for nursing advanced degrees and specialty certifications within their dept. Provide opportunities for growth and advancement. Recognize employees' special and/or unique needs. Develop avenues to communicate effectively and efficiently in deal with RN-MD, RN-RN, RN-outside agencies i.e., paramedics, other nurses, and other doctors/vendors, RN-allied healthcare worker, RN-Manager, and RN-patient issues/problems in order to keep and retained trained clinically competent nurses. Have a clear career pathway, or ladder for career advancement, Develop incentives for special work situations i.e., working overtime, going beyond what is expected. Offer highly competitive salaries with extra incentives i.e., significant shift/weekend differentiate, bonus pay, and sign-on/relocation packages for professional staff.

Provide a generous and comprehensive benefit employee package i.e., in- house day care center, free parking, 30% discount in the gift shop/cafeteria, tuition assistance/ loan repayment option for professional staff.

Foster pride pertaining to the mission, value statement, core standards, and facility/dept philosophy in the healthcare organization. Establish effective policies to deal with verbally abusive physicians. Provide budget resources to the Staff Development dept so the department may offer staff education courses.

It is a unit manager's job to make the workplace safe and free of intimidation and/or sexual harassment. If a case goes to court and testimony reveals that the manager knew of the harassment but did nothing to stop it, that manager will be found at fault. The organization will be found at fault as an additional result.

Leadership Success Strategy

Communicate Often

Hold your ground, but when you are playing tug-of-war with a tiger, let the tiger take the pull-toy before he takes your arm.

Stress can kill.

Principle(s)

Profit from failure (Napoleon Hill).

> "When the going gets rough, get as rough as the job."
>
> Dr. Norman Vincent Peale

Cultivate an inner emotional calm through the storm.

> "The world can take everything away from you but one thing-your dignity"
>
> Kaile Warren

"You can never change your image with people who are against you by backing down for them. *You'll never make them like you anyway.* So, if you believe you're right, stand up to the opposition and hit hard for your convictions" Bishop Fred Pierce Corson.

> "Get mad, then get over it"
>
> Colin Powell

Theory Guiding Practice

Nursing

Patricia Benner's Theory of Novice to Expert is a mid-range theory to define stages of function in the field of nursing:

1) Novice
2) Advanced Beginner
3) Competent
4) Proficient
5) Expert

Non-Nursing

1) *Bowling and Beehr's research introduced an Attribution-and Reciprocity-Based Workplace Harassment Model* that examines the link between harassment and it's consequences that was found to be negatively correlated to the well-being of employees and their organizations. A meta-analysis of workplace harassment was also done by the authors.

2) *Salovey and Mayer's Theory of Emotional Intelligence* involves a unique set of intellectual skills designed to appraise and express emotion appropriately and alter the affective reactions of others.

Evidence-Base

Bowling, N., and Beehr, T. (2006). Workplace harassment from the victim's perspective: A theoretical model and meta-analysis. *J Appl, Psychol*(91), 5.

Jenkins, R., Sredl, D., Hsueh, H., Ding, C. (2007). Evidence-based nursing process (EBNP) consumer culture attribute identity: A message-based persuasion strategy study among nurse executives in the U.S *Journal of Medical Sciences, 27*(2), 55-62.

LEADERSHIP STRATEGY SITUATION # 8.2

Darlene Sredl

When the Harassment Comes from the Top

It had been a difficult winter at the luxurious nursing home where I worked as Director of Nurses. The flagrant affair between the Administrator and the Dining Room Supervisor had finally been brought to an abrupt end when the Administrator's wife discovered where the secret lay one quiet Saturday morning. The Dining Room Supervisor was conspicuously absent on Monday and the reason why traveled fast.

The staff was relieved. Now, we thought, we could get our collective attention back to our real mission of running a nursing home and caring for the residents- not that we didn't do this before the affair was exposed, but day-to-day activities were certainly accompanied by a lot of gossip.

What I did not realize at the time was that once a man has turned to philandering, the loss of a regular partner does not necessarily signal the loss of desire. Oftentimes his amorous net is simply cast into uncharted waters hoping to find another catch. Little did I realize at the time that the uncharted waters he would be fishing next were mine!

The situation climaxed at a day-long educational seminar held at a local hotel. Several members of the administrative team were scheduled to attend. Mr. Administrator sat next to me at a long table covered with an equally long beige linen tablecloth. Each place was furnished with a note pad, pencil and water glass. Midway through the first speaker's session, I felt a hand on my thigh. Thinking that surely this was a mistake, I shifted uncomfortably in my chair and the hand dropped off. But… moments later, the hand returned- this time with a squeeze- unmistakable in its intent.

"What am I going to do?" I thought frantically. "This cannot be allowed to continue…I have to nip this in the bud right now. But…How? I have to definitively let him know that I am *not* a candidate for whatever he has in mind. How can I do it without totally smashing his male ego? But,…I also want to keep my job. This is the best job I have ever had. If I don't handle this right I might not have it very long."

Using the circumstances and things within reach, I took the pencil and drew a long line from top to bottom on the linen tablecloth.

Curious, "What are you doing?" He asked.
Looking him straight in the eye, I hissed, "I am drawing the line."

Analysis

Using communication tools of puns or a twist of words can inject some subtle humor into a pensive situation. The situation must be dealt with IMMEDIATELY because any non-refutational delay will be perceived as consent in the mind of the perpetrator and the situation will become more and more encumbered with innuendo and overt acts of touching.

Leadership Strategy
You are the guardian of your own body. Use your critical thinking skills to defuse a potentially explosive emotional situation as soon as you perceive it.

Principle(s)

"With God's help you live through life's storms-even the one that may be buffeting you now."

Dr. Norman Vincent Peale

Every problem contains the seeds of it's own solution-find them.

Theory Guiding Practice

Nursing
Roux's Inner Strength in Women Model focuses on the phenomenon of inner strength in women studied with various chronic illnesses. It is appropriate in this situation also because a woman who has been sexually harassed has to exhibit resources of inner strength in order to continue in the present and plan for the future with the new context of harassment looming in the picture. Five constructs support the infrastructure:

1) Knowing and searching;
2) Nurturing through connection;
3) Dwelling in a different place by creating the spirit within;
4) Healing through movement in the present; and,
5) Connecting with the future by living a new normal.

Cogin and Fish's research examins the prevalence of sexual harassment in nursing from a mixed method research methodology. Questionnaire data suggest that patients are the most likely perpetrators but interview data named physicians as the most likely perpetrators among a sample of 538 completed questionnaires and 23 in-depth structured interviews. Results indicate that leadership behaviors, unbalanced job gender ratios, and no prior socialization are positively associated with sexual harassment.

Non-Nursing

Magley's Framework of Women's Coping with Sexual Harassment provides insight into a complicated problem requiring complex coping skills. Using multidimensional scaling, clustering and confirmatory factor analysis across eight data sets, four cluster factors emerged: behavioral engagement, behavioral disengagement, cognitive engagement, and cognitive disengagement.

Evidence-Base

Cogin, J., and Fish, A. (2009). Sexual harassment-- a touchy subject for nurses. *J Health Organ Manag, 23*(4), 442-462.

Dingley, C., Bush, H., and Roux, G. (2001). Inner strength in women recovering from coronary heart disease: A grounded theory. *Journal of Theory Construction and Testing, 6*(1), 4-5.

Magley, V. (2002). Coping with sexual harrassment: Reconceptualizing women's resistance. *J. Pers Soc Psychol, 83*(4), 930-946

Roux, G. (1998). *Inner Strength in Women: A Grounded Theory*. Paper presented at the Qualitative Health Research International Conference

Roux, G., and Dingley, C. (1997). *A Grounded Theory: Inner Strength in Women*. Paper presented at the Scientific Session of Sigma Theta Tau International Convention.

Roux, G., Dingley, C., and Bush, H. (2002). Inner strength in women: Metasynthesis of qualitative findings in theory development. *Journal of Theory Construction and Testing, 6*(1), 4-15.

LEADERSHIP STRATEGY SITUATION #8.3

Darlene Sredl

Turnabout is Fair Play

The proper, strait-laced, and very married head of one of the hospital's major medical departments came bursting into the nurses' packed lunchroom one day demanding to speak to Nurse X. Angrily waving a pack of documents he issued forth a tirade of epithets ending with..." and she is so stupid! Nurse X, the object of his usual wrath, was in the lunchroom at the time-but this time she was ready for him. She looked up from her sandwich and calmly purred, "That ain't whatcha said last night, honey". Whoops of raucous laughter followed as the surprised Doctor, in light of this unexpected turn of events, hastily left.

Analysis

It is difficult to confront someone with a God-complex head-on and win, but this nurse did just that. She had analyzed this man's vulnerable spots and was obviously ready for the time a situation like this might erupt.

No one took her words seriously but they were high enough in emotional impact to defuse the situation and send the doctor packing until some later time when the incident that brought this about could be dealt with civilly.

This doctor intentionally sought to sully the professional actions of Nurse X. And, like O'Tooles Corrolary to Murphy's Law- he chose the worst possible time (for highest possible impact)- when most of the unit's staff had congregated together for lunch. Nurse X's words ricocheted around the room, puncturing the pompous doctor and flattening his malicious intent.

Leadership Strategy
Painting a verbal picture is worth 1000 words.

Principle(s)

Emotional Intelligence is acting (not reacting) with a cool frame of mind.

> "He (she) who steps on the stone he/she stumbled on, rises in the world."
> Dr. Norman Vincent Peale.

Theory Guiding Practice

Nursing
Peplau's Interpersonal Relations Model (1952) views nursing as a maturing process that develops over four phases: Orientation, identification, exploitation, and resolution, through which a power-shift occurs.

Non-Nursing
Gutheil and Gabbard's Boundary Theory focuses mainly on defensive postures concerning sexual misconduct that occur with boundary violations during psychotherapy

Evidence-Base

Fitzgerald, L., and Shullman, S. (1993). Sexual Harassment: A research analysis and agenda for the 1990s. *Journal of Vocational Behavior,, 42*, 5-27.

Fitzgerald, L., Gelfand, M., and Drasgow, F. (1995). Measuring sexual harassment: Theoretical and psychometric advances. *Basic and Applied Social Psychology, 17*, 425-445.

Magley, V., Hulin, C., Fitzgerald, L., and DeNardo, M. . (1999). Outcomes of self-labeling sexual harassment *Journal of Applied Psychology, 84*, 390-402.

Pryor, J., and McKinney, K. . (1995). Research on sexual harassment: Lingering issues and future directions. *Basic and Applied Social Psychology, 17*, 605-611.

LEADERSHIP STRATEGY SITUATION #8.4

Darlene Sredl

Trust Your Nursing Intuition

I was a newly hired V.P. of Nursing at a 200+ bed Midwestern hospital when the Director of Maintenance suggested that I accompany him to the hospital basement where he would show me how to turn off all the important valves for gas, water, and electricity in the event of an emergency during which I might be the only member of administration in the facility and would have to deal with the emergency single-handedly..

While I mentally acknowledged the probable need for this knowledge in my position, I felt uneasy about the prospect of going into the basement with a man I did not know. The validity of this suspicion was borne out a short time later when my secretary cautioned me about being alone with "Mr. F" as he had earned a reputation for being an opportunistic womanizer. I had an 'AH-HA! Moment' and scheduled the 'basement field trip' for the following week to give myself some time to think.

Gradually an idea began to take hold. I asked my secretary for the names of the 10 most recently hired RNs and found that 5 of them were scheduled to work on the date of the 'field trip'. I then requested that the 5 recently hired nurses complete their shift assignments by 1:30 PM on the day in question and report to my office at 1:45 PM for additional orientation.

When Mr. F arrived, he found he now had 6 newly- hired nurses to show the main valve turnoffs to. I do believe he was turned off as well.

Analysis

Starting a position at any level is challenging. There is so much to take in and assimilate- policies, procedures, and learning personality traits about the various co-workers one will be working with. Although one always hopes that your co-workers are made of fine and upstanding ethical principles, this is not always the case. Listen to your intuition and, when in doubt, devise a plan to include others in dubious situations. Extra witnesses on hand will work in your favor IF the situation turns out to be not so fine and ethically upstanding as you imagined. It is a unit manager's job to make the workplace safe and free of intimidation and/or sexual harassment. If a case goes to court and testimony reveals that the manager knew of the harassment but did nothing to stop it, that manager will be found at fault. The organization will be found at fault as an additional result.

Leadership Strategy

There is safety and an intact reputation in numbers!

Strategy

Intimidation by sexual harassment must be confronted immediately, and prevented from happening again.

Principle(s)

Rothbard's Law-everyone specializes in his own area of weakness.
Rotten attitudes, left alone, ruin everything

Theory Guiding Practice

Nursing

Martha Roger's Science of Unitary Human Beings is a complex and futuristic paradigm that introduced a new worldview to nursing. She also developed another Theory of Paranormal Phenomena. Her theory contains a tenet that human beings are possessed of electrical energy patterns since energy is everywhere, constantly shifting and changing and, in fact, pandimensional. Rogers said that 'paranormal' experiences are actually changing energy field patterns, Human and environmental energy fields are integral with each other Rogers felt. Rogers also identified a state she called 'beyond waking' which included hyperawareness, tacit knowing, *intuition,* clairvoyance and other mystical experiences.

Non-Nursing

1) Matusitz and Breen's Use of Innoculation Theory in the Prevention of Sexual Harassment in the Medical Workplace deals with indices of extreme behavior in the workplace.
2) Howard Gardner's Theory of Multiple Intelligences- Existential Intelligence is one of the ten 'intelligences' that Dr. Gardner explains with which we grasp information and learn. This Existential intelligence includes Extra Sensory Perception (ESP), Clairvoyance, Premonitions, and other paranormal phenomena that cannot be explained logically, but that do happen to some people to give them advance knowledge or warning of an event about to happen that could not be explained through normal channels of communication.

Evidence-Base

Butcher, H. (2004b). Nursing's distinctive knowledge. In H. B. L. Haynes, and T. Boese (Ed.), *Nursing in Contemporary Society: Issues, Trends and Transition to Practice.* Upper Saddle River, NJ: Prentice-Hall.

Fendrich, M., Woodward, P., and Richman, J. (2002). The structure of harassment and abuse in the workplace: A factorial comparison of two measures. *Violence and Victime, 17*(4), 491-505.

Matusitz, J., and Breen, G. (2005). Prevention of sexual harassment in the medical setting: Apply inoculation theory. *J. Health Soc Policy, 21*(2), 53-71.

In: Evidence-Based Leadership Success Strategies …   ISBN: 978-1-62081-104-7
Editor: Darlene Sredl   © 2012 Nova Science Publishers, Inc.

Chapter 9

CULTURAL CONSIDERATIONS

SITUATION 9.1. THE MOST USEFUL TOOL IN CROSS CULTURAL CARE (THAT YOU ALREADY KNOW HOW TO DO)

Barbara Bogomolov[*]

Clinical Manager: Refugee Health Service, Center for Diversity
and Cultural Competence, Barnes-Jewish Hospital, Washington
University Medical Center, St. Louis, MO, US

Introduction

Some 20 years ago, I acquired responsibility for the small interpreter service of our large academic medical center in the Midwest. The three interpreters were worried about working under a nursing administrator and moving from their previous home in social work. I heard through the grapevine that they were especially concerned that I had a working command of their language. I didn't think that was problematic, but it didn't take long to discover that the interpreters had a legitimate concern.

While working the desk in one of the clinics I managed, I overheard a physician telling a patient that the biopsy on her lung showed that she had a *cancer*. My stomach clenched as I heard the Russian interpreter say that the biopsy showed a *growth*. Russian has a word for cancer, *Rok,* but, the interpreter had not used that word. As I listened, I realized that the interpreter was covertly editing the physician in other ways, sharply modifying and reducing the import of his words. When the patient and interpreter approached the desk to schedule follow-up appointments and testing, the interpreter met my eyes and her expression became guarded. Her attitude elevated to defensive in my office an hour later when I called her in to talk about what had happened. She blurted out. "This is why we didn't want to work for you. We knew that we would be forced to do things to hurt our patients!" Stung, I asked hotly just how accurate interpretation of the physician's words constituted "hurting the patient." The

---

[*] Email: bob6753@bjc.org.

interpreter jutted her chin and fired back, "You may understand *Russian*, but you do not understand *Russians*. You do not know our culture. Good doctors, caring doctors, do not speak straight of things like cancer to the patient. It would be cruel and wrong and the patient would very likely give up, go home and die. By speaking the way I do, she will get the care that she needs, but will not have to be crushed by the word, 'Rok'".

The interpreter was essentially correct that I had only the vaguest notion of traditional Russian cultural imperatives around medical truth telling. Still, even as a very green administrator, I knew quite a bit about the Western medical construct of informed consent. Added to that conflict, I also knew that an interpreter editing a speaker (without informing the speaker that the editing was occurring) was committing the worst kind of ethical breach. As the interpreter and I squared off, I could see her waiting for the metaphorical ax to fall. I think we both were surprised when what came out of my mouth next was, "Tell me more."

Our discussion ultimately took some months and pulled in patients and providers, interpreters and Russian community members, hospital risk managers and our multidisciplinary ethics committee. The three Russian interpreters shifted from evasive action to active participants in our search for a way to reconcile the medical center's need to obtain informed consent with our growing recognition that there were individuals in many cultures who held that our level of physician truth- telling could do more harm than good. These cultures placed the burden for serious health care decision making with the doctor or the patient's family.

With everyone pulling in the same direction, we carved out an approach that balanced the expectation that competent adults participate in the informed consent process with the universal medical mandate to "do no harm." With a nod to Wisconsin case law, we created something called the *waiver process*. Working under this concept, the physician needing to discuss the difficult information approaches the patient and, through the interpreter, offers that, for instance, "tests results are back and important findings need to be discussed and crucial decisions made." The doctor then asks the patient if that is something that the patient wishes to do for himself, or if there is someone else he wishes to receive this information who can, and will, make care-planning decisions for him. At first, the interpreters feared that even this was too much disclosure, but they committed to transparency and accuracy in their role. Our physicians expected that patients given this much choice would say, "Give it to me straight, Doc." What actually happened was that many immigrant patients exercised their autonomy by choosing to opt out of informed consent. They delegated the responsibility to loved ones, to informed friends…once even to a rabbi. The only option closed to them was to tell the physician, "No, you decide." Someone, other than a member of the care team, had to be chosen by the patient to hear, and to decide. If the patient opted out, they were kept informed of next steps and of what to expect from procedures and therapies. But the diagnosis and prognosis, always available to them if they asked, was never unloaded, unasked for, where it might "crush." Over time and thoughtfully applied, this approach won support from diverse immigrant community members and hospital lawyers grappling with HIPAA. Our interpreter service now numbers 37 individuals who provided or facilitated over 41,000 interpreted encounters in 81 languages at our complex last year. The majority of patients, from around the world, chose to hear. Some patients, including those born and raised in the shadow of our medical center, chose to leave that burden to others whom they trusted. As head of our hospital's Refugee Health Service, a part of our Center for Diversity and Cultural Competence, I still have ultimate responsibility for our interpreter team, although it is now directly supervised by the woman who held her ground that day in my office. I have learned a great deal about the rich diversity of health beliefs over the course of my career; and I will be learning still more in the future, as we continue to design patient-centered care that treats people the way they wish to be treated, not the way you would wish to be treated in their place. The powerful tool that supports my continued growth is the same one that I stumbled upon in my office those many years ago... three little words—"Tell me more."

LEADERSHIP STRATEGY; Always respond to the *presupposition,* NOT to the sequence it is hidden in. ("definition-a presupposition is something that a native speaker of a language knows is part of the meaning of a sequence of that language, even if it not overtly present in the sequence". (Elgin, 1980), p15).

ANALYSIS: Knowing a language is not the same as understanding the culture of the people who speak that language. A good administrator always keeps tight reins on her/his emotional intelligence keeping discussions on an even keel. By asking the open-ended question, "Tell me more" the author advanced not only the conversation but the relationship that ultimately led to a smoothly running department in which all employees felt that their voices were heard and their beliefs respected.

PRINCIPLE(S): Be open to learning about new and different points of view

Learning, threatening to the self (with new attitudes or perspectives), is more easily assimilated when external threats are kept to a minimum

Theory Guiding Practice

Nursing

Madeleine Leininger, originated the Transcultural Theory of Nursing, a Grand Theory envisioned as a possible means for promoting relationships between people from different cultures. The study of specific cultural health practices helps to maintain health, promote healing, and prevent illness or disease, while aiding in the recovery process. Culturally based care results in the ability to know, explain, interpret, and predict beneficial congruent care practices. Leininger devised a "Sunrise Enabler" graphic to demonstrate the many rays of caring within her theory. The theory is holistic, incorporating cultural background, socioeconomic status, religion, political views, values regarding lifespan, kinship, and philosophy of living.

Non-Nursing

The Speech Codes Theory by Gerry Philipsen evolved from ethnographic studies determining what meanings are shared within a culture. The Speech Codes Theory contains five propositions:

1 A distinctive culture contains distinctive speech coded.
2 The speech code contains culturally distinctive psychology, sociology and rhetoric.
3 Communication interpretation depends upon the speech codes used by both speakers and listeners in creating and interpreting their meaning in the communication.
4 Speech codes are always on display.
5 Shared speech codes can be used artfully for predicting, explaining and controlling the conversational conduct.

Evidence-Base

Elgin, S. (1980). *The Gentle Art of Verbal Self Defense*. US: Dorset Press.

Helms, J. (1993). Black and White Racial Identity: Theory, Research, and *Practice*. Westport: Praeger.

Jenkins, R., Sredl, D., Hsueh, H., Ding, C. (2007). Evidence-based nursing process (EBNP) consumer culture attribute identity: A message-based persuasion strategy study among nurse executives in the U.S. *Journal of Medical Sciences, 27*(2), 55-62.

SITUATION 9.2. CULTURAL COMPETENCE

Marge Phillips [*]

Lutheran School of Nursing, St. Louis, MO

Introduction

When working in a foreign country, nurses must first realize that differences exist between cultures and must genuinely appreciate the new culture they are exposed to. Don't try to change everything.

Work alongside the nurse and, at appropriate times, begin to show them your tips on getting a particular procedure done. You have to learn their culture first.

Americans tend to think ethnocentrically- that our way is the best; but unfortunately, that's not always true. Never belittle or speak negatively about their ways; instead, concentrate on building rapport. You may not meet your expectations but at least you've got a start. Don't rush. Americans are the only ones in a hurry. Be patient.

LEADERSHIP STRATEGY: Transformative nursing involves building relationships not just accomplishing a goal.

ANALYSIS: Cultural competence occurs at many levels. Building a relationship around trust is an important starting point. When one is a guest in another's home one does not take liberties.

The situation described above is like being a guest-only in another's workplace in another's culture. Keeping in mind the communication differences between Western and Eastern countries one must measure words wisely before speaking.

Communication tactics that we, in Western civilization, take for granted (like making eye contact, shaking hands and speaking assertively) are not endearing to nurses practicing in Eastern countries. Go slow.

PRINCIPLE(S) Aspire to higher things or a higher purpose

---

[*] Email: majormarge@aol.com.

Theory Guiding Practice

Nursing

Campinha-Bacote's Cultural Competence in the Delivery of Healthcare Services Model contains five constructs within it: Cultural awareness; cultural knowledge; cultural skill; cultural encounters, and cultural desire.

Non-Nursing

Ponterotto's Theory of the Multicultural Personality. Ponterotto hypothesized that the individual possessed of a multicultural personality may experience higher levels of psychological well-being than those who do not possess this personality trait. Ponterotto cited three important aspects of the Multicultural Personality model as being:

1   An openness to and appreciation of multicultural issues;
2   Strong multicultural intra and interpersonal traits; and,
3   Physical and psychological well-being with an interrelationship among these traits.

Evidence-Base

Hong, G. (2009). Familiarity, preference, and utilization of ethnic items among Asian Americans. *Asian Nursing Research,* 3(4), 186-195.

SITUATION #3 9.3. COMMUNICATION HELP

Kuei-HsiangHsueh [*]

College of Nursing, University of Missouri St. Louis, St. Louis, MO

Introduction

"Arriving from Taiwan to accept a faculty position in a major Midwestern university, I felt very insecure speaking the limited English that I knew. I discovered two ways that American culture helped me improve my language skills." The first way was going to the library and reading books and journals in my field. When I came across a passage I didn't understand, I would ask the person sitting next to me (or in close proximity) to explain what was meant by the passage. I watched body language to determine how many questions like this I could ask that person before the person left (or moved) in exasperation. The second method that I used to help improve my language skills involved engaging tele-marketers in conversation. When I answered such a call, I would feign interest in the product or service that the telemarketer was promoting just to keep them on the line and talking. By asking

[*] hsuehk@umsl.edu.

questions and pondering their answers, I learned some of the colloquisms that are used so often in America. The telemarketers, in turn, usually were only used to having brief solicitation calls- but when they talked to me they spoke a long time indeed."

LEADERSHIP STRATEGY: Use the resources freely available to you to perfect your communication skills. ANALYSIS: This author first used critical thinking skills as she became aware of common American goings-on that could be put to constructive use in helping perfect her communication skills. She then applied her decision to expand on conversations that could benefit the fine- tuning of her conversation skills.

PRINCIPLE(S) Problems contain the seeds of their own solution- find them!

Theory Guiding Practice

Nursing

Wiedenbach's Prescriptive Theory is a situation-producing theory which aims to direct action towards a specific goal. It causes the user to implement a plan of action necessary to bring about results related to the central purpose (usually of acquiring information).

Non-Nursing

McClelland's Motivational Needs Theory. This theory recognizes three distinct motivational needs: Achievement motivation, authority/power motivation, and affiliation motivation. Achievement motivation centers about the need to attain challenging but realistic goals. The authority/power motivation drives a personal need to be influential or in nursing, to make a difference. The need for affiliation speaks to the 'team player' in us all- a need to be liked and respected by one's peers.

Evidence-Base

Griffin, E. (1997). *A First Look at Communication*. New York: McGraw-Hill.

SITUATION 9.4. GROWING UP FAST

Esther Christian

Introduction

As a new registered nurse who had just passed NCLEX, I was full of excitement and enthusiasm. Very quickly, however, I got indoctrinated into a culture-unbalanced world. Though it happened years ago, I remember it as if it happened yesterday.

I was working on a medical-surgical unit in a 500+ bed hospital located in the southern region of the United States. Demographically the city is comprised of more than 60% African Americans. I am one of them. The shift had just begun and I was busy getting change-of-shift report and chart reviews. I was anxious to "get down the hall" and begin direct patient care. Three other licensed personnel were assigned eight patients each, as I was, and we each had a nursing assistant assigned to help. As I went from room to room completing my assessments, administering medication, and documenting, I also assisted some of the patients with their personal hygiene. This was my normal routine as a nurse and I felt confident in what I was doing.

Rounds were almost completed when the nursing assistant reported that one of the older female patients had just called her name using the "N" word. This was the first inter-racial conflict that I had to face without the back-up of having my instructor or other student peers to advise me through. Hurriedly, I reviewed my notes on the patient in question as I had just visited her. I did not find anything abnormal, such as a change in mental status or abnormal lab values that might alter the thought process potentially sparking such behavior. I knew I had to collect all the information from the nursing assistant. The nursing assistant was very upset and stated that she would not be treated that way by anybody-sick or not. I again searched up and down the hall for another of my peers but did not see anyone. I tried to calm the nursing assistant down but her continued vocal outrage made me feel that I was doing more harm than good. To this equation I should add that I was just 23 years old while the nursing assistant was in her mid-50s. How could I, I wondered, a novice and emotionally immature nurse, handle such a conflict?

I decided to go back to the patient and find out what *she* felt was going on. The patient was very upset when I approached her. She did not seem to remember me though I had just assessed her with no problem. She said, "N' you better not put your dirty hands on me". Obviously she was not the same darling patient I had previously assessed. Now she was very upset and outspoken. I tried to re-introduce myself as the nurse who had just assessed her. I told her that I wanted to help her. For some inexplicable (to me) reason this seemed to make the situation worst.

The charge nurse had just completed her rounds and, hearing the loud confrontation, came into the room. The charge nurse was a Caucasian as was the patient. The charge nurse took over. She sent me out of the room on the pretense of getting some supplies. While I was out of the room, she investigated further (I later found) and discovered that the patient felt that her life was in danger because of the way the nursing assistant had talked to her. Tearfully, the patient said that she had been incontinent and that the nursing assistant accused her of soiling herself on purpose!

The nursing assistant also asserted that the patient knew how to call for help, or she could have just 'held it'. The nursing assistant finished, the patient alleged, by saying that if she did it again she was going to 'whip her.' When she left the room told the patient that she was going to get help to clean her up.

When I, another African-American, came into the room the patient may have thought that I was the 'help' that was going to whip her! She was upset with me because she thought I was going to follow-up with the previous threat from the nursing assistant.

The charge nurse handled the situation from this point on and found a course of action that brought about a positive change in the situation. After the charge nurse got this important information from the patient, she reinforced our goal to provide care for the patient.

The charge nurse agreed that the nursing assistant's choice of words, if that was indeed what she said, was inappropriate, but also added that in African-American culture, statements such as "hit you upside the head" and 'gonna whip you" are commonly used by Black mothers and grandmothers in dealing with their children/ grandchildren and that these expressions of speech were not always intended to be followed up with physical manifestations.

The charge nurse assured the patient that such behavior would be investigated further, not be tolerated if indeed it did happen (the nursing assistant denied saying this), and that appropriate action would be taken upon the conclusion of the investigation. This solution was agreed upon by the patient, the nursing assistant, and myself and was put into writing and initialed by all of us.

The conflict resolution also included a re-demonstration on how to use the call-light to request bathroom (or, any kind of) assistance, the patient's agreement to continue with my professional care, and a change of assignment for the nursing assistant. The three of us went back into the patient's room and everybody apologized to each other.

This first conflict as a registered nurse was a growing up experience because I had to handle much of it by myself. In truth, my initial response was just as bad as the nursing assistant's. When the patient had called me a defamatory name, I wanted to retaliate! The memory still brings a feeling of despair to this day. However, this experience also taught me that there is always more to a story than initially appears.

The patient should always be treated with respect. I learned that there can be no such thing as retaliation within the health care profession. I was, and am, morally bound to provide professional care regardless of the situation. In any situation involving conflict, more data (data provided by people from both sides of the argument) needs to be collected before a sound decision can be made.

LEADERSHIP STRATEGY: Resolving conflict involves hearing BOTH sides of the story. ANALYSIS: Multi-cultural conflict situations may escalate tensions very quickly. Sometimes a third party is required before any sense can be made of the situation.

PRINCIPLE(S): Support holes in your knowledge-base with colleague's knowledge

Theory Guiding Practice

Nursing

Rosemary Parse's Human Becoming Theory is based on nine assumptions:

1. The human is coexisting while co-constituting rhythmical patterns with the universe.
2   The human is open, freely choosing meaning in situation, bearing responsibility for decisions.
3   The human is unitary, continuously co-constituting patterns of relating.
4   The human is transcending multi-dimensionally with possibilities.
5   Becoming is unitary human-living-health.
6   Becoming is a rhythmically co-constituting human-universe process.
7   Becoming is the human's patterns of relating value priorities.
8   Becoming is an inter-subjective process of transcending with the possibilities.
9   Becoming is unitary humans emerging

Non-Nursing

Helm's Black and White Racial Identity Theory was dev eloped around 3 factors and their associated traits in understanding human behavior.

The three factors that emerged from study are: degree of racial comfort; attitudes toward racial equality; and, attitudes of racial curiosity.. Janet Helms also developed the White Racial Identity Scale (WRIS).

Evidence-Base

Bosher, S. and Pharris, M. (Editors). (2009). *Transforming Nursing Education: The Culturally Inclusive Environment*. New York: Springer Publishing Company.

Helms, J. (1993). Black and White Racial Identity: Theory, Research, and Practice. Westport, CT: Praeger.

Lucas, J., Ivnik,R., Smith, G., Ferman, T., Willis, F., Petersen, R., et al., (2005). A brief report on WAIS-R Normative data collection in Mayo's older African Americans normative studies. *Clinical Neuropsychologist,* 19(2), 184-188.

Ponterotto, J., Gretchen, D., Utsey, S., Stracuzzi, T., and Saya, R., Jr. (2003). The Multigroup Ethnic Identity Measure (MEIM): Psychometric review and further validity testing. *Education and Psychological Measurement, 63,* 502-515.

Van Der Zee, K. and Van Oudenhoven, J. (2000). The Multicultural Personality Questionnaire: A multidimensional instrument of multicultural effectiveness. *European Journal of Personality,* 14, 291-309.

Williams, D., Neighbors, H. and Jackson, J. (2003). Racial/ethnic discrimination and health. Findings from community studies. *American Journal of Public Health,* 93(2), 200-208.

SITUATION 9.5. FOREIGN NURSES: BARRIERS TO ACHIEVING U.S. LICENSURE

Joyce Parrone[*]

Nursing Education, Lutheran School of Nursing, St. Louis, MO

Introduction

It seemed like a relatively simple solution to the nursing shortage. At least, so it seemed for our inner city hospital affiliated with a diploma school of nursing. The solution? Hire an international recruiting agency to recruit and screen for English language proficiency, BSN-educated nurses who were willing to relocate to the United States and work here for a 3-year period commitment. We brought in 65 nurses from the Philippines and 2 from India.

[*] jparrone@yahoo.com.

As I said, our plan was simple: we pay the agency; the agency does the work; we will then house the foreign nurses in the school of nursing dormitory; have them participate in a three-week review course, then WHOLA! They pass the NCLEX and go to work. No more nursing shortage!? Or, was there?

Somehow, as the nurses arrived, nothing seemed more complicated. Symptomatically, on arrival it was obvious that they were experiencing the effects of jet lag. Then, there was the problem that they came from a tropical climate wearing very light clothing into the middle of a Midwestern winter. They refused to eat our unfamiliar food. They cried a lot. The initial impact of this culture shock seemed overwhelming.

Although by contract they knew that they must participate in the review course, it was obvious that very little 'learning' was taking place. Although they spoke English, they were not familiar with our language idioms and their thick accents made communication all the more difficult.

The faculty of the school of nursing were initially at a loss as to what to do until they personalized the plight of the foreign nurses mentally putting themselves in their place. They soon realized that these nurses left behind their husbands, babies, young children, parents, homes-everything in fact that was dear to them-all for an opportunity to earn an income that they could send back to their families to improve their living conditions at home. They were, in a word-HOMESICK!

Once this fact was realized a new plan emerged to help relieve this homesickness.

The foreign nurses were housed in the spacious 8-story student nurse's dormitory with each nurse allocated a private room. Room arrangements were changed so that all the foreign nurses were clustered on the same floors. They had more access to talk to each other with this move. Each floor also had a small kitchen so the foreign nurses could cook rice and other foods that they preferred. Some of the faculty members offered to drive them to local grocery stores and were successful in asking the store managers to order certain foods that the foreign nurses were used to preparing. The administration at the school then provided computers so the foreign nurses could email their families and friends as often as they wanted. By special arrangement with a telephone company they were also allowed to make long-distance calls at no cost to themselves. The faculty brought in gently-used winter-appropriate clothing of their own and gave it to the foreign nurses. Local ethnic support groups were invited in to maintain a further reminder of their culture and interests. Faculty also took many to churches that were located near the school and hospital.

By waiting until the initial manifestations of homesickness had passed, and by providing manifestations of caring in all the ways described above, the faculty found that they became more than teachers-in fact, friends and confidants to the foreign nurses.

Although the U.S. NCLEX national average pass rate for foreign nurses was 50% at that time, this initiative saw all 67 foreign nurses pass by their second attempt with 59 passing on the first attempt!

LEADERSHIP STRATEGY: One can never push an intellectual task through a highly charged emotional state.

ANALYSIS: By leaving their home countries and all that they held dear these foreign nurses felt alone and abandoned. The faculty recognized this and, by providing the tangible help that they did, made the foreign nurses feel cared for-something they very much needed. Once familiarity settled in and their basic needs were met the foreign nurses were able to turn their attention to the intellectual task of completing the 3 week remedial course that was their ticket to passing the NCLEX licensure exam.

PRINCIPLE(S): If a higher-order need is frustrated, an individual may regress to increase the satisfaction of a lower-order need which appears easier to satisfy. This is known as the *frustration-regression principle*.

Theory Guiding Practice

Nursing

Jean Watson's Caring Theory is the only nursing theory (*Grand Theory*) to incorporate the spiritual needs of the patient at the theory's inception. Watson's theory is based on the following ten Carrative Factors:

1   A humanistic-altruistic system of values;
2   Enabling faith and hope;
3   Realizing a sensitivity to self and others;
4   Developing a helping/trusting/caring relationship;
5   Freedom to express positive and negative feelings and emotions;
6   Developing a creative, individualized problem-solving caring nursing
7   process;
8   Application of transpersonal teaching-learning;
9   Supportive, protective, and/or corrective mental, physical, societal and
10   spiritual environment;
11   Assisting with gratification of human needs while preserving dignity
12   and wholeness;
13   Being open to existential-phenomenological and spiritual forces.

Non-Nursing

Maslow identified the Hierarchy of Needs and placed levels of need in a triangle graphic. Basic subsistence needs of food, water, shelter, etc were at the broad base of the triangle. The top was devoted to self-actualization. Maslow theorized that one must have the lower level needs met before one can aspire to self actualization.

This is a *Grand Theory* that identifies the universal human physiological needs of food, water, air, and rest shared by all in the graphic base of an isosceles triangle. The hierarchy has five layers which include:

- Physiological needs
- Safety and security needs
- Love and belonging needs
- Esteem needs
- Self-actualization

As attention moves up from the base, those most basic physiological needs, the next level of needs that must be met is security/safety, then a sense of belonging, feelings of increased self-esteem, and finally-self-actualization. These basic human needs MUST be met before a person can aspire toward self-actualization, or goal attainment.

Evidence-Base

Hogan, M. and Nickitas, D. (2009). *Nursing Leadership and Management: Reviews and Rationales*. Upper Saddle River: Pearson/Prentice Hall.

Hong, G. (2009). Familiarity, preference, and utilization of ethnic items among Asian Americans. *Asian Nursing Research,* 3(4), 186-195. (Descriptive exploratory methodology, N=224).

International Journal of Cultural Diversity in Organisations (sic), Communities and Nations, 8(4), p 171-176.

Parrone, J., Sredl, D., Miller, M., Donaubauer, C. (2006). Overcoming cultural change anxiety before coming to America. *Philippine Journal of Nursing,* 76(2), p17 (ISSN =0048-3818).

Parrone, J., Sredl, D., Miller, M., Phillips, M., Donaubauer, C. (2008). An evidence-based teaching/learning strategy involving the HESI Exam as a predictor of success for foreign nurses. *Journal of Teaching and Learning in Nursing,* 3(1), p 35-40.

Parrone, J., Sredl, D., Miller, M., Phillips, M., Donaubauer, C. (2008).Charting the 7 C's of cultural change affecting foreign nurses: Competency, (Jenkins, 2007) *Journal of Cultural Diversity: An Interdisciplinary Journal,* 15(1), p3-6.

Sredl, D. and Dickerman, J. (2008). Fostering a culturally congruent acceptance of critical thinking among nursing professionals in an extended care setting.

In: Evidence-Based Leadership Success Strategies …   ISBN: 978-1-62081-104-7
Editor: Darlene Sredl   © 2012 Nova Science Publishers, Inc.

Chapter 10

CONTEMPORARY ISSUES

Frederick J. Brown[*]

SITUATION #10.1. TWENTY-FIRST CENTURY AMERICA'S EFFORTS AT LEGAL REFORM-PRO AND CON

Introduction

A popular topic of current debate (until the Healthcare Insurance Reform Law was passed) was the potential for all US citizens to be able to obtain universal healthcare (UHC-which means health care coverage extended to all eligible residents of a governmental region and is publicly funded via taxes). This type of system is already in place in various settings, such as military hospitals for active duty and retired high ranking commission officers and their immediate family members, veteran's administration medical centers for veterans who have served in times of war and/or if they are service- connected, Indian Health Service hospitals, and local state/county run facilities (e.g., psychiatric hospitals, county medical centers, and city government funded hospitals). Some American citizens do not realize that they already pay for this semblance of a UHC system via their high healthcare insurance premiums, which may increase annually at their place of employment.

In addition, hospitals write off unpaid care as charity or bad debt for tax purposes, therefore, taxpayers actually pay for these services already. Although it is already passed into law, should UHC be instituted in the United States of America? Critics of UHC suggest that this type of system will increase wait times and cause healthcare rationing and unnecessary deaths. The US already has an established system of indigent care in the state-funded Medicaid healthcare system.

Additionally, the heavy effects of foreign illegal aliens' utilization of emergency rooms have taken a toll because they must be screened per the federal government guidelines in The Emergency Medical Treatment and Active Labor Act (EMTALA), which is a United States

---

[*] Email: fbrown1149@gmail.com.

Act of Congress, passed in 1986 as part of the Consolidated Omnibus Budget Reconciliation Act. This act requires hospitals and ambulance services to provide care to anyone needing emergency treatment regardless of citizenship, legal status, or ability to pay, with no reimbursement provisions included. Because of this act, patients requiring emergency treatment can be discharged only under their own informed consent or when their condition requires a transfer to a hospital that is better equipped to administer treatment. EMTALA applies to "participating hospitals," i.e., those that accept payment from the Department of Health and Human Services or the Centers for Medicare and Medicaid Services (CMS) under the Medicare program. However, in practicality, EMTALA applies to virtually every hospital in the U.S. with exception for Shriners' Hospitals for Children, Indian Health Service hospitals, and Veterans Affairs hospitals. Due to the prevalence of Medicare and Medicaid, (the combined payments of which were $602 billion in 2004 or roughly 44% of all medical expenditures in the U.S.), not participating in EMTALA becomes impractical for nearly all hospitals. EMTALA's provisions apply to all patients, not just Medicare patients. In most instances, the federal government does not directly cover the cost of emergency care required by EMTALA. One wonders how this will change with the law's proposed cuts to the Medicare system? It is also difficult to comprehend a healthcare system that now takes up one-sixth of the US Gross Domestic Product (GDP) not growing by leaps and bounds when millions upon millions of newly eligible (and possibly some ineligible) people enter the healthcare utilization arena.

Case Study

The previous background information was included to set the stage for the story about Doug. Doug recently decided to work as a freelance agent and pay for his own healthcare insurance. Initially, he applied for insurance through a well known national insurance company; however, they denied coverage because of his sleep apnea.

This company knew about his prior health situation because healthcare insurance companies share patients' health histories with one another via a common database. Therefore, he applied to another healthcare insurance company, but they denied him for reasons that were not divulged to him. He began to worry while applying to the third insurance company, who incidentally also denied him, and the fourth, which is affiliated with the second company he applied to, both of which also denied him.

Finally, the fifth healthcare insurance company told him that they would give him a quote and consider insuring him, but he had to sign his HIPAA rights away. By doing so, he dropped the privacy of his medical history information protection. Therefore, the insuring company did a nationwide pharmacy search of their databases, which are associated with the big four chain drug stores (CVS, Walgreens, Wal-Mart pharmacy, and Rite Aid Pharmacies) and obtained a detailed list of every drug that he had ever taken. It does not sound like HIPAA privacy will endure with all the inter-sharing that is destined to occur under the new Healthcare Insurance Reform Law.

Doug thought that the insurance company was not very concerned with his more serious heath issues of hypertension or sleep apnea; it seemed like they were more interested in his sexual history. Apparently, he has herpes simplex II (i.e., the common cold sore), for which the treatment of choice is 1000mg of Valtrex®. This medication keeps the virus at bay, reducing flare ups by 90 to 100% if taken regularly.

The drug, however, was expensive (i.e., for a 30-day supply, the cost averaged at $33 per pill). The insurance company informed him that if he wanted to establish healthcare and pharmacy coverage, they would make him sign a waiver so that they could place an inhibiting pharmaceutical rider on his policy, effectively preventing him from obtaining insurance benefit coverage for the one drug that works well with his body system.

While it is Utopian to want to believe that under the new Healthcare Insurance Reform law this drug would be permitted, the fact is that under the new Healthcare Insurance Reform Law restrictions like the one above are expected to become commonplace because the government can easily establish restrictive generic formularies. Only the drugs on the generic formulary will be covered.

Finally, health care systems throughout the world face sustainability challenges that may require far-reaching changes in national policy. UHC is provided in most developed countries, in many developing countries, and is the trend worldwide. Whether a government-mandated system of UHC should be actually implemented, or the law repealed in the U.S. remains a hotly debated political topic. However, it will be nursing leaders such as yourself who will help decide that issue in the future.

ANALYSIS: The new Healthcare Insurance Reform Act has recently been passed by Congress into law. At the time of this publication it is too new to have many of the provisions within it enacted. What is interesting, however, is that the humanitarian effort that purportedly supported this movement is not realized in this law. The resultant law is one of Healthcare Insurance Reform, not the one originally designed to reduce healthcare costs. The net result will be either a stasis or an escalation of healthcare costs. The other result will be higher costs to US citizens who will have to pay additional taxes to cover the government's entitlement legislation.

LEADERSHIP STRATEGY: Vote! Vote! Vote! YOU can change policies that you do not agree with or support those that you do agree with by voting.

PRINCIPLE(S): "One should think less about himself and his feelings and more about the principles in which he believes-and get back into the fight." Dr. Norman Vincent Peale.

Theory Guiding Practice

Nursing

Patterson and Zderad's Humanistic Nursing Communication Theory identifies trust-promoting behaviors of nursing especially as they apply to communicative interactions. Today's contemporary reliance on technology has often precluded reliance on the nurse-patient relationship as a focus of understanding.

Non-Nursing

Soren Ventegodt's (MD) Quality of Life Theory is operationalized in his Quality of Life Questionnaire that seeks to identify ethnographically tenets of high quality of life of a specific population or patient group as compared to the general population.

Evidence-Base

Eberhardt, G. D., B. (1989). Trusting the hospice nurse. *American Journal of Hospice and palliative Medicine,* 6(6), 29-32.

Sredl, D. (2004). Health-related quality of life: A concept analysis. *West African Journal of Nursing,* 15(1), 9-19.

Sredl, D. (In Press). The QALY vs DALY Quandary. *Common Ground Publishing.*

Tumulty, K. (2009). Where did reform go? *Time,* 174(23), 54-55.

Ventegodt, S. (1996). *Measuring the Quality of Life from Theory to Practice.* Copenhagen: Forskingscentrets Forlag.

Ventegodt, S., Flensborg-Madsen, T., Andersen, N., and Merrick, J. (2008). Which factors determine our quality of life, health, and ability? Results from a Danish population sample and the Copenhagen perinatal cohort. *Journal of the College of Physicians and Surgeons Pakistan.*

SITUATION #10.2. MOVING NURSING FROM INVISIBLE TO INVINCIBLE

Leah Nguyen[*]
Neurology ICU, Barnes-Jewish
Hospital, St. Louis, MO

Introduction

Nursing is invisible! Wrapped up in the invisibility cloak of the 'room rate' a patient bill does not give the patient any idea of the amount of work done by, and the expertise of, the nurses who cared for him/her in the hospital. Physician bills reflect the procedures that the physician has performed on the patient. If the doctor has done a thorocentesis or a chest-tube insertion, the physician's bill reflects that procedure as an example of a higher complexity effort expended on the patient's behalf.

Nurses may also perform more complex tasks (like IV starts, PICC line insertion, ABG blood draws, etc.), but the current method of billing never indicates that a higher level of practice has occurred or been expended on the patient's behalf. Many of these procedures require additional education and clinical training under an advanced practitioner.

Many procedural skills also require that the nurse go through an annual re-certification process to demonstrate that her skill level of expertise is still proficient. Because of this invisibility, nursing does not receive the respect it deserves from either administration or the general public it serves.

We, as nurses, must think of a way to change top administration's thinking that the Department of Nursing is a cost center to thinking of it as a profit center. The present system

[*] Email: tanv94@umsl.edu.

of patient billing, lumping nursing services in the daily room rate along with housekeeping, dietary, and grounds maintenance, encourages administrators to see nursing as a cost center. The Department of Nursing has the largest number of employees, hence the largest payroll. If there were a nursing charge in plain view on the bill, and not just the total daily fee, then this might be viewed differently.

Administration might be more able to see that nurses actually help produce the hospital's profit. There should also be a way to track the patient's retention rate, or, the likelihood of the patients to come back to the same hospital as the result of the excellent nursing care provided. This research would also help the nurses to be viewed as profit makers. In order to track the patients returning to the same hospital over and over again there needs to be surveys that the patients could fill out.

The survey could ask repeat patients the following questions "What make you choose to go back to this hospital?" To make response easier the question could also provide multiple choice answers, such as…

A) Because of the nursing services this hospital provided. _____ (Add a special Nurse's name if applicable).
B) The doctors services this hospital provided _____ (Add a special Doctor's name if applicable).
C) The advance in technology of this hospital

If the answer that the patients chose is "A- because of the nursing services provided", this will let the administrator know that the nurses actually help to bring in patients and thereby help the hospital generate more profit. Research leads the effort towards making nursing less invisible by collecting data that shows how the nurses at a particular hospital help to decrease hospital costs by having patients develop less in-patient hospital ulcers, less medications errors, using less of the budget resources, wasting less (of whatever) than the other hospital's thus contributing to the hospital overall profits while reducing hospital costs.

But, this plan demands a commitment from nursing administration; who must strongly advocate for these changes. The nurse administrator, or Chief Nursing Executive (CNE) sets the tone for how the Department of Nursing is perceived in the facility. If the CNE presents a strong case for showcasing the efforts of nursing instead of hiding them, then nursing can make the successful move from invisibility to invincibility!

ANALYSIS: The situation described above shows one of the reasons that nursing is thought of as a 'cost center' rather than a 'profit center' by hospital administration. The Department of Nursing has the largest number of employees, hence the largest payroll. When thinking only of numbers, it is easy to see why administration seeks to make budget cuts from the Department of Nursing when crunch time comes. But…cutting positions in professional nursing means that less educated people will be hired to fill the vacated professional positions. This, then, means that those less educated people will have tasks, treatments, medication passes, etc. delegated to them. Since they are less educated, their scope of experience will probably not be adequate to assess for problems that may arise as they attempt to fulfill their delegated duties.

It is not unreasonable to forsee adverse patient outcomes, even death, arising from this inevitable situation. Adverse patient outcomes may lead to lawsuits. Lost lawsuits that will lead to depletions of hospital revenue-possibly even to economic collapse!

In addition to the above, the new Healthcare Insurance Reform Law of 2010 mandates that Medicare reimbursement will be cut across the board and eliminated entirely unless the hospital has put in place a statistical way of tracking patient care outcomes. Bad outcomes = bad reimbursement= bad outcomes-a vicious cycle.

LEADERSHIP STRATEGY: Nursing is one of the world's best kept secrets. This must change! Publicize and showcase the success of nurses at your facility!

PRINCIPLE(S): Utilize the principle of "Learning from your successes" When you do a thing well, study your success and print your method and state of mind at the time firmly in your consciousness. Your mind will tend to repeat a successful procedure quite as successfully as a mistaken one." Dr. Norman Vincent Peale.

Theory Guiding Practice

Nursing

Bloom's Taxonomy, or Domains of Learning (1956) identifies three domains of learning, each with a hierarchial classification within that calls for behaviors from simple to complex that demonstrate that learning has occurred. These domains are: cognitive, affective and psychomotor. Within the cognitive domain are six intellectual skills that include: remembering, understanding, applying, analyzing, evaluating, and creating. The affective domain includes: feelings, emotions, interests, attitudes, and appreciations, and ranks according to receiving, responding, valuing, organizing, and internalizing. The psychomotor domain adds motor skills into the mix, such as: imitation, manipulation, precision, articulation, and naturalization. In learning a new and specialized clinical technique a nurse must be able to combine motor skill with the requisite intellectual functions. Adding a skill like this should receive more compensation than care that does not have and apply this technique.

Non-Nursing

Stone's Return on Investment (ROI) Model of Pay for Performance. Return on investment is a cost benefit analysis conducted from the health care decision maker (investor's) point of view. A facility's 'costs' are the amount of money an organization has to invest in order to implement a policy or service. 'Benefits' are the amount of money saved by implementing the policy. When the 'costs' are subtracted from the 'benefits', the return on investment (ROI) is the ratio (expressed as a percentage) of money saved to money spent. Breakeven is determined by calculating how much money must be spent on the new process/service before it yields profits.

Evidence-Base

Bartel, A. (2000). Measuring the employer's return on investments in training: Evidence from the literature. *Industrial Relations,* 39, 502-524.

Bodrock, J., Mion, L. (2008). Pay for performance in hospitals: Implications for nurses and nursing care. *Quality Management in Health Care,* 17(2), 102-111.

Donabedian, A. (1966). Evaluating the quality of medical care. *Milbank Quarterly,* 83(4), 691-729.

Lindenaur, P., Remus, D., Roman, S., et al. (2007). Public reporting and pay for performance in hospital quality improvement. *New England Journal of Medicine,* 356, 486-496.

Needleman, J., Buerhaus, P., Mattke, S., Stewart, M., and Zelevinsky, K. (2002). Nurse-staffing levels and the quality of care in hospitals. *New England Journal of Medicine,* 346(22), 1715-1722.

Petersen, I., Woodard, L., Urech, T., Daw, C., and Sookanan, S. (2006). Does pay for performance improve the quality of health care? *Ann. Intern. Med.,* 145(265-272).

Rosenthal, M. F., R. (2006). What is the empirical basis for paying for quality in health care? *Med. Care Res. Rev.,* 63, 135-157.

Rowe, J. (2006). Pay for performance and accountability: Related themes in improving health care. *Ann. Intern. Med.,* 145, 695-699.

Sautter, K., Bokhour, B. and White, B., et al. (2007). The early experience of a hospital-based pay-for-performance program. *Journal of Healthcare Management,* 52(2), 95-107.

Sredl, D. and Peng, N. (In Press). CEO-CNE Relationships: Building the evidence-base of Chief Nursing Executive Replacement Costs. *International Journal of Medical Sciences.*

Stone, P. (2002). Using economic evidence in clinical practice. *Journal of Medical Practice Management,* 17, 272-277.

Stone, P. (2005). Return on investment models. *Applied Nursing Research,* 18(3), 186-189.

Stone, P., Bakken, S., Curran, C. and Walker, P. (2002). Evaluation of studies of health economics. *Evidence-Based Nursing,* 5, 100-104.

SITUATION #10.3. INTERNATIONAL COLLABORATION THROUGH BUILDING EDUCATIONAL EXCHANGE PROGRAMS

*Rita Csapso-Sweet**

Department of Theater, Dance, and Media Studies, Fulbright Center for International Studies, University of Missouri St. Louis

Introduction

Croatia is next in line to join the European Union (EU). The EU has standards that Croatia must meet if it is ultimately allowed to join. According to European Union rules, the hospital must employ 2,000 nurses by the time of Croatia's inclusion in the EU. At present, the University of Dubrovnik and the Regional Hospital of Dubrovnik are only the two institutions available for this educational metamorphosis. In order to meet the objective of training so many nurses, the University of Dubrovnik must build up its faculty in a number of areas…quickly. The Regional Hospital of Dubrovnik, desperately in need of nurses, serves a large sector of Southern Dalmacia. The hospital is large, modern, and, despite sporadic

* Email: dadsweet@earthlink.net.

nursing shortages provides excellent care. Currently Croatia has only 1,000 nurses and the EU has a requirement that the country produce a total of 5,000 nurses before they can join.

Since the University of Dubrovnik's current priorities are nursing and music, among others, these are the colleges that must be enhanced first, with nursing at the forefront. The University of Dubrovnik hopes that the University of Missouri at St. Louis (UMSL)'s College of Nursing can help them train the nurses they need to fill the EU quota. Croatian nurses are required to speak English and modern nurses' training in Dubrovnik is in English.

Asynchronous online/distance education may be the vehicle to accomplish this. UMSL's President's emphasis on increasing online education delivery is expanding with new distance educational offerings produced every year. Another opportunity for multi-cultural clinical training in St. Louis is the budding emergence of one of Barnes-Jewish's facilities as a "Teaching Extended Care" facility that offers sub-acute Intensive Care training along with Geriatrics. The Barnes-Jewish Hospital system is the largest employer in the state of Missouri and is world-renowned for the health care opportunities it provides.

My Role

Establishing initial contact with the University of Dubrovnik (UD) occurred in the spring of 2006 when I traveled to Dubrovnik for a film festival. At the time, I decided to investigate the possibilities of cross-cultural academic exchanges with the University of Dubrovnik by visiting classes in communication studies and having extensive meetings with faculty members of the Department of Communication, the Rector's Office and the Office of International Relations. That is where I found that the two highest priorities at the University of Dubrovnik are building up the departments of nursing and contemporary music. By this visit, I visualized a perfect 'match' with their needs and the opportunities that I knew were available at the University of Missouri @ St. Louis (UMSL). By the end of 2007, UMSL had signed agreements with three universities: Sarajevo, and Tuzla in Bosnia, and Dubrovnik, in Croatia. The importance and urgency of these academic partnership programs to UMSL is that St. Louis has one of the highest Bosnian/Serbo-Croatian speaking populations in the United States. Over 50,000 Bosnian refugees were settled in the St. Louis area during and after the Balkan wars in the 1990s.

At my urging, by the fall of 2007, UMSL's Chancellor and the University of Dubrovnik's Rector had signed an official 'Memorandum of Understanding' between our universities, inaugurating the official student/faculty exchange program of this historic agreement in 2009-2010. UMSL is the FIRST American university to successfully negotiate an exchange program with the University of Dubrovnik and is their sole educational partner in the United States. Although the University of Dubrovnik has exchanges with many European universities and is part of the Bologna Agreement, to date, UMSL is the only American university to have taken this step with one of Europe's oldest and most prestigious academic institutions. (Technically, the Bologna Agreement does not have a direct connection to the E.U. It is an attempt to standardize higher education in Europe and has been signed by most countries in Europe including Bosnia and Herzogovina, and Croatia).

The University of Missouri is a state institution with an academically substantial offering of disciplines among the four campuses and a comprehensive nursing program awarding degrees at the Baccalaureate, Masters, Ph.D., and DNP levels. A trend in universities in the regional areas of the former Yugoslavia that makes cross-cultural cooperation easier is the emphasis on shifting to courses and training in English. As Bosnia and Croatia prepare to join the EU, teaching and research in post secondary education is increasingly taking place in English.

There are several areas where I see potential for continued successful collaboration. The first and the most immediate need for the University of Dubrovnik is the nursing program. It would be worth pursuing government funding on both sides of the Atlantic for medical/nursing training. The University of Dubrovnik could send their students to UMSL, offer them distance education via online delivery, or we could prepare a team of consulting faculty to go to Dubrovnik and provide training there.

The reason the relationship with the University of Missouri is so important for the University of Dubrovnik results from a situation that occurred with another American university following the Balkan War in the late 1990s. That war destroyed a great deal of property in Dubrovnik. It also put development of economic progress and relationships with the west in a deep freeze for nearly a decade. The war in Croatia ended before the Dayton Agreement ended the war in Bosnia. However, fighting in the region delayed progress in Croatia for a full decade compared to countries like Hungary and the Czech Republic that started integration with the west in the early 1990s.

The faculty and administration at the University of Dubrovnik were guarded when I first began to discuss forming an ongoing academic relationship with UMSL. They were very honest about their naivety in doing business with, and reluctant to blindly trust, another American university. Over the last four years however, our negotiations have been open, direct, and very productive. It took nearly two years for UMSL to sign the joint "Memorandum of Understanding," but now we have proceeded to a level where we are discussing both faculty and student exchanges in addition to an equally exciting plan to have the University of Missouri be the sole American university to train UD faculty as they create and build the University of Dubrovnik to full "Universitas" status.

The administration at The University of Dubrovnik feel they can find everything they need academically at the University of Missouri and they are comforted by the maturity and stability of our institution. It is also an advantage that they can conduct negotiations with the Director of the Center for International Studies, which has been supporting my research in Bosnia and Croatia for years. The partnership with UMSL will allow Croatian students from Dubrovnik and elsewhere in Southern Dalmacia to participate in an affordable American education. A trend in universities in the regional areas of the former Yugoslavia that makes cross-cultural cooperation easier is the emphasis on shifting to courses and training in English.

As Bosnia and Croatia prepare to join the EU, teaching and research in post secondary education is increasingly taking place in English, through their enrollment at the University of Dubrovnik, and hopefully they will be able to educate enough nurses to meet the mandate of the European Union. By the end of 2007, UMSL had signed the Agreements with all three universities: Sarajevo, Tuzla, and Dubrovnik.

Moving forward with these plans, March of 2010 saw Dr. Mato Brautovic, Professor of Mass Communications at UD, visited the UMSL campus to tour the UMSL campus including the School of Nursing. His visit was the first official event to formally inaugurate the faculty/student exchange program between our two institutions.

Dr. Brautovic was able to have a series of extensive meetings with administration and faculty at the College of Nursing, the Center for International Studies, and the College of Fine Arts and Communication, including the Department of Music. There was significant progress with the Department of Music to move the exchange program forward in the coming academic year. Hopefully this UMSL/UD collaboration will yield many benefits to both countries. Not the least of them, the education of many new Croatian nurses!

ANALYSIS: What did it take to bring about the Agreement with Dubrovnik? It began with a vision. I have been working in Eastern Europe (mostly Hungary) for decades. Although my work is primarily in the arts, my father was a scientist and a physician and his ongoing research was in the field of medicine (OBandGYN). He was born and raised in Hungary and even during the height of the Cold War he would bring young Hungarian physicians to Washington University. in St. Louis to work for a year in his labs. I suppose I grew up seeing how powerful international educational exchange can be. My father trained an entire generation of Hungary's OBs.

In 1995, The Director of International Studies and Associate Provost for Academic Affairs at UMSL and I wrote a State Department grant for $80,000 to bring four students from the University of Debrecen in Hungary to UMSL for a year, and for four UMSL students to study there. The grant would have continued for five years had the US Congress not reduced funds for the State Department at the end of the first year of the program.

By 2010, I can reflect a bit on what was involved in creating this program at UMSL from scratch. It began with a broader vision of the power of international collaboration, which is greatly enhanced by the fact that my husband (who is also in the OB Department at Wash U) shares the vision.

We can get a tremendous amount accomplished since we work together as a team. The other factor of course, is support from the Center for International Studies (CIS) at UMSL. Support from CIS has averaged about $2,000 a year towards the program. Unfortunately, there were no funds in 2009 because of the financial crisis, just as the program was reaching a critical point. So I guess beyond the vision, I have had to make a commitment that no matter what happens financially in terms of institutional support, we will keep the process going.

Lastly, it does take perseverance to keep enthusiasm going for international programs at UMSL during a time of severe financial stress. But my vision for what lies beyond sustains me. If through these programs UMSL can (in addition to student and faculty exchange): design the modern dance curriculum for universities throughout Bosnia; or positively effect healthcare in the region by helping to build the Nursing Program at the University of Dubrovnik and Dubrovnik Hospital; I am convinced that the effort is worth it.

LEADERSHIP STRATEGY: Identify a unique niche that nobody else seems to notice…then work to fill it!

PRINCIPLE(S): Utilize Dr. Norman Vincent Peale's 8 P Plan:

1   Plan purposively
2   Prepare prayerfully
3   Proceed positively, and,
4   Pursue persistently.

Theory Guiding Practice

Nursing

The Leadership Initiative for Nursing Education (LINE) by Helene Fuld Trust Fund authored by: Bellack, J., Morjikian, R., Berger, S., Strachota, E., Fitxmaurice, J., Lee, A., Kluzik, T., Lynch, E, Tsao, J., O'Neil, E., was undertaken to enhance basic leadership competencies of BSN students. To date, 26 BSN programs and their clinical partners have participated in LINE development. The emotional intelligence and social competence frameworks underpin the LINE structure.

Non-Nursing

Reigeluth's Elaboration Theory deals primarily with macro-strategies for organizing instruction. The order of instruction should proceed from an ever increasing order of complexity-simple to complex sequencing strategies.

Evidence-Base

Bellack, J., Morjikian, R., Barger, S., Strachota, E., Fitzmaurice, J., Lee, A., Kluzik, T., Lynch, E., Tsao, J., and O'Neil, E. (2001). Developing BSN leaders for the future: The Fuld Leadership Initiative for Nursing Education (LINE). *Journal of Professional Education,* 17(1), 23-32.

Reigeluth, C. M. (1999). The elaboration theory: Guidance for scope and sequences decisions. In: E. R.M. Reigeluth (Ed.), *Instructional-design Theories and Models: A New Paradigm of Instructional Theory, Vol. II* (Vol. II, pp. 425-454). Mahwah, NJ: Lawrence Erlbaum Associates.

Wilson, B. C., P. (1992). A critical review of elaboration theory. *Educational Technology Research and Development,* 40(3), 63-79.

In: Evidence-Based Leadership Success Strategies …
Editor: Darlene Sredl

ISBN: 978-1-62081-104-7
© 2012 Nova Science Publishers, Inc.

Chapter 11

GATHER INSPIRATION

SITUATION #11.1. THE SOUTHERN CROSS

*Beth Vesper**
St. Louis, MO, US

Introduction

As dawn broke over the Andes, I looked groggily into the hopeful eyes of my new husband. I was sicker than I had ever been, just barely beginning to shake off a night of the kind of food poisoning that only strikes on the opposite side of the equator. Even in my haze, I agreed that I was going to do what I came to do. This was the Inca Trail, and this was our honeymoon. An hour later, with backpacks packed, I chugged down two bottles of Spanish-language-labeled Pedialyte and committed myself to the task. Regardless of the difficulty, I was even hoping to enjoy it.

At the same time, I was also tackling big challenges in other parts of my life. I had abandoned a successful 12-year career in Information Technology to return to school, I was getting married many years after a failed first marriage, and we had scheduled our wedding for the short break just three months into my accelerated BSN program.

Although happy about my choices, I was feeling uprooted from the professional identity that had defined my life throughout my twenties and thirties. In addition to submitting myself to the rigors of a baccalaureate program all over again, I felt the uncertainty that comes with giving up comfortable success. My life still held all of the normal furnishings of mid-life – a mortgage, family and personal obligations, a familiar lifestyle, and certain freedoms. I knew that I had a nagging desire to try something different, but the foundation of my profession was no longer there to ground me.

Having just completed a demanding first semester, I was relieved to celebrate our wedding and take a trip away from the intensity of school. Because we both love adventure, we chose a vacation that provided us with challenges of its own. In preparation, I had read

---

* Email: busybeth@sbcglobal.net.

about high altitude sickness, and I had given respectful attention to the fearsome symptoms of HAPE (High Altitude Pulmonary Edema) and HACE (High Altitude Cerebral Edema). Both my husband and I are, after all, lowlanders from the middle of the U.S. We had come to Peru prepared with Diamox for altitude and Cipro for our bellies, and, as it turned out, we would need them both.

As our hike took us higher and higher into the mountains, my sickness gradually subsided. As miserable as I felt at the trailhead, the stunning Andean Mountains, like emerald green shark's teeth, provided me with all the distraction and motivation that I needed to keep moving forward. My husband's difficulties, however, were just beginning. Although he had managed to evade whatever I had ingested, his body found the elevation more and more taxing as we climbed higher. By the time we reached camp on the second night at well over 12,000 feet, I was feeling nearly as good as new, and my husband was crawling into the tent with a churning belly and a pounding head.

That night I saw the most amazing things in the sky above our camp, which was situated on a deep ledge cut into the steep mountainside. As we arrived earlier that evening, we were almost completely socked in by bloated gray clouds. Our view was limited to only the closest of neighboring mountains. My husband wanted to stay in our tent for dinner, so I stayed in to help him get a little soup down and to offer what comfort I could.

By the time I emerged to join our group for dessert in the small, makeshift dining tent, the sun had set. I was astonished to see, however, that the sky had actually grown *lighter* than before sundown. Sinking along with the sun, the thick gray clouds had settled snuggly into the giant valley below us. Now I found myself standing above the clouds, gazing at row after row of mountaintops illuminated by the moon and stars for as far as I could see.

Our guide pointed out the Southern Cross above us. Shaped like an old-fashioned kite, I gazed up at an imposing and beautiful constellation that I had never (*could* never have) seen before. I knew that the constellations would look different from below the equator. My husband and I had even tried to find a planisphere to bring along at the last minute, but could not find a southern hemisphere edition in time. But in my northern-hemisphere-centric life, it had never occurred to me that if you are travelling in the southern hemisphere, you cannot navigate by the North Star. You are in such a different place, that you cannot even see it. You have to use the Southern Cross.

Even if I had known that I was looking for a fresh way to navigate through a difficult new world, I could not have invented a more perfect metaphor, 'The Southern Cross'. It had always existed, and I had never even known it was there. I had to travel to the other side of the world to discover it for myself, and I could not have been in a better place at a better time – above the clouds, after sundown, on the southeast face of a steep Andean mountainside. It was one of those rare moments in life that feels like serendipity. Truly, I was standing at a crossroads in my life in so many ways, and those monolithic stars burned above me without a care for what lay below them on earth.

On the next day, as the trail began to descend into the valley below, my husband and I both found a new spring in our step. Feeling healthy and invigorated, we were energized for the last day of hiking before arriving at the ancient city of Machu Picchu. When our trip was over, I resolved not to lose touch with what I had learned about the limitless resources that the universe provides. Just as I had prepared for our hike, I turned my attention back to my class work with a determination to learn and prepare, look to the stars, and hike on.

ANALYSIS: Nursing is such a demanding profession it can literally sap a person of all emotional reserves. The end of a shift (be it 8, 10 or 12 hours) signals the body that it needs rest and signals the mind that it, too, needs soothing. It is imperative that nurses recognize their need to 'fill themselves up' by engaging in whatever type of activities provide comfort and stress-relief for them. Few will tell you this at your place of employment. Emphasis is usually on filling the next shift and, if that means staying over your usual quitting time, so be it- they will ask you to stay over.

Recreation provides that stress-relief. Whether it is hiking and mountain climbing like the contributing author of this essay, riding a bicycle, or joining friends for a workout at the gym, the exercise challenges your muscles and, in doing so, releases toxins and stress. Creative recreation like watching movies, concerts, reading soothes your psyche and sometimes instills new insights that you can tap into and use later on. Sometimes majestic experiences in nature like the one shared by the author above provide a spiritual perceptivity that would be impossible to arrive at just keeping to the daily grind.

Jack Nicholson and Morgan Freeman starred in a movie titled 'The Bucket List". This improbably- titled movie concerned two aging men discussing all the things they had wanted to do (but had not accomplished) in their lifetimes. At the time of this discussion, an impending incapacitating illness was advancing for both so the men knew that they would have to act quickly if they were to achieve the goals of their 'bucket list". If you have compiled a similar 'bucket list', start achieving it now. It is much easier (and infinitely more enjoyable) to accomplish physical goals when you are young than when you are older.

"Ultimately, the only real tragedy in life is allowing ambitions to remain unfulfilled. One day you awaken knowing the thief of time stole as you slept, forever robbing you of opportunities; and that your chances of trading on youth, beauty, and brains are now over. Youth is gone. Beauty has faded. The brains are not quite as quick-witted as once they were; and the body is now too frail, too pained, to answer the door should opportunity even dare to knock." (Sredl, Prologue, Pilot Quest, 2007)

LEADERSHIP STRATEGY: Probably NO ONE will tell you to take some time to pursue your own interests-you have to take it for yourself. And...do not apologize to anyone for doing so!

PRINCIPLE(S): First you must climb the mountain in order to appreciate the view. Dr. Norman Vincent Peale.

Theory Guiding Practice

Nursing: Engel (1962)/Solomon (1964)/Ader (1981) Psychoneuroimmunology (Pni) Theory

This theory as originally proposed by Engel, later improved by Solomon and Ader, and most recently promoted by Dr. Mary Bennett studies the interactions of one's perception of the world around them, their behavior, cognizance of the way their brain functions and the strength of their immune system. The psychological portion is the 'Psycho' portion; the central nervous system is the "Neuro" portion; and the endocrine interplay comprises the "Immunology" portion of the theory.

Non-Nursing

Clayton Alderfer's ERG Theory is a grand theory that consists of (E) Existence needs, (R) Relatedness needs, (G) and Growth needs.

Existence needs refer to all people's concerns with basic material existence motivators-physiological and safety needs, example, hunger, thirst, oxygen.

Relatedness refers to the motivation we have for establishing and maintaining close interpersonal relationships and is concerned with external personal esteem; examples include family relationships, friends, colleagues.

Growth refers to a desire for personal achievement similar to Maslow's pinnacle which is self-actualization; an example includes personal development toward a goal.

A general 'hardiness' indicates an aptitude for taking action.

Evidence-Base

Overmier, B. and Gahtan, E. (2007). Psychoneuroimmunology: The final hurdle. *Integrative Psychological and Behavioral Science*, 33(2), 137-140.

Sredl, D. (2007). *Pilot Quest.* Frederick, MD: PublishAmerica

SITUATION #11.2. INSPIRATION FROM LONG AGO

A letter from Eileen Phillips

Eileen Phillips, BSN, RN, Infection Control Professional,
University of Missouri Health System, Columbia, Missouri

Introduction

Dear Dr. Sredl,

I ran across your name in something I just received from the Missouri League of Nursing on upcoming conferences in 2010. I was interested in the one you are presenting on critical thinking. When I saw your name, I remembered you!

Long ago, I worked as a CMT and a CAN at the Westchester House in Chesterfield when you were the Director of Nursing. You told me that I was a leader and had talent. When I left Westchester House to go to work at St. Luke's Hospital as a Unit clerk around 1984, I had no idea I would later become a nurse and leader that you thought I could become. I graduated with an AND in 1991 from Lewis and Clark Community College in Godfrey. I am just about finished with my BSN from Mizzou and have lived here and worked for the University of Missouri for the last 16 years. Currently, I am a clinical educator for this system.

You gave me a copy of your book on airborne patient care management and many kind words to get me motivated to believe in myself to become a nurse. Thanks for your words of encouragement so many years ago. Don't worry, I am paying it forward!

Thanks,

Eileen Phillips, B.S.N., R.N.Infection Control Practitioner, University of Missouri

ANALYSIS: Words are powerful. They have the potential to inspire and to depress. Always remember that your words, as a nursing administrator, can have far reaching effects. The above letter was written 25 years after the conversation took place! Yet, my words of believing in this colleague and pointing out some of her talents and abilities had profound effects.

One of the reasons why YOUR words are so impressionable is because you are in a pedigreed position. By 'pedigree' I mean that you have achieved a high position in nursing. It is assumed that you are a person of high ethical caliber, and very knowledgeable in nursing. These, no doubt, are some of the reasons you were chosen to fill the administrative position. The ability to recognize talent in others is assumed to be also within your skill-set. So, if you complement a person on a unique personality characteristic or talent it is taken as verifiable fact that that is true.

Coaching one's colleagues then becomes more important---and, may have life-long lasting benefits.

LEADERSHIP STRATEGY: Be lavish with sincere praise-you never know when what you say will be exactly what another person needs to hear.

PRINCIPLE(S): Tell others about the goodness you see in them.

"Jesus, let my words be a source of inspiration for others." Dr. Norman Vincent Peale

Theory Guiding Practice

Nursing

Feil's Validation Theory was originally designed as a method of communicating with Alzheimer's patients. It fosters an attitude of respect and empathy and utilizes simple, practical techniques to restore personal dignity. This theory projects the basic premise that all people are valuable and must be accepted non-judgmentally. This theory has broad application in nursing especially in interactions with nursing colleagues in which a culture of motivation can be established.

Non-Nursing

Prochasca and Diclemente's Transtheoretical Model of Behavior identifies four levels or stages in the change process: pre-contemplative (in which the person is resistant to initiating a change, or even of recognizing that a problem exists that needs resolution); Contemplation (in which the person is aware of a distressing problem and wondering if it is resolvable); Action (in which the person is actively working on the change); and Maintenance (in which the person has made the change and is seeking to consolidate gains).

Evidence-Base

No Author. (2007). The role of nursing leadership in creating a mentoring culture: Inspirational motivation. *Nursing Economics, 25*(3), 143-148.

SITUATION #11.3. TURNING A NEGATIVE INTO A POSITIVE

C. Betz [*]

Cecily Betz, Ph.D., R.N., Editor-in-Chief,
The Journal of Pediatric Nursing

Introduction

Many years ago, I was required to pass comprehensive exams at the conclusion of my graduate studies to obtain my Master's Degree in Nursing. It was a very stressful period as I was juggling many activities besides studying for this examination. As it turned out, I failed the research portion of the exam. I was absolutely devastated as this was a very disappointing outcome and it was extremely humbling to disclose to my family and friends that I had not passed.

Subsequently, I met with the professor to review the failed research section of the exam and to obtain recommendations to prepare for the next one. As we reviewed my essay composition, the professor reminded me that drafting an *outline* for the subsequent exam essays would be helpful in organizing my thoughts that I wanted to convey to the reader. A LIGHT went on in my head with that simple suggestion. I was struck by the simplicity of the recommendation and in that very same moment realized that I had forgotten a very simple lesson I had learned in English composition when I was in grammar school! I remember that moment vividly as I eased back in the chair I was sitting in and experienced the absolute release of tension and the rush of relaxation throughout my body.

That very simple recommendation was the impetus for an enormous change in my life on many different levels. First, applying that suggestion to my subsequent study preparation for the next round of the comprehensive exam was the key to my passing it and completing my Master's degree in Nursing. More importantly, that apparent experience of failure opened new doors and opportunities in my personal and professional life.

I discovered with that experience, that an apparent "failure" can be the important pivotal moment to overcome the challenge and move forward. I learned that "failure" does not mean an end, a cessation of effort. I learned that "failure" means that the outcome I had hoped for did not occur and I needed to consider what my next steps forward would be. This particular lesson, learned so many years ago has been a driving force in my life ever since. Knowing that there are always options, even in the face of disappointment and "defeat," I came to firmly believe that there are other alternatives and opportunities are "out there" whether available now or later.

As an example, when I first approached a publisher about starting a new journal in pediatric nursing, I was very hopeful that our efforts were going to be successful. Ultimately, the publisher decided that it was not a project his company wanted to pursue. However, not long afterwards, a representative from another publisher approached me to talk about a development effort for a textbook. I declined but indicated I would be interested in starting a

[*] Email: CLBetz@aol.com.

nursing journal. Obviously, this was the opening door for starting the *Journal of Pediatric Nursing* over twenty-five years ago!

I might add that now I share my story of failure frequently with students and colleagues alike as an example that those of us who have been successful in nursing have encountered "bumps in the road." I find sharing the story particularly amusing now, as those who hear about this experience are surprised by it given the fact that I founded and have served as the Editor-in-Chief of the *Journal of Pediatric Nursing* for the past twenty-five years and have conducted NIH-funded research.

ANALYSIS: If you give up at the first speed-bump you will never accomplish what you have set out to do. Any goal worth pursuing is worth pursuing aggressively, and taking risks for. When the Wright brothers first locked up their bicycle repair shop to try to invent a machine that would make them 'fly like the birds' they were ridiculed. But...they kept seeing those flying birds and knew that there must be a way for man to fly also if the body-mass of birds could be kept aloft somehow. Finally that dream was realized when one of their inventions stayed aloft for 23 seconds and they knew they had accomplished their objective.

This author's inherent talent was magnified by help from a concerned teacher. A simple but forgotten technique brought to her attention made all the difference between success and failure for her in the future.

LEADERSHIP STRATEGY: If at first you don't succeed, try, try again. PRINCIPLES; "See and constantly picture good outcomes. By envisioning good things you actually bring good influences into play both within yourself and in the world around you. Life tends to develop your long mental image of yourself." Dr. Norman Vincent Peale.

Think of success as a journey-not a destination

Theory Guiding Practice

Nursing

Reed's Theory of Self-Transcendence is based upon the supposition that when a person is faced with a life-threatening illness, or experiences an awareness of acute vulnerability, there may be a readiness to transcend the self boundary and integrate necessary changes in order to re-achieve a sense of well-being.

Non-Nursing

Napoleon Hill's "Profit from Failure" tenet of his fifteen Personality Characteristics of Successful People poses the thought that we all fail every day. If a person can analyze what caused the failure, then analyze what needs to change, then make the change, that person is well on his/her way to turning the failure into a success.

Evidence-Base

Hill, N. (1979). *The Law of Success*. Chicago: Success Unlimited, Inc.

Reed, P. (1991). Toward a nursing theory of self-transcendence: Deductive reformulation using developmental theories. *Advances in Nursing Science, 13*(4), 64-77.

Reed, P. (1996). Transcendence: Formulating nursing perspectives. *Nursing Science Quarterly,* 9(1), 2-4.

Reed, P. (1997). Nursing: The ontology of the discipline. *Nursing Science Quarterly,* 10(2), 76-79.

In: Evidence-Based Leadership Success Strategies ...
Editor: Darlene Sredl

ISBN: 978-1-62081-104-7
© 2012 Nova Science Publishers, Inc.

Chapter 12

REFRAMING A DIFFICULT SITUATION

SITUATION #12.1. THE CASE – THE PREDICAMENT OF STUDENT INCIVILITY

Claudia Horton[*]

Graceland University, School of Nursing, Independence, MO, US

Introduction

Shortly my title will be changed to Associate Dean and official Chair of the BSN-RN Nursing Program (undergraduate generic nursing program). The nursing program is small with approximately 35 seniors and 33 juniors. This fall there was an incident that led to a student grade appeal, that was only recently resolved by the appeals committee not supporting the student's petition.

I feel the need to reflect on my involvement as Program Chair and the circumstances that led to the appeal. In doing so, I want to answer the following questions. What was my official role in the process? Did I act appropriately with the student and the instructor? What kind of support did I need from the Dean? What kind of support did I get from the Dean? What is the perception of my role by the faculty in these situations? Does the nursing faculty think I acted appropriately? Did I give sufficient support to the instructor? Did I influence the instructor to do what was best for her, the student, the class, and the faculty as a whole? What lessons did I learn and how will I deal with a similar situation in the future?

The Situation

Junior students took their first exam in the health assessment (HA) class, and over half the class failed. In fact, many of the students thought to be "B" students did very poorly.

---

[*] Email: horton@graceland.edu.

Mary, the instructor, and we (five faculty) were all fairly shocked. Upon review, the exam and didn't seem unusually difficult. The test analysis did not indicate that it was a bad test, even though more than half the students missed many of the same questions.

I asked Mary what she wanted to do. She said she was willing to accept two answers for some of the questions which would increase some grades. She made the adjustment, but students continued to complain and we met again.

She wanted to accept more answers as correct since she could see why some of the students would have chosen them as correct also. Mary also voiced the concern that possibly some of the questions were beyond the students' level of comprehension.

We looked over the questions again and I thought there were some that she should not change. Mary decided to make the adjustments and required the students to complete definitions of the terms they missed on the exam. Even with the adjustments some of the students failed the exam again. They still had the potential to raise their grades with the following exams.

When I met with Mary I had mixed emotions. I wanted to support her but I didn't want the students to fail the exam to the degree that they would be unable to pull themselves out of a big hole.

The students thought the first exam was very difficult and very confusing. They stated that the exam covered information that was not covered in class. (Students had been told that the instructor cannot possibly cover all information in class and that they were also responsible for the assigned readings which covered other important material).

Some of the students came to my office to complain about Mary, saying that "she talks too fast", "uses the book to lecture from", and "doesn't use enough real life examples to help them learn" like one of the other instructors does. Students also complained that in class Mary focuses on normal assessment findings but tests on the abnormal findings. One student stated that she knew that Mary was a new faculty member but that it wasn't fair that the student's were failing because of that. I asked the student if she asked Mary to speak more slowly and to provide more examples?

The student agreed to meet with Mary and discuss those issues. Following that meeting with Mary, the student told me that she was now speaking more slowly and providing more examples during class.

I attended one of Mary's classes in the latter part of the semester and found that she was teaching appropriately. I also noted that several of the students were chatting during class. This class includes a hands-on lab where students are supervised by faculty as they practice and must demonstrate proficiency of the skills taught in class.

Following exam 1, Mary put copies of her power point presentations in the library prior to the lecture and encouraged students to stop her during lecture if they had any questions. She also emphasized specific pages in the textbook with pictures of techniques to assist them in following the lecture content.

The students were instructed to review the vocabulary terms in the textbook and Mary provided vocabulary lists as well. She also gave them practice questions at the end of each class session.

On the second exam she gave more knowledge- based questions rather than application questions. She also provided a test blue-print with specific tables and page numbers to review. She did the same for the final exam.

One generally good student came to me crying after failing two exams and wanting to know how to study for the final exam. I asked her how she studied, who she studied with, and how her study partners did on the exams.

She met with Mary and went over the exams and asked questions. This student caused me to question Mary's ability. This same student did not do as well as I expected, however, in another course either.

She did pass the final exam in both Mary's and the other course. Now I questioned my own ability. How much did this student affect me? It is hard to know when students are being honest and how to judge their ability. Many times they complain and then finally share that they didn't study as much as they should have.

For example, another student who also did poorly on the exam and blamed the instructor, finally confessed to hunting all weekend and studying very little- a fact that she didn't share with the other students either.

The majority of students improved overall on the last two exams but one failed all three exams and wound up appealing her course grade. I felt frustrated writing this realizing all the things that Mary did to facilitate the students' learning.

We have been struggling the last year to decrease grade inflation letting the students reap the consequences of their actions -yet here we were doing just the opposite. Since this particular course is a prerequisite for future courses we had to consider the economic impact on the school if half the students failed the course. They would have to drop classes until the next semester.

The Appeal Process

The appeal process begins informally. The student meets with the faculty member trying to resolve the problem. The student who met with Mary learned that Mary would not change the grade or give another exam. I also met with this student and her mother at their request asking me what I could do.

I explained that Mary has the final say on her exams and that I could not change the student's grade. Her mother asked "If the student's last name was Bush, would you change her grade?" It took me a minute to understand the sarcasm intended.

I asked if she meant that if she was related to President Bush would that make a difference, and said, "No, I'm not sure where you're coming from by saying that".

She said "You got it." At that point I suggested that if they wanted to continue the appeal they should see the Dean who might be able to answer questions better than I could since this was my first appeal process.

I felt particularly frustrated and inadequate since it truly was my first experience with the appeal process and I felt I should have been better prepared to deal with the situation. I was also somewhat shocked by the mother's question and demeanor. Actually, I felt I was in over my head.

After Linda failed the course, they both visited Mary again.

Mom's opening remark to Mary was "How much responsibility are you going to take for her F"?

To which Mary replied "none".

Her mother responded "Really, that is unbelievable!"

The student, her mother and stepfather met with Mary two more times each time reviewing each exam question trying to press her to change the grade. She did accept two more questions but it resulted in very little change in the grade. I told Mary that she did not have to meet with them again; she could refer them to the Dean.

By that time they had already scheduled a meeting with the Dean after the holidays but still wanted to go over the exams with Mary again.

The student readily admitted to not understanding some of the questions as she moved through the exams. She said "now, I understand" when discussing some of the content but it was clear to Mary that during the conversation that the student still did not understand some of the major concepts.

The meeting with the Dean did not result in a grade change either. A follow-up letter sent by the Dean stated:

1) Each exam question was analyzed once again and deemed by the faculty to be valid on all of the exams.
2) All of your exams were re-graded by hand and no errors were found.
3) The spreadsheet summarizing all grades was rechecked for potential errors and none were found.
4) Policies regarding grading were reviewed and no violations were found.
5) Grading for all class members was reviewed with consistency of *grading verified*.

The Dean then referred the student to the policy for the formal appeal process. I feel like the letter should have come from me and that I should've had guidance in writing it.

The Formal Appeal

The student submitted documentation supporting her position to the Dean of Faculty who convened an appeals committee. The committee did not support the student's appeal.

Additional Information

The Dean and I discussed the appeal process and resolved that I would be the one handling future appeals.

Mary is still concerned because the mother is a paralegal and could potentially initiate a lawsuit.

During the appeal process when I asked how we could have supported Mary, one teacher replied "Mary needed support when the students failed the first exam." This teacher thought Mary shouldn't have changed the scores on the first exam and that the students should have had to study harder to pass the other exams. The teacher thought I didn't give enough support to Mary to stand by her first exam scores.

Other questions to consider are: Is something wrong when more than half the class fails an exam? I asked an instructor at another school what his thoughts on this issue were. He thought we needed to look at the situation and consider some other options because she was a fairly new instructor.

So, we are left with a number of questions needing answers. Where is the wrong? Is the teacher wrong? Is the exam poorly constructed? Are the students doing their share of the work? Should the exam be tossed and the students given another exam; or the same exam over again? If so, what kind of precedent would we be setting? Should the instructor be expected to teach everything that's going to be on the test in lecture? Isn't that called, 'teaching to the exam'? What is the student's responsibility in reading and understanding the text? One can admit them into a school but only the student can decide to admit the information into her/his brain by studying.

Should all instructors be expected to use study guides if one does? What about test blueprints- do we formalize those too? What is the limit for meeting with a hostile parent, or for meeting with an immature student? If the students don't like us, can they still respect our teaching and our methods? I want to become a stronger leader and be better equipped to handle similar situations in the future.

Conclusion

As a result of this experience we made some changes to support the faculty in situations like this. Faculty have attended workshops on item writing and test construction. We have better test analysis software that facilitates objective decisions on individual items. Consequently, faculty state that they are much more comfortable in standing by their exam questions.

In addition, we offered a workshop to faculty on student incivility. We are now offering faculty development sessions on conflict management which may assist them in preventing negative confrontations. We have not encountered another student/family experience such as the one just described. We hope that implementing these prevention activities will better prepare all of us to deescalate confrontational situations.

ANALYSIS: From this situation one can readily see that much soul-searching goes into every decision a leader must make whether that leader is a teacher, a clinical supervisor, or the VP of the entire facility. This re-checking of our own thoughts, values, and priorities ultimately makes for sound decisions.

LEADERSHIP STRATEGY: Support the people you have entrusted with doing the job.

PRINCIPLE(S): Sayre's Law- "In any dispute the intensity of feeling is inversely proportional to the value of the issues at stake" The law adds a corollary, "that is why academic politics are so bitter."

Theory Guiding Practice

Nursing

Barbara Dossey's Theory of Integral Nursing is a grand theory designed to guide the science and art of nursing on multiple levels of practice, research, education, and health care policy. Built upon Nightingale's foundation the Theory of Integral Nursing attempts to organize human experienced phenomena and reality from four perspectives: (1) The physiological-behavioral, or individual exterior; (2) the personal-intentional or, individual interior; (3) the shared cultural, collective interior; and (4) the systems-structure collective exterior.

As with all theories, the Theory of Integral Nursing has intentions, three of them. It aims to encompass the unitary whole person along with the health care complex; to explore possibilities of directly applying the integral process and integral worldview; and, to expand nurse's capabilities as new-age Florence Nightingales, health care advocates, health care diplomats, and integral health care coaches-local to global.

Non-Nursing: Cognitive Reframing Model (Milton Erickson)

Milton H. Erickson (the Father of Hypnosis) has been regarded as one of the most eclectic, pragmatic, and innovative family therapists of the 20th century. Major concepts such as, the utilization approach, brief therapy, strategic therapy, the naturalistic approach, depathologizing, cognitive reframing, and use of metaphor both within and without the hypnotic state are included.

Conclusions drawn from the above topics are applied to the science and art of nursing in general, and of family nursing specifically. There are two basic reframing modes that can alter our internal representations of situations so that the person can experience the situation in other ways.

The two ways are CONTEXT reframing and CONTENT reframing.

CONTEXT reframing takes a negative (possibly an anxiety-causing) situation and presents how the behavior or experience within the situation can actually be useful. Making lemonade out of lemons such as we saw in Situation 1.4. Context reframing allows the mind to hold multiple viewpoints that can later be used as perceptual filters through which to view those distressing situations.

For example, a nursing home, wishing to beautify the resident's common gathering places asked a local mortuary what they did with the flowers after a funeral. They found out that the mortuary threw them away. The Activity Director asked if the nursing home could have them and was granted that permission. The Activity Director carefully took apart the arrangements, threw out the Gladiolas (synonymous with funeral flowers) and remade the most beautiful table decorations for the dining room, and large centerpieces for the entry foyer. She had reframed the context within which the original flowers were used.

CONTENT reframing is changing the meaning of a situation. In politics this is known as 'spin'-idealizing an event or situation to satisfy one's interpretation. The person who sets the frame, defines the situation. Hypnosis utilizes this technique by adding the power of positive suggestion while a person is receptive to accepting the hypnotist's proposed 'frame'.

Evidence-Base

Berne, E. (1972). *What do you say after you say hello? The Psychology of Human Destiny.* Grove Press. New York.

Cade,B., O'Hanlon, W. (1993). *A Brief Guide to Brief Therapy.* W. W. Norton and Co. London.

Erickson, M. and Rossi, E. (1979). *Hypnotherapy: An Exploratory Casebook.* New York: Irvington Publishers, Inc.

Erickson, M., Rossi, E. (1980). The hypnotic and hydrotherapeutic investigation and determination of symptom function.. In: Rossi, E., Sharp, F., O'Loghlin, Ryan, M. (Eds). *The collected papers of Milton H. Erickson on hypnosis*, Vol. 4. Irvington Publishers, New York.

Erickson, M., Rossi, E., Rossi, S. (1976). *Hypnotic Realities: The Induction of Clinical Hypnosis and Forms of Indirect Suggestion.* Irvington Publishers, Inc. New York.

Fisch, R. (1990). *The Broader Implications of Milton H. Erickson's Work.* Brunner/Mazel. New York

Gordon, D. and Mayers-Anderson, M. (1981). *Phoenix: Therapeutic Patterns of Milton Erickson.* Cupertino, CA: Meta Publications.

Guilligan, S. (1987). *Therapeutic trances: The Cooperation Principle in Ericksonian hypnotherapy.* Brunner/Mazel. New York.

Haley, J. (1963). *Strategies of Psychotherapy.* New York: Grune and Stratton.

Haley, J. (1986). *Uncommon Therapy: The Psychiatric Techniques of Milton H. Erickson, M. D. W. W. Norton and Co.* New York.

Haley, J. (1990). *Conversations with Milton H. Erickson, M. D. Vol. I, Changing Individuals.* W. W. Norton and Co. New York.

Haley, J. (1990). *Conversations with Milton H. Erickson, M. D., Vol. III, Changing Children and Families.* W. W. Norton and Co. New York.

Haley, J. (Ed). (1967). *Advanced Techniques of Hypnosis and Therapy: The Selected Papers of Milton H. Erickson, M.D. Grune and Stratton.* New York.

Havens, R. A. (1992). *The Wisdom of Milton H. Erickson,* (Vol. II). Irvington Publishers, Inc. New York.

http://en.wikipedia.org/wiki/List_of_eponymous_laws

Imber-Black, E. (1993). *Secrets in Families and Family Therapy.* W. W. Norton and Co. New York.

Karpel, M. (1980). *Family secrets. Family Process,* 19: 295-306.

Lankton, S. (1985). *Elements and Dimensions of an Ericksonian Approach.* Brunner/Mazel Publishers. New York.

Lankton, S. (1987). *Central Themes and Principles of Ericksonian Therapy.* Brunner/Mazel Publishers. New York.

Lankton, S., Lankton, C., Matthews, W. (1991). *Ericksonian Family Therapy, a Chapter in Handbook of Family Therapy, Vol. II.* (Gurman, N., Kniskern, D., Eds). Brunner/Mazel. New York.

Lovern, J. (1991). *Pathways to Reality: Ericksonian-inspired Treatment Approaches to Chemical Dependency.* Brunner/Mazel. New York.

Rosen, S. (1982). *My VoiceWill Go with You: The Teaching Tales of Milton H. Erickson.* W. W. Norton and Co. New York.

Rossi, E. (1980). *The CollectedPpapers of Milton H. Erickson. Vol. III: Hypnotic Investigations of Psychodynamic Processes.* Irvington Publishers, Inc. New York.

Zeig, J. (1980). *A Teaching Seminar with Milton Erickson.* Brunner/Mazel. New York.

Zeig, J. (1985). *Experiencing Erickson: An Introduction to the Man and His Work.* Brunner/Mazel. New York.

Zeig, J. (1994). *Ericksonian Methods: The Essence of the Story.* Brunner/Mazel. New York.

Zeig, J., Lankton, S. (1988). *Developing Ericksonian Therapy: States of the Art.* Brunner/Mazel. New York.

SITUATION #12.2. CREATING A VIRTUAL NURSING RESEARCH ENVIRONMENT

Lee Williams[*]

Sr. Library, Graceland University

Introduction

A few years ago, I became director of a small university library serving a nursing program of online graduate students and on-campus undergraduates. Coming from a community college system with multiple libraries and access points, I was surprised to find over 200 paper journal subscriptions doing little more than gathering dust on the current periodical shelves. Space in the stacks was also a scarce commodity.

Why was there no push toward electronic subscriptions with such a large online graduate program, I wondered? The out-going library director subsequently told me that if the online subscriptions or databases cost more than the paper journals themselves, she was not permitted to purchase them. This narrow view of resource utilization had to change, I felt! I began researching journals available in electronic collections (with consortium pricing) and prepared a report for my supervisors. In the report, I asserted that print journals in all cases would be less expensive than buying them online, but the overhead costs of labor and storage must also be associated with print subscription costs. In addition, a resource instantly available to students online was much more likely to be used than a paper journal that has to be retrieved, scanned, emailed and re-shelved. A few years later, we've added three new (well-utilized) electronic journal databases for students and have cut labor costs to the point of being able to reduce a full-time staff member to a half-time document delivery person. We are still, however, pitching out miles of old paper journals!

ANALYSIS: Even when confronted with the semblance of an economic 'pinch' you can still achieve your objective if you plan well and couch your proposal in terms that will appear evident to long-term cost saving.

LEADERSHIP STRATEGY: Worthwhile goals are usually progressively realized-especially when pursued with confidence and backed-up with facts.

PRINCIPLE(S): Weiner's Law of Libraries-there are no answers, only cross-references.

Theory Guiding Practice

Nursing

Eichelberger's Evolution of Nursing Theory on the Internet has led the way for the further development of the nursing specialty of 'Nursing Informatics".

---

[*] leawilli@graceland.edu.

Non-Nursing

Fisher, Ury and Patton's Seven Strategies for Treating Framing Problems specifies that the first rule of principled negotiations is to separate relationship issues from substantive issues and examine and deal with each individually. The authors identify seven steps to use in dealing with 'framing, or perception' problems.

1   Try to view the situation from your opponent's point of view.
2   Don't adopt a suspicious attitude based on your own fears.
3   Avoid the blame game.
4   Discuss each other's perceptions.
5   Seek opportunities to act inconsistent with your opponent's (mis)perceptions.
6   Think of a way to give your opponent a stake in the outcome.
7   Propose a plan consistent with the professional/personal self image of your opponent.

Evidence-Base

Gyeszly, S. (2001). Electronic or paper journals?: budgetary, collection development, and user satisfaction questions. *Collection Building, (AN ISTA3600873)*, 20(1), 5-10.

http://en.wikipedia.org/wiki/List_of_eponymous_laws

Lee, M. and Baron, S. (2008). Common Practices for Interlibrary Loan and Document Delivery at a Small Private University: We Want It and We Want It Now *Journal of Interlibrary Loan, Document Delivery and Information Supply* 18(2), 205-218.

Lingle, V. and Robinson, C. (2009a). Conversion of an Academic Health Sciences Library to a Near-Total Electronic Library: Part 1. *Journal of Electronic Resources in Medical Libraries,* 6(3), 193-210.

Lingle, V. and Robinson, C. (2009b). Conversion of an Academic Health Sciences Library to a Near-Total Electronic Library: Part 2. *Journal of Electronic Resources in Medical Libraries,* 6(4), 279-293.

Williams, T., Lindsay, J., Burnham, M., Judy, F. (2006). Online vs. Print Journals: New Challenges for Academic Medical Libraries. doi:DOI: 10.1300/J383v03n01_01; (AN 21820957)

SITUATION #12.3. COMMUNITY ISSUES: GOING THE EXTRA MILE

Betty Sawyer

Introduction

I was working as the Operations Manager in a Midwest Skilled Nursing facility while preparing to take my Nursing Home Administrator's exam. One of my duties for the facility was to collect intake admission information from potential patients, when one day a very tired looking, distraught lady came to see me.

She was extremely upset because no one would help her wherever she went, and she threatened that if she didn't get some help soon she was going to take her Dad downtown to the Division of Aging office and leave him there. She said they could either take care of him or get her some help!

As she spoke, the whole problem came to light. She had visited several nursing facilities hoping to place her father, who had dementia and was becoming increasingly more incontinent. No one would accept him because he was named on a "Life Estate Document" in another state on a property wherein he shared ownership with other family members. Her father was living with her, and she and her husband had already changed their work schedules so that someone was always at home with him. Now, however, they could no longer sleep, as Dad was getting up during the night and urinating in corners of her living room and sometimes trying to cook on the stove with disastrous results while they slept. He needed nursing home placement and he needed it quickly!

Several other facilities she had visited would not accept him as a pending Medicaid patient because they were unsure of how the "Life Estate" issue would affect his Medicaid eligibility that held he could have no more than $999 in total assets. As I looked at this lady, I knew I could not send her away but MUST find a way to help her even though I did not know the ramifications of a 'Life Estate" document either. I informed her that by the end of the day we would know if this 'Life Estate' issue was a (monetary) asset that might hinder his Medicaid eligibility, and if we could admit him to our facility.

Then, my work really began. I called the Division of Aging main office in our Capital city and spoke with several people to no avail, until I finally reached the right person knowledgeable to discuss this dilemma. After research, I was told that he *could* qualify for Medicaid and that this "Life Estate" was not considered a monetary asset that might disqualify his estate according to Medicaid rules. We could admit the patient the following day.

The family was so grateful and happy that they were able to find a facility that went the extra mile. Now, he would have a caring place to live. The very next day "Dad" came to live at our facility. Eventually as an Administrator, I moved to a position at another facility not far from my previous employment.

One day the phone rang and it was the same lady asking if she could move Dad to my new place of employment. After much conversation and sharing my concern that this would be disruptive to her Dad, she still wanted to bring him to the new location. About a week later he arrived and stayed with us until he eventually passed away.

To this day, this is one of the things I feel really good about. I was able to help the family and the resident cope with some of the hardest days of their life.

ANALYSIS: Sometimes you have to search through a lot of uninformed opinions until you get one that is informed. Yes, it takes time, but like in the situation described above, it is worth it.

LEADERSHIP STRATEGY: Research is knowledge with a fist.

PRINCIPLE(S): Stretch out of your comfort zone.

Every problem contains the seeds of its own solution- look for it.

Theory Guiding Practice

Nursing

Marilyn Ann Ray's Theory of Bureaucratic Caring combines caring from a cultural, technological, political, economic, and administrative point of view as practiced in complex healthcare organizations. As the identification of the final theory emerged, qualitative research using three methodological approaches were used: ethnography, phenomenology, and the grounded theory method. Her latest research conducted with Dr. Marian Turkel used both quantitative and qualitative research methods to study caring and its effects on economic and patient-related outcomes in hospitals.

Non-Nursing

Gagne's Information Processing Theory (1974) identifies eight levels of intellectual skill involved in new learning:

1 Signal or cue;
2 Response to the signal;
3 Chaining, or connecting two signals;
4 Verbal association, or assembling prior knowledge;
5 Discriminating among the various signals;
6 Concept formation;
7 Principle formation of applying a principle made up of at least 2 or more concepts (hypothesis).
8 Problem solving by processing 2 or more principles to achieve a higher level principle

Evidence-Base

Manworren, R. (2008). *A pilot study to test the feasibility of using human factors engineering methods to measure factors that compete or influence nurse's abilities to relieve acute pediatric pain (Application of the Bureaucratic Caring Theory).* University of Texas at Arlington, Arlington.

Ray, M. and Turkel, M. (1994a). Complex caring dynamics: A unifying model of nursing inquiry. *Theoretic and Applied Chaos in Nursing*, 1(1), 23-32.

Ray, M. and Turkel, M. (1999). *Econometric analysis of the nurse-patient relationship*: Qualitative Data Analysis Grant. Bethesda, MD: Department of Defense, TriService Nursing Research Program.

Ray, M. T., M. (1993). A study of care processes using Total Quality Management as a framework in a USF regional hospital emergency service and related services. *Military Medicine*, 158(6), 396-403.

Ray, M., Turkel, M. and Marino, F. (2002). The transformative process for nursing in workforce redevelopment. *Nursing Administration Quarterly*, 26(2), 1-14.

Swanson, K. (1991). Empirical development of a middle-range theory of caring. *Nursing Research*, 40, 161-166.

Turkel, M. (1997). *Struggling to find a balance: A grounded theory study of the nurse-patient relationship in the changing healthcare environment.* Unpublished doctoral dissertation. University of Miami, Florida.

Turkel, M. and Ray, M. (2001). Relational complexity: From grounded theory to instrument development and theoretical testing. *Nursing Science Quarterly*, 14(4), 281-287.

Turkel, M. and Ray, M. (2003). A process model for policy analysis within the context of political caring. *International Journal for Human Caring*, 7(3), 26-34.

Wiggins, M. (2006). Clinical nurse leader. Evolution of a revolution. The partnership care delivery model. *Journal of Nursing Administration*, 36(7/8), 341-345.

SITUATION #12.4. BEST MANAGEMENT PRACTICE

Teresa M. Bovia[*]

University School of Nursing, New Orleans, Louisiana

Introduction

I am the Director of Critical Care at a small rural hospital. There are 10 ED beds and 8 ICU beds. Staffing and communicating with that staff has always been a challenge as only two or three nurses work on any given day. When I arrived, there was a new CEO in place and we were tasked with moving the department forward quickly. This included everything from approaching environmental issues to providing quality care and patient satisfaction. After about thirty days on the job, I identified the informal leaders of the group and convened a charge nurse informational session. During this session nurses were asked to prepare an informal paper on what they could bring to the organization, and in particular to the Emergency Department. Six of the group stepped up to the plate-some with more significant contributions than others.

These six nurses were promoted and designated permanent charge nurses. As such, one of those six, was always scheduled to be on duty. The next step was to begin mentoring this group and brainstorming on the best way to move the department forward. We began by writing a mission statement for the ED. This draft was refined by the rest of the ED staff and is now hanging prominently in the nurses' station to remind staff on their respective shifts of the new practices.

This group of six has faithfully met every other month to brainstorm and address the tough issues that come up. Each has a core role (schedule preparation, payroll submission, policy and procedure review, etc) and takes the lead and the accountability in their respective areas. If just-in-time procedures or practices need to be implemented I am able to communicate with those six charge nurses and explain the reasoning behind the concept. They are able to help remind staff on their respective shifts of the new practice.

[*]Email: tbovia2012@yahoo.com.

The results: We have eliminated agency usage; have a permanent full time staff; and, have increased our productivity and patient satisfaction within the last six months. I have recently been given the responsibility of the ICU and am planning to implement this same strategy.

ANALYSIS: Although every institution has formal leaders (those who have a position conferred upon them by a higher authority) there can also be found 'informal' leaders-those who, when called upon to assist in some collaborative effort, will do so. In this situation six managers emerged as informal leaders who were ultimately rewarded with positions of formal leadership as well.

LEADERSHIP STRATEGY: Transformational behaviors can be cultivated through relationship building.

Spread the credit around 'Enlist team spirit" Charles Garfield.

PRINCIPLE(S): Praise effort

Reward strong performance

Innovators embrace change

Communicate often

Be open and flexible

Theory Guiding Practice

Nursing

Meleis's Transitions Theory involves mega-changes manifested in fundamental life patterns. Transitions cause changes in identities, roles, relationships, mentorship and patterns of behavior. Negotiating successful life transitions are dependent upon health interactions and solidifying trusting relationships. "professional nursing practice is based on critical thinking, mastery of knowledge and skill, integration of theories and research, and a commitment to lifelong learning, Ongoing professional development is necessary to maintain excellent nursing care, promote the nurse's growth, and continue the advancement of the nursing profession." (Schumacher, K. and Meleis, A. (1994). Transitions: A central concept in nursing. IMAGE: Journal of Nursing Scholarship, 26(2), 119-127.)

Non-Nursing

Napoleon Hill's fifteen characteristics of successful people apply here-especially, "Always do more than you are paid for". The extra effort usually gets noticed in ways that may not be immediately apparent.

Evidence-Base

DiClemente, R., Crosby, R. and Kegler, M. (Ed). (2002). *Emerging Theories in Health Promotion Practice and Research: Strategies for Improving Public Health*. San Francisco.

Hill, N. (1979). The Law of Success. Chicago: Success Unlimited, Inc. Schumacher, K. and Meleis, A. (1994). Transitions: A central concept in nursing. *IMAGE: Journal of Nursing Scholarship*, 26(2), 119-127.

Schumacher, K., Jones, P. and Meleis, A. (1999). Helping elderly persons in transition: a framework for research and practice. In: L. S. T. T. R. (Eds) (Ed.), *Advances in Gerontological Nursing: Life Transitions in the Older Adult* (Vol. 3, pp. 1-26). New York: Springer Publishing.

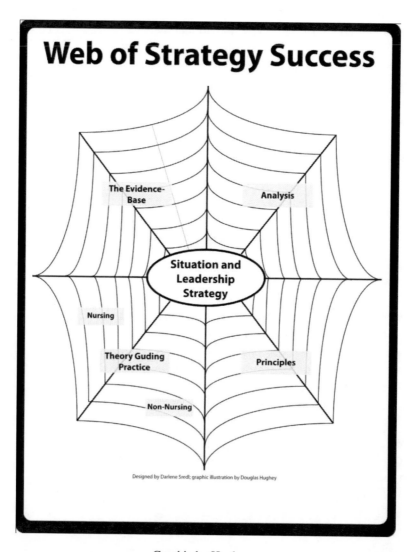

Graphic by Hughey.

REFERENCES

12Manage. ((n.d.)). heory of needs (David McClelland). Retrieved from http://www.12 manage.com.

Alligood, M. M., B. (2000). A nursing theory of empathy discovered in King's personal system. *Nursing Science Quarterly, 13*(3), 243-247.

Alligood, M. T., A. (2006). *Nursing Theory: Utilization and Application.* St. Louis: Mosby/Elsevier.

American Nurses Credentialing Center, and http://www.nursecredentialing.org/.

Amerson, R. (2006.). Energizing the nursing lecture: Application of the theory of multiple intelligence learning. *Nursing Education Perspectives, 27*(4), 194-196.

Army, U. S. (unknown). The Communication Initiative Network: Commitment to Change Model. from http://www.comminit.com/en/node/27210/36.

Association, A. N. (2007). Infections and deaths down, quality up: Evidence for having appropriate nurse staffing mounts. *American Journal of Nursing, 107*(4), 19.

Auerbach, D., Buerhaus, P., and Steiger, D. (2007). Better late than never" Workforce supply implications of later entry into nursing. *Health Affairs, 26*(1), 178-185.

Ausubel, D. Retrieved from www.davidausubel.org.

Baianu, I. (2006). Robert Rosen's work and complex systems biology. *Axiomathes, 16*(1-2), 25-34.

Banning, M. (2005). Conceptions of evidence, evidence-based medicine, evidence-based practice and their use in nursing: independent nurse prescribers' views *Journal of Clinical Nursing, 411-417.*

Barney, J. C., D. (2007). *Resource-based Theory: Creating and Sustaining Competitive Advantage.* Oxford, Great Britain: Oxford University Press.

Barrett, E. (1996). Canonical correlation analysis and its use in Rogerian research. *Nursing Science Quarterly, 9*, 50-52.

Barrett, E., and Caroselli, C. (1998). Methodological ponderings related to the power as knowing participation in change tool. *Nursing Science Quarterly, 11*, 17-22.

Bartel, A. (2000). Measuring the employer's return on investments in training: Evidence from the literature. *Industrial Relations, 39*, 502-524.

Becker, G. (1993). Human Capital: A Theoretical and Empirical Analysis, with Special Reference to Education.

Bellack, J., Morjikian, R., Barger, S., Strachota, E., Fitzmaurice, J., Lee, A., Kluzik, T., Lynch, E., Tsao, J., and O'Neil, E. (2001). Developing BSN leaders for the future: The

Fuld Leadership Initiative for Nursing Education (LINE). *Journal of Professional Education, 17*(1), 23-32.

Berne, E. (1972). *What Do You Say After You Say Hello? The Psychology of Human Destiny.* New York: Grove Press.

Berwick, D., Godfrey, A., and Roessner, J. (2002). *Curing healthcare: New strategies for quality improvement.* Hoboken, NJ: Jossey-Bass.

Bhola, H. S. ((1994)). The CLER Model: Thinking Through Change. *Nursing Management, 25* (5), 59, 62-63.

Block, V., and Sredl, D. (2006). Nursing education and professional practice: A collaborative approach to enhance retention. *Journal for Nurses in Staff Development, 22*(1), 23-30.

Bodrock, J., Mion, L. (2008). Pay for performance in hospitals: Implications for nurses and nursing care. *Quality Management in Health Care, 17*(2), 102-111.

Boeree, C. G. (2006). http://wwebstace.ship.edu/cgboer/skinner.html.

Borckardt, J., Nash, M., Hardesty, S., Herbert, J., Cooney, H., and Pelic, C. (2006). How unusual are the 'unusual events' detected by control chart techniques in healthcare settings? *Journal for Healthcare Quality: Promoting Excellence in Healthcare, 28*(4), 4-9.

Bosher, S., and Pharris, M. (Editors). (2009). *Transforming Nursing Edication: The Culturally Inclusive Environment.* New York: Springer Publishing Company.

Bowling, N., and Beehr, T. (2006). Workplace harassment from the victim's perspective: A theoretical model and meta-analysis. *J Appl, Psychol*(91), 5.

Brodie, S., and Biley, F. . (1999). An exploration of the potential benefits of pet-facilitated therapy. *Journal of Clinical Nursing, 8,* 329-337.

Brooks, E., and Thomas, S. (1997). The perception and judgment of senior baccalaureate nursing students in clinical decision making. *Advances in Nursing Science, 19,* 50-69.

Brunner, J. Constructivist Theory http://carbon.cudenver.edu/~mryder/itc_data/ constructivism.html.

Buerhaus, P. (2009). *The Future of the Nursing Workforce in the United States: Data, Trends, and Implications.* Sudbury, MA: Jones and Bartlett Publishers.

Butcher, H. (1994). The unitary field pattern portrait method: Development of research method within Roger's science of unitary human beings. In Madrid and Barrett's (Ed.), *Roger's Scientific Art of Nursing Practice* (pp. 397-425). New York: National League for Nursing.

Butcher, H. (1998). Crystallizing the process of the unitary field pattern portrait research method. *Visions: The Journal of Rogerian Nursing Science, 6,* 13-26.

Butcher, H. (2004b). Nursing's distinctive knowledge. In H. B. L. Haynes, and T. Boese (Ed.), *Nursing in Contemporary Society: Issues, Trends and Transition to Practice.* Upper Saddle River, NJ: Prentice-Hall.

Butcher, H. (2005). The unitary field pattern portrait research method: Facets, processes and findings. *Nursing Science Quarterly, 18,* 293-297.

Butcher, H., and Parker, N. (1988). Guided imagery within Martha Rogers' science of unitary human beings: An experimental study. *Nursing Science Quarterly, 1*(103-110).

Cade, B., and O'Hanlon, W. (1993). *A Brief Guide to Brief Therapy.* London: W.W. Norton and Co.

Caldwell, C. (2006). Lean- Six Sigma: Tools for rapid cycle cost reduction. *Healthcare Financial Management, 60*(10), 96-98.

Campbell, P., and Rudisill, P. (2005). Servant leadership: A critical component for nurse leaders. *Nurse Leader, 3*(3), 27-29.

Catlin, D., and Murray, T. . (1996). Drug testing in sport: Bayes Theorem meets advanced technology. *JAMA, 276*(18), 1471-1472.

Chen, J. (2004). Theory of multiple intelligences: Is it a scientific theory? . *Teachers College Record, 106*(1), 17-23.

Chongde, L., and Tsingan, L. . (2003). Multiple intelligence and the structure of thinking. . *Theory and Psychology, 13*(6), 829-845.

Cogin, J., and Fish, A. (2009). Sexual harassment-- a touchy subject for nurses. *J Health Organ Manag, 23*(4), 442-462.

Collins, A. (1983). A cognitive approach to inquiry teaching *Reigeluth, C.M. (Ed). Instructional Design Theories and: an Overview of their Current Status* (pp. 247-277). Hillsdale, NJ: Lawrence Erlbaum Associates, Publishing.

Conti-O'Hare, M. (1996). A descriptive analysis of the therapeutic use of self with addicted clients in early recovery: The expert nurse's perspective *Journal of Addictions Nursing, 8*, 81-84.

Conti-O'Hare, M., and O'Hare, J (June 18, 2001). Don't participate in horizontal violence. *Nursing Spectrum, 13*(12), 6.

Conti-O'Hare, M. (2002, May 20). Walking wounded to wounded healer. *Nursing Spectrum, 14*(10), 26-27.

Conti-O'Hare, M., O'Hare, A., Scarolla, L., Greco, P. and Murray, T. . (2000). Transforming nursing with love: Nurses caring for themselves and each other *Beginnings: The Official Newsletter of the American Holistic Nurses' Association, 20*(4), 1, 13.

Corley, M. (2002). Nurse moral distress: a proposed theory and research agenda *Nursing Ethics, 9*, 636-650.

Corley, M., Elswick, R., Gorman, M. et al,. (2001). Development and evaluation of a Moral Distress Scale. *Journal of Advanced Nursing, 33*, 250-256.

Cory, C. Retrieved from http://www.motivation-articles.com/motivate/equity-theory-and-employee-motivation.html.

Covey, S. (1991). *Principle-Centered Leadership.* New York: Summit Books.

Curley, M. (1996). Patient-nurse sypatient outcomes. *American Journal of Critical Care, 7*(1), 64-72.

DiClemente, R., Crosby, R., and Kegler, M. (Ed). (2002). *Emerging Theories in Health Promotion Practice and Research: Strategies for Improving Public Health.* San Francisco.

Dingley, C., Bush, H., and Roux, G. (2001). Inner strength in women recovering from coronary heart disease: A grounded theory. *Journal of Theory Construction and Testing, 6*(1), 4-5.

Donabedian, A. (1966). Evaluating the quality of medical care. *Milbank Quarterly, 83*(4), 691-729.

Donaldson, N., Bolton, L., Aydin, C., Brown, D., Elashoff, J., and Sandhu, M. (2005). Impact of California;s licensed nurse-patient ratios on unit-level staffing and patient outcomes. *Policy Polit Nurs Pract, 6*(3), 198-210.

Donohew, L., Palmgreen, P., and Duncan, J. (1980). An activation model of information exposure. *Communication Monographs, 47*, 295-303.

Dossey, B. (2010). Barbara Dossey's Theory of Integral Nursing. In M. P. M. Smith (Ed.), *Nursing Theories and Nursing Practice*. Philadelphia: F.A. Davis.

Duck, J. (2002). *The Change Monster: The Human Forces that Fuel or Foil Corporate Transformation and Change*. New York: Crown Business.

Eberhardt, G. D., B. (1989). Trusting the hospice nurse. *American Journal of Hospice and palliative Medicine, 6*(6), 29-32.

Ehrenberger, H., Alligood, M., Thomas, S., Wallace, D., and Licavoli, C. . (2002). Testing a theory of decision-making derived from King's Systems Framework in women eligible for a cancer clinical trial. *Nursing Science Quarterly, 15*(2), 156-163.

elisabethkublerross.com. Retrieved from Retrieved from http://www.elisabethkublerross.com.

Erickson, M., and Rossi, E.,. (1979). *Hypnotherapy: An Exploratory Casebook*. New York: Irvington Publishers, Inc.

Erickson, M., Rossi, E., and Rossi, S. (1976). *Hypnotic Realities: The Induction of Clinical Hypnosis and Forms of Indirect Suggestion*. New York: Irvington Publishers, Inc.

Erickson, M. R., E. (1980). The hypnotic and hydrotherapeutic investigation and determination of symptom function. In S. Rossi, O'Loughlin, and Ryan (Ed.), *The Collected Papers of Milton H. Erickson on Hypnosis* (Vol. 4). New York: Irvington Publishers, Inc.

Evidence-Informed management decision making: Is it a possibility in healthcare? (2007, June 7). Paper presented at the International Conference on Evidence-Based Best Practice Guidelines.

Fendrich, M., Woodward, P., and Richman, J. (2002). The structure of harassment and abuse in the workplace: A factorial comparison of two measures. *Violence and Victime, 17*(4), 491-505.

Ferrucci, L., Baldasseroni, S., DeAlfieri, W., Cartei, A., Calvani, D., Baldini, A., Masotti, G., and Marchionni, N. (2000). Disease severity and health-related quality of life across chronic conditions. *Journal of the American Geriatrics Society, 48*(11), 1490-1495.

Festinger, L., and Carlsmith, J. , and (1959). Cognitive Consequences of Forced Compliance. *Journal of Abnormal and Social Psychology http://psychclassics.yorku.ca/Festinger/, 58*, 203-210.

Fisch, R. (1990). *The Broader Implications of Milton H. Erickson's Work*. New York: Brunner/Mazel.

Fisher, R., Ury, W., and Patton, B. (1991). Seven Strategies for Treating Perception-or Framing-Problems *Getting To Yes* (pp. 22-40). New York: Penguin Books.

Fitzgerald, L., and Shullman, S. . (1993). Sexual Harassment: A research analysis and agenda for the 1990s. *Journal of Vocational Behavior, 42*, 5-27.

Fitzgerald, L., Gelfand, M., and Drasgow, F. . (1995). Measuring sexual harassment: Theoretical and psychometric advances. *Basic and Applied Social Psychology, 17*, 425-445.

Flint, A., Farrugia, C., Courtney, M. and Webster, J. (2010). Psychometric analysis of the Brisbane Practice Environment Measure (B-PEM). *Journal of Nursing Scholarship, 42*(1), 66-75.

Freeley, N., and Gottleib, L. (2000). Nursing approaches for working with family strengths and resources. *Journal of Family Nursing, 6*(1), 9-24.

French, B. (2005). The process of research use in nursing *Journal of Advanced Nursing* 125-134.

Gardner, H. (1999). Are there additional intelligences? The case for naturalistic, spiritual, and existentialist intelligences. In J. Kane (Ed.), *Education, Information and Transformation*. Englewood Cliffs, CA: Prentice-Hall.

Gawlinski, A. (2008). The Power of Clinical Nursing Research: Engage Clinicians, Improve Patients' Lives, and Forge A Professional Legacy. . *American Journal of Critical Care* 315-326.

Gordon, D., and Mayers-Anderson, M. (1981). *Phoenix: Therapeutic Patterns of Milton Erickson*. Cupertino, CA: Meta Publications.

Gottlieb, L., and Feeley, N. (1995). Nursing intervention studies: issues related to change and timing. *Canadian Journal of Nursing Research, 27*(1), 13-29.

Gottlieb, L., and Feeley, N. (1996). The McGill model of nursing and children with a chronic condition: Who benefits, and why? *Canadian Journal of Nursing Research, 28*(3), 29-48.

Greenleaf, R. (1991). *The Servant as Leader*. Indianapolis: Robert K. Greenleaf Center.

Griffin, E. (1997). *A First Look at Communication*. New York: McGraw-Hill.

Griffin, E. (2009). *A First Look at Communication Theory*. New York: McGraw-Hill.

Grojean, M., Resick, C., Dickson, M. et al. (2004). Leaders, values, and organizational climate: examining leadership strategies for establishing an organizational climate regarding ethics. *Journal of Business Ethics, 55*, 223-241.

Guilligan, S. (1987). *Therapeutic Trances: The Cooperation Principle in Ericksonian Hypnotherapy*. New York: Brunner/Mazel.

Gutierrez, K. (2005). Critical care nurses' perceptions of and responses to moral distress. *Dimensions of Critical Care Nursing 24*, 229-241.

Gyeszly, S. (2001). Electronic or paper journals?: budgetary, collection development, and user satisfaction questions. *Collection Building, (AN ISTA3600873), 20*(1), 5-10.

Halcomb, E., Davidson, P., Caldwell, B., Salamonson, Y., and Rolley, J. (2010). Validation of the Professional Practice Environment Scale in Australian general practice. *Journal of Nursing Scholarship, 42*(2), 207-213.

Haley, J. (1963). *Strategies of Psychotherapy*. New York: Grune and Stratton.

Haley, J. (1986). *Uncommon therapy: The Psychiatric Techniques of Milton H.Erickson, M.D.* New York: W.W. Norton and Co.

Haley, J. (1990a). *Conversations with Milton H. Erickson, M.D. -Changing Couples* (Vol. II). New York: W.W. Norton and Co.

Haley, J. (1990b). *Conversations with Milton H. Erickson, M.D. Changing Individuals* (Vol. I). New York: W.W. Norton and Co.

Haley, J. (1990c). *Conversations with Milton H. Erickson, M.D., Vol III, Changing Children and Families*. (Vol. III). New York: W.W. Norton and Co.

Haley, J. E. (1967). *Advanced Techniques of Hypnosis and Therapy: The Selected Papers of Milton H. Erickson, M.D.* . New York: Grune and Stratton.

Hamel, G. (1998). Strategy innovation and the quest for value. *Sloan Management Review, Winter*.

Hart, S. (2005). Hospital ethical climates and registered nurses' turnover intentions. *Journal of Nursing Scholarship, 37*, 173-177.

Havens, R. (1992). *The wisdom of Milton H. Erickson, (Vol. II)* New York: Irvington Publishers, Inc.

Helms, J. (1993). Introduction: Review of racial identity terminology. In J. Helms (Ed.), *Black and White Racial Identity: Theory, Research and Practice*. Westport: Praeger.

Helms, J. (1994). The conceptualization of ethnic identity and other 'racial constructs'. In R. W. E. Thicket, and E. Birman. (Ed.), *Human Diversity: Perspectives on People in Context*. San Francisco: Jossey-Bass.

Helms, J. (1995). An update of Helms: White and people of color racial identity models. In J. C. J. Ponterott, L. Suzuki, and C. Alexander. (Ed.), *Handbook of Multicultural Counseling*. Thousand Oaks,: Sage.

Hill, N. (1979). *The Law of Success*. Chicago: Success Unlimited, Inc.

Hodge, D. (2007). A Systematic Review of the Empirical Literature on Intercessory Prayer *Research on Social Work Practice 17*, 174-187.

Hodges, B. (1997). Hodges' Health Career Model.

Hogan, M., and Nickitas, D. (2009). *Nursing Leadership and Management: Reviews and Rationales*. Upper Saddle River: Pearson/Prentice Hall.

Hong, G. (2009). Familiarity, preference, and utilization of ethnic items among Asian Americans. *Asian Nursing Research, 3*(4), 186-195.

Huang, M., Courtney, M., Edwards, H., and McDowell, J. (2009). Psychometric evaluation of the Chinese version of the diabetews coping measure scale. *Journal of Nursing Scholarship, 41*(4), 385-390.

Hupcey, J. (2000). Feeling safe: the psychosocial needs of ICU patients. *Journal of Nursing Scholarship, 32*(4), 361-367.

Imber-Black, E. (1993). *Secrets in families and family therapy* New York: W.W. Norton and Co.

Jarvis, G., and Northcott, H. (1987). Religion and differences in morbidity and mortality. *Social Science and Medicine, 25*, 813-824.

Jenkins, R., Sredl, D., Hsueh, H., and Ding, C. . (2007). Evidence-based nursing process (EBNP) consumer culture attribute identity: A message-based persuasion strategy study among nurse executives in the U.S *Journal of Medical Sciences, 27*(2), 55-62.

Jha, A., Duncan, B., and Bates, D. (2002). Evidence report/technology assessment, No 43: Making healthcare safer of patient safety practice from www.ahcpr.gov/ clinic/ptsafety/index.

Jones, P. (2004). Viewpoint: Can informatics and holistic multidisciplinary care be harmonised? *British Journal of Healthcare Computing and Information Management, 21*(6), 17-18.

Kalyuga, S. (2006). Cognitive Load Factors in Instructional Design for Advanced Learners *Instructing and Testing Advanced Learners: A Cognitive Load Approach*. New York: Nova Science Publishers, Inc.

Kass, R. (1995). Bayes Factors *Journal of the American Statistical Association, 90*(430), 773-795.

Kerfoot, K. (1997). Leadership Principles: Lessons learned. *Dermatology Nursing, 9*(4), 279-280.

King, I. (1981). *A theory for nursing: Systems, Concepts, Process*. New York: John Wiley and Sons.

Koenig, H. (1997). *Is Religion Good for your Health? The Effects of Religion on Physical and Mental Health*. New York: The Hawarth Press.

Kovner, A., Elton, J., Billings, J. (2000). Evidence-based management. *Frontiers of Health Services Management, 16*(4), 3-24.

Lee, M., and Baron, S. (2008). Common Practices for Interlibrary Loan and Document Delivery at a Small Private University: We Want It and We Want It Now *Journal of Interlibrary Loan, Document Delivery and Information Supply 18*(2), 205-218.

Lehman, K. J. (2008). Change Management: Magic or Mayhem? *Journal for Nurses in Staff Development, 24*(4), 176-184.

Leibovici, L. (2001). Effects of remote, retroactive, intercessory prayer on outcomes in patients with bloodstream infection: randomised controlled trial. *British Medical Journal, 323*, 1450-1451.

Lenz, E., Suppe, F., Gift, A., Pugh, L., and Milligan, R. (1995). Collaborative development of middle-range nursing theories: Toward a theory of unpleasant symptoms. *Advances in Nursing Science, 17*(3), 1-13.

Levin, J. (1994). Religion and health: Is there an association, is it valid, and is it causal? *Social Science and Medicine, 38*, 1475-1482.

Lewin, K., and Lippitt, R. (1938). An experimental approach to the study of autocracy and democracy: A preliminary note. *Sociometry, 1*, 292-300.

Lewin, K., Lippitt, R., and White, R. . (1939). Patterns of aggressive behavior in experimentally created social climates. *Journal of Social Psychology, 10*, 271-301.

Lindenaur, P., Remus, D., Roman, S. et al. (2007). Public reporting and pay for performance in hospital quality improvement. *New England Journal of Medicine, 356*, 486-496.

Lingle, V., and Robinson, C. (2009a). Conversion of an Academic Health Sciences Library to a Near-Total Electronic Library: Part 1. *Journal of Electronic Resources in Medical Libraries, 6*(3), 193-210.

Lingle, V., and Robinson, C. (2009b). Conversion of an Academic Health Sciences Library to a Near-Total Electronic Library: Part 2. *Journal of Electronic Resources in Medical Libraries, 6*(4), 279-293.

Locsin, R. (2005). *Technological competency as caring in nursing: A model for practice.* Indianapolis: Sigma Theta Tau International.

Locsin, R., and Campling, A. (2005). Techno sapiens and posthumans: Nursing, caring and technology. In R. Locsin (Ed.), *Technological Competency as Caring in Nursing: A Model for Practice.* Indianapolis: Sigma Theta Tau International.

Lucas, J., Ivnik,R.,Smith, G.,Ferman, T.,Willis, F., Petersen, R., et al.,. (2005). A brief report on WAIS-R Normative data collection in Mayo's older African Americans normative studies. *Clinical Neuropsychologist, 19*(2), 184-188.

Magley, V. (2002). Coping with sexual harrassment: Reconceptualizing women's resistance. *J. Pers Soc Psychol, 83*(4), 930-946.

Magley, V., Hulin, C., Fitzgerald, L., and DeNardo, M. . (1999). Outcomes of self-labeling sexual harassment *Journal of Applied Psychology, 84*, 390-402.

Manworren, R. (2008). *A pilot study to test the feasibility of using human factors engineering methods to measure factors that compete or influence nurse's abilities to relieve acute pediatric pain (Application of the Bureaucratic Caring Theory).* University of Texas at Arlington, Arlington.

Marchionni, C., and Richer M. (2007). Using appreciative inquiry to promote evidence-based practice in nursing: The glass is more than half full. *Nursing Research, 20*(3), 86-95.

Marker, C. (1987). The marker umbrella model for quality assurance: Monitoring and evaluating professional practice. *Journal of Nursing Quality Assurance, 1*(3), 52-63.

Maslow, A. (1943). A Theory of Human Motivation *Psychological Review, 50*(4), 370-396.

Matthews, D., McCullough, M., Larson, D., Koenig, H., Swyers, J., and Milano, M. (1998). Religious commitment and health status: A review of the research and implications for family medicine. *Archives of Family Medicine, 7*(2), 118-124.

Matusitz, J., and Breen, G. (2005). Prevention of sexual harassment in the medical setting: Apply inoculation theory. *J. Health Soc Policy, 21*(2), 53-71.

Maxwell, J. (2003). *Attitude 101: What Every Leader Needs to Know*. Nashville: Thomas Nelson Publishers.

May, B. (2000). *Relationship Among Basic Empathy, Self-Awareness, and Learning Styles of Baccalaureate Pre-Nursing Students within King's Personal System.* Unpublished Dissertation Abstracts International, University of Tennessee, Tennessee.

McCarthy, J., and Deady, R. (2008). Moral Distress Reconsidered. *Nursing Ethics, 15*(2), 254-262.

McEwen, M. W., Evelyn. (2011). *Theoretical Basis for Nursing* (Third ed.). Philadelphia: Wolters Kluwer/Lippincott/Williams and Wilkins.

Melnyk, B. (2002). Strategies for overcoming barriers in implementing evidence-based practice. *Pediatric Nursing, 28*(2), 159-161.

Melnyk, B., Fineout-Overholt, E. (2005). *Evidence-based Practice in Nursing and Healthcare*. Philadelphia: Lippincott Williams and Wilkins.

Miller, E., and Conti-O'Hare, M. . (1998). An evaluation of a patient centered care model *Federal Practitioner, 4*, 52-61.

Morgan, T. (2000). Toward evidence-based statistics *Annals of Internal Medicine 132*(6), 507.

Needleman, J., Buerhaus, P., Mattke, S., Stewart, M., and Zelevinsky, K. (2002). Nurse-staffing levels and the quality of care in hospitals. *New England Journal of Medicine, 346*(22), 1715-1722.

Neuringer, A. (2002). Operant variability: evidence, functions, and theory. *Psychonometric Bulletin and Review, 9*(4).

Newbold, D. (2007). The production economics of nursing. *Int J Nurs Stud, 45*(1), 120-128.

Newhouse, R. (2007). Creating infrastructure supportive of evidence-based nursing practice: Leadership strategies. *Worldviews on Evidence-Based Nursing, 4*(1), 21-29.

Newhouse, R., Dearholt, S., and Poe, S. (2007). Organizational Change Strategies for Evidence-Based Practice *JONA* 552-557.

Neylan, T. (1998). Hans Selye and the Field of Stress Research. *Neuropsychiatry Classics, 10*(230-231).

No Author. (2007). The role of nursing leadership in creating a mentoring culture: Inspirational motivation. *Nursing Economics, 25*(3), 143-148.

Olaniyan, D., and Okemakinde, T. (2008). Human Capital theory: Implications for Educational Development. *European Journal of Scientific Research, 24*(2), 157-162.

Overmier, B., and Gahtan, E. (2007). Psychoneuroimmunology: The final hurdle. *Integrative Psychological and Behavioral Science, 33*(2), 137-140.

Parker, M., and Smith, M. (2010). *Nursing Theories and Nursing Practice* (3 rd ed.). Philadelphia: F.A.Davis.

Parrone, J., Sredl, D., Miller, M., Donaubauer, C. . (2006.). Overcoming cultural change anxiety before coming to America. . *Philippine Journal of Nursing, 76*(2), 17.

Parrone, J., Sredl, D., Miller, M., Phillips, M., and Donaubauer, C. (2008). An evidence-based teaching/learning strategy for foreign nurses involving the Health Education

Systems Incorporated examination as a predictor for National Council Licensure Examination for Registered Nurse success. *Teaching and Learning in Nursing, 3*, 35-40.

Perdrizet, G. (1997). Hans Selye and beyond: responses to stress. *Cell Stress and Chaperone, 2*(4), 214-219.

Petersen, l., Woodard, L., Urech, T., Daw, C., and Sookanan, S. (2006). Does pay for performance improve the quality of health care? *Ann. Intern. Med., 145*(265-272).

Pfeffer, J. S., R. (2006). Act on facts, not faith: How management can follow medicine's lead and rely on evidence, not on half truths. Retrieved from http://www.ssireview.org/images/articles/2006SP_feature_Pfeffer_Sutton.pdf.

Ponterotto, J., Gretchen, D., Utsey, S., Stracuzzi, T. and Saya, R., Jr. (2003). The Multigroup Ethnic Identity Measure (MEIM): Psychometric review and further validity testing. *Education and Psychological Measurement, 63*, 502-515.

Porter-O'Grady, T., and Malloch, K. (2002). *Quantum Leadership: A Textbook of New Leadership*. Gaithersburg, MD: Aspen.

Pryor, J., and McKinney, K. . (1995). Research on sexual harassment: Lingering issues and future directions. *Basic and Applied Social Psychology, 17*, 605-611.

Purnell, M. J. (2006). Development of a model of nursing education grounded in caring and application to online nursing education. *International Journal for Human Caring 10*, 8-16.

Quine, L. (1999). Workplace Bullying in NHS Community Trust: Staff Questionnaire Survey,. *British Medical Journal 318*(7178), 228-232.

Rashevsky, N. (1969). Outline of a unified approach to physics, biology, and sociology. *Bulletin of Mathematical Biophysics, 31*, 159-198.

Ray, M., and Turkel, M. (1994a). Complex caring dynamics: A unifying model of nursing inquiry. *Theoretic and Applied Chaos in Nursing, 1*(1), 23-32.

Ray, M., . and Turkel, M. (1999). Econometric analysis of the nurse-patient relationship: Qualitative Data Analysis Grant. Bethesda, MD: Department of Defense, TriService Nursing Research Program.

Ray, M., Turkel, M., and Marino, F. (2002). The transformative process for nursing in workforce redevelopment. *Nursing Administration Quarterly, 26*(2), 1-14.

Ray, M. T., M. (1993). A study of care processes using Total Quality Management as a framework in a USAF regional hospital emergency service and related services. *Military medicine, 158*(6), 396-403.

Ray, M. T., M. (2010). Marilyn Anne Ray's Theory of Bureaucratic Caring. In M. P. M. Smith (Ed.), *Nursing Theories and Nursing Practice*. Philadelphia: F.A. Davis.

Reed, P. (1991). Toward a nursing theory of self-transcendence: Deductive reformulation using developmental theories. *Advances in Nursing Science, 13*(4), 64-77.

Reed, P. (1996). Transcendence: Formulating nursing perspectives. *Nursing Science Quarterly, 9*(1), 2-4.

Reed, P. (1997). Nursing: The ontology of the discipline. *Nursing Science Quarterly, 10*(2), 76-79.

Reeves, K. (2007). New evidence report on nurse staffing and quality of patient care. *MEDSURG Nursing, 16*(2), 73-74.

Reigeluth, C. M. (1999). The elaboration theory: Guidance for scope and sequences decisions. In E. R.M. Reigeluth (Ed.), *Instructional-design Theories and Models: A New*

Paradigm of Instructional Theory, Vol II (Vol. II, pp. 425-454). Mahwah, NJ: Lawrence Erlbaum Associates.

Rosen, R. (1960). A quantum-theoretic approach to genetic problems. *Bulletin of Mathematical Biophysics, 22*, 227-255.

Rosen, R., and Brown, P. (1996). *Leading People: Transforming Business from the Inside Out* New York: Viking Penguin.

Rosenthal, M. F., R. (2006). What is the empirical basis for paying for quality in health care? *Med Care Res Rev, 63*, 135-157.

Roux, G. (1998). *Inner Strength in Women: A Grounded Theory*. Paper presented at the Qualitative Health Research International Conference.

Roux, G., and Dingley, C. (1997). *A Grounded Theory: Inner Strength in Women*. Paper presented at the Scientific Session of Sigma Theta Tau International Convention.

Roux, G., Bush, H., and Dingley, C. (2000, Fall). Inner strength: A concept analysis. *Journal of Theory Construction and Testing, 4*(2), 36-39.

Roux, G., Dingley, C., and Bush, H. (2002). Inner strength in women: Metasynthesis of qualitative findings in theory development. *Journal of Theory Construction and Testing, 6*(1), 4-15.

Rowe, J. (2006). Pay for performance and accountability: Related themes in improving health care. *Ann Intern Med, 145*, 695-699.

Rudebusch, G., Wu, T. (2002). Macroeconomic models for monetary policy. *Federal Reserve Bank of San Francisco Economic Review, 02-11*, 75-77.

Sare, M., and Ogilvie, L. (2010). *Strategic Planning for Nurses: Change Management in Health Care*. Boston: Jones and Bartlett Publishers.

Sautter, K., Bokhour, B., and White, B. et al. (2007). The early experience of a hospital-based pay-for-performance program. *Journal of Healthcare Management, 52*(2), 95-107.

Scannell-Desch, E., and Doherty, M. (2010). Experiences of U.S. military nurses in the Iraq and Afghanistan Wars, 2003-2009. *Journal of Nursing Scholarship, 42*(1), 3-12.

Schiemann, D. (2006). Expert Standards in Nursing as an Instrument for Evidence-based Nursing Practice *Journal of Nursing Care and Quality* 172-179.

Schumacher, K., and Meleis, A. (1994). Transitions: A central concept in nursing. *IMAGE: Journal of Nursing Scholarship, 26*(2), 119-127.

Schumacher, K., Jones, P., and Meleis, A. (1999). Helping elderly persons in transition: a framework for research and practice. In L. S. T. T. R. (Eds) (Ed.), *Advances in Gerontological Nursing: Life Transitions in the Older Adult* (Vol. 3, pp. 1-26). New York: Springer Publishing.

Sherwood, G. (1997). Metasynthesis of qualitative analysis of caring: Defining a therapeutic model of nursing. *Advanced Practice Nursing Quarterly, 3*(1), 32-42.

Sieloff, C. (1991). *Imogene King: A Conceptual Framework for Nursing*. Thousand Oaks, CA: Sage.

Sieloff, C. (1995). Development of a theory of departmental power. In M. S. Frey, C (Ed.), *Advancing King's Systems Framework and Theory of Nursing* (pp. 46-65). Thousand Oaks, CA: Sage.

Smith, J., Winkler, R., Fryback, D. . (2000). The first positive: Computing positive predictive values at the extremes *Annals of Internal Medicine 132*(10), 804-809.

Somnath, S. S., S. (2006). *The rationale for diversity in the health professions: A review of the evidence*. Retrieved from http://www.hrsa.gov/.

Sredl, D. (1979a). Acceleration phenomena: Effect on pregnant women *Point of View 16*(4), 6-7.

Sredl, D. (1979b). Night flight sight and stress *Private Pilot, Oct.*

Sredl, D. (1979c). Top flight care in the air. *Emergency, 11*(11), 58-60.

Sredl, D. (1979). Up in the air. *Nursing '79, 8*(10), 110-116.

Sredl, D. (1980). Aerohemodynamics. *Point of View, 17*(3), 11.

Sredl, D. (1981). Aviation opportunities for occupational health nurses. *Occupational Health Nursing 29*(4), 20-21.

Sredl, D. (1983). *Airborne Patient Care Management: A Multidisciplinary Approach.* St. Louis: Medical Research Associates Publications.

Sredl, D. (2004). Health-related quality of life: A concept analysis. *West African Journal of Nursing, 15*(1), 9-19.

Sredl, D. (2005). Evidence-based nursing practice (EBNP) meta-paradigm: A crystallized synthesis of apperceptions, beliefs and efforts toward EBNP implementation among contemporary nurse executives in the United States of America (pp. 166). St. Louis, MO: Doctoral Dissertation, University of Missouri- Saint Louis.

Sredl, D. (2006). The Triangle Technique: Pilot study and construct of a new evidence-based educational tool for pediatric medication calculations. . *NLN's Nursing Educational Perspectives, 27*(2), 84-88.

Sredl, D. (2007). *Pilot Quest* Frederick, MD: PublishAmerica.

Sredl, D. (2008a). Conceptual Model: The Aerohemodynamics Meta-Theory. *Journal of Teaching and Learning in Nursing, 3*, 115-120.

Sredl, D. (2008b). What contemporary nurse executives in the United States Really think about Evidence-Based Nursing Practice (EBNP). *Nurse Researcher, 15*(4), 51-67.

Sredl, D. (2009). Multi-attribute Multidisciplinary concept analyses related to the Aerohemodynamics Conceptual Model *Journal of Teaching and Learning in Nursing 4*(3), 98-103.

Sredl, D. (In Press-a). Evidence-Based Process (EBP) Considerations of Hypoxia During Flight for Flight Nurses: The Aerohemodynamics Theory Revisited *Airline Industry: Strategies, Operations and Safety.*

Sredl, D. (In Press-b). The QALY vs DALY Quandary. *Common Ground Publishing.*

Sredl, D., and Peng, N. (2010). CEO-CNE Relationships: Building the evidence-base of Chief Nursing Executive Replacement Costs. *International Journal of Medical Sciences. Available from http://www.medsci.org/v07p0160.htm 7*, 160-168.

Sredl, D., and Peng, N. (In Press). CEO-CNE Relationships: Building the evidence-base of Chief Nursing Executive Replacement Costs. *International Journal of Medical Sciences.*

Sredl, D., Aukamp, V. (2006). Evidence-Based Nursing Care Management for the Pregnant Woman With an Ostomy. *Journal of Wound, Ostomy and Continence Nursing, 33*(1), 42-49.

Sredl, D., Dickerman, J., and Bess, F. (2008). Fostering a culturally congruent acceptance of critical thinking among nursing professionals in an extended care facility. *In Press-International Journal of Cultural Diversity in Organizations, Communities and Nations.*

Sredl, D., Melynk, B., Jenkins, R., Hsueh, K., Ding, C., and Durham, J. (In Press). Healthcare in crisis! Can evidence-based nursing practice (EBP) be a key solution to healthcare reform? *Journal of Teaching and Learning in Healthcare.*

Sredl, D., Parrone, J., Donaubauer, C., Miller, M. (2006). Overcoming cultural change anxieties before coming to America. *The Philippine Journal of Nursing*.

Sredl, D., Werner, T., Springhart, D., Watkins, D., Shaner, M., McBride, G. (2003). Evidence-based practice in action. An evidence-based pilot study exploring relationships between psychologic and physiologic factors in post-lung transplant adolescents with cystic fibrosis. *Journal of Pediatric Nursing: Nursing Care of Children and Families, 18*(3), 216-220.

Stein, H. (2007). *Insight and Imagination: A Study in Knowing and Not-Knowing in Organizational Life*. Lanham: University Press of America, Inc.

Stone, P. (2002). Using economic evidence in clinical practice. *Journal of Medical Practice Management, 17*, 272-277.

Stone, P. (2005). Return on investment models. *Applied Nursing Research, 18*(3), 186-189.

Stone, P., Bakken, S., Curran, C. and Walker, P. (2002). Evaluation of studies of health economics. *Evidence-Based Nursing, 5*, 100-104.

Stone, P., Stone, C., Curran, C. and Bakken, S. (2002). Economic evidence for evidence-based practice. *Journal of Nursing Scholarship, 34*, 277-282.

Sullivan, E., and Decker, P. (2009). *Effective Leadership and Management in Nursing (7th Edition ed.)*. Upper Saddle River, NJ: Pearson:Prentice-Hall.

Swanson, K. (1991). Empirical development of a middle-range theory of caring. *Nursing Research, 40*, 161-166.

Taylor, E. (2002). *Spiritual Care: Nursing Theory, Research and Practice*. Upper Saddle River: Prentice Hall.

Taylor, E., Highfield, M. and Amenta, M. (1994). Attitudes and beliefs regarding spiritual care: A survey of cancer nurses. *Cancer Nursing, 17*(6), 479-487.

Titler, M. (2002). Use of research in practice. In J. Haber (Ed.), *Nursing Research* (5th ed.). St. Louis: Mosby-Yearbook, Inc.

Titler, M., and Everett, L. (2001). Translating research into practice: Considerations for critical care investigators. *Critical Care Clinics of North America, 13*(4), 587-604.

Torres, V. (1996). *Empirical Studies in Latino/Latina Ethnic Identity*. Paper presented at the National Association of Student Personnel Administrators National Conference.

Tumulty, K. (2009). Where did reform go? *Time, 174*(23), 54-55.

Turkel, M. (1997). Struggling to find a balance: A grounded theory study of the nurse-patient relationship in the changing healthcare environment. Unpublished Unpublished doctoral dissertation. University of Miami, Florida.

Turkel, M., and Ray, M. (2001). Relational complexity: From grounded theory to instrument development and theoretical testing. *Nursing Science Quarterly, 14*(4), 281-287.

Turkel, M., and Ray, M. (2003). A process model for policy analysis within the context of political caring. *International Journal for Human Caring, 7*(3), 26-34.

Turley, J. (2007). Toward a model for nursing informatics. *Journal of Nursing Scholarship, 28*(4), 309-313.

U.S. Dept of Health, E., and Welfare,. *Ethical Principals and Guidelines for the Protection of Human Subjects of Research (The Belmont Report). Publication no. OS 78-0012*.

Van Der Zee, K., and Van Oudenhoven, J. (2000). The Multicultural Personality Questionnaire: A multidimensional instrument of multicultural effectiveness. *European Journal of Personality, 14*, 291-309.

Van Der Zee, K., and Van Oudenhoven, J. (2001). The Multicultural Personality Questionnaire: Reliability and validity of self- and other ratings of multicultural effectiveness. *Journal in Research in Personality, 35*, 278-288.

Ventegodt, S. (1996). *Measuring the Quality of Life from Theory to Practice.* Copenhagen: Forskingscentrets Forlag.

Ventegodt, S., Flensborg-Madsen, T., Andersen, N., and Merrick, J. (2008). Which factors determine our quality of life, health, and ability? Results from a Danish population sample and the Copenhagen perinatal cohort. *Journal of the College of Physicians and Surgeons Pakistan.*

Watson, J. (1996). Watson's theory of transpersonal caring. In P. Walker (Ed.), *Blueprint for Use of Nursing Models: Education, Research, Practice and Administration* (pp. 141-184). New York: National League for Nursing.

Weiss, C., Murphy-Graham, E., Petrosino, A., and Gandhi, A. (2008). The fairy godmother-and her warts: Making the dream of evidence-based policy come true. *American Journal of Evaluation, 29*(1), 29-47.

Wiedenbach, E. (1969). *Meeting the Realities in Clinical Teaching.* New York: Springer.

Wiggins, M. (2006). Clinical nurse leader. Evolution of a revolution. The partnership care delivery model. *Journal of Nursing Administration, 36*(7/8), 341-345.

Williams, D., Neighbors, H., and Jackson, J. (2003). Racial/ethnic discrimination and health. Findings from community studies. *American Journal of Public Health, 93*(2), 200-208.

Williams, T., Lindsay, J., Burnham, M., Judy, F. . (2006). Online vs. Print Journals: New Challenges for Academic Medical Libraries. doi:DOI: 10.1300/J383v03n01_01; (AN 21820957).

Wilson, B. C., P. (1992). A critical review of elaboration theory. *Educational Technology Research and Development, 40*(3), 63-79.

Wimpenny, P., Johnson, N., Walter, I., and Wilkinson, J. . (2008). Tracing and Identifying the Impact of Evidence-Use of a Modified Pipeline Model *Worldviews on Evidence-Based Nursing* 3-12.

Wittmann-Price, R., and Bhattacharya, A. (2006). Exploring the subconcepts of the Wittmann-Price Theory Of Emancipated Decision-Making in women's health care. *Journal of Nursing Scholarship, 38*(4), 377-382.

Wojmer, A. (2002). Capturing error rates and reporting significant data. *Critical Care Nursing Clinics of North America, 14*(4), 375-384.

Wyer, R., Albarracin, D. (2005). Belief formation, organization, and change: Cognitive and motivational influences. In D. Albarracin, Johnson, B., Zanna, M. (Ed.), *The Handbook of Attitudes.* Mahwah, NJ: Lawrence Erlbaum Associates Publishers.

Yinger, J. (1976). Ethnicity in complex societies In L. Coser (Ed.), *The Uses of Controversy in Sociology.* New York: Free Press.

Zeig, J. (1994). *Ericksonian Methods: The Essence of the Story* New York: Brunner/Mazel.

Zerwekh, J., and Claborn, J. (2009). *Nursing Today: Transition and Trends* (6 ed.). St. Louis: Saunders/Elsevier.

Zuzelo, P. (2007). Exploring the moral distress of registered nurses. *Nursing Ethics, 14*(3), 344-359.

INDEX

D

E

F

G

J

K

L

M

N

O

P

Q

R